MAKING LEMONADE
OUT OF LEMONS

JOSÉ M. ALAMILLO

Making Lemonade
Out of Lemons

MEXICAN AMERICAN LABOR AND
LEISURE IN A CALIFORNIA TOWN,
1880–1960

UNIVERSITY OF ILLINOIS PRESS

URBANA AND CHICAGO

∞ This book is printed on acid-free paper.

Library of Congress Cataloging-in-Publication Data

Alamillo, José M., 1969–
   Making lemonade out of lemons : Mexican American labor and leisure in a
California town, 1880–1960 / José M. Alamillo.
       p. cm. — (Statue of Liberty-Ellis Island Centennial series)
   Includes index.
   ISBN-13: 978-0-252-03081-9 (cloth : alk. paper)
   ISBN-10: 0-252-03081-8 (cloth : alk. paper)
   ISBN-13: 978-0-252-07325-0 (pbk. : alk. paper)
   ISBN-10: 0-252-07325-8 (pbk. : alk. paper)
       1. Mexican Americans—California—Corona—History.   2. Mexican Americans—
California—Corona—Social conditions.   3. Agricultural laborers—California—
Corona—History.   4. Agricultural laborers—California—Corona—Social
conditions.   5. Corona (Calif.)—History.   6. Corona (Calif.)—Social conditions.
I. Title.   II. Series.
F869.C79A53   2006
979.4'970046872—dc22   2006003047

For Leilani

Contents

Acknowledgments

This book could not have been written without the people of Corona who invited me to their homes and shared their memories and photographs with me. I owe a huge debt to the late Frances Martínez who worked tirelessly to make Corona a better place for all and encouraged me to document the city's Mexican roots. Thanks also to Rudy Ramos for driving me around town and taking pictures, and introducing me to many of the residents. Thanks also to Rey Aparicio, Onias Acevedo, Manuel Cruz, Juanita Ramírez, Emily and Jim "Chayo" Rodríguez, Tito Cortez, Lupe Avalos, Fred and Dolores Salgado, Ruth Cortez, Guadalupe R. Delgadillo, Teresa E. Lopez, Manuel Muñoz, Margaret Rosales, David Felix, and Ray Delgadillo. Thanks also to Angelo Lunetta, Kate Hyett, Edward Willits, Carl Hercklerath, Donald McGaffin, Sylvia Barnett, and many other Coronans. At Corona Public Library's Heritage Room, Gloria Scott went out of her way to help me find documents and encouraged me to expand the library's oral history collection. A wonderful group of librarians—Vera Garcia, Chris Smith, and Sandra Falero—also provided invaluable assistance.

At the University of California, Irvine, I received support from a host of individuals, groups, and institutions. Gilbert G. González, my dissertation adviser and impeccable mentor, always took time to meet with me and, when my graduate program dissolved, made sure I received encouragement, guidance, and support. Additional committee members Raúl Fernandez, Dorothy Fujita Rony, Heidi Tinsman, and Jeff Garcilazo all provided invaluable advice and were generous with their time as I rushed to complete my dissertation. Dorothy Fujita Rony read the entire manuscript in a timely manner, offered incisive comments, and continues to be a constant source of support and encouragement. My work also benefited from the dynamic discussions at the Labor Studies research group, especially from Nancy Naples, Judith Stepan-Norris, Hector Delgado, John Liu, Rodolfo Torres, and David Smith. I was saddened by the loss of two mentors and colleagues, Jeff Garcilazo and Lionel Cantú, whose personal integrity, innovative research, and commitment to social justice continue to inspire me. The Chicano/Latino Studies Program became a second home to me. Stella Ginez made me feel welcome and kept me going with her wise counsel and lively conversations. Special thanks to students Oscar Cerna, Armando Garibay, and Federico Orozco, who helped me collect data. Thanks also to Glen Mimura, Daniel Tsang, and June Kurata, Augusto Espiritu and Anna Gonzalez.

As a graduate student at UC Irvine I was lucky to have met graduate students, many of them members of the Graduate Students of Color Collective and the Dissertation Liberation Army, who became an important source of support as I stumbled, often tripped and fell, but ultimately survived graduate school. Thanks to Brian Chiu, Robert Hayden, Nick Bhatt, Freddy Heredia, Jaime Ruiz, John Rosa, Mike Masatsugu, Enrique Buelna, Alonso Nichols, Grace Talusan, Carl Almer, Charlene Tung, Adrienne Hurley, Julio Moreno, Mariam Beevi, John Rosa, Theo Gonzalves, Jocelyn Pacleb, Charlene Tung, Chiou-ling Yeh, Michelle Madsen-Camacho, Ester Hernandez, Leslie Bunnage, Vivian Price, Clare Weber, and Chrisy Moutsatsos. Special thanks to Wilson Chen and Jane Hseu who continue to be great friends, colleagues, and *compadre* and *comadre*, respectively.

I was fortunate to have participated in a two-week summer seminar on Latino Studies sponsored by the Smithsonian Center for Latino Initiatives and the Inter-University Program for Latino Research (IUPLR). The seminar helped sharpen my research and most of all allowed me to meet dynamic scholars and graduate students from around the country. Thanks to Magdalena Mieri, Gilberto Cardenas, and Amelia Malagamba for their gracious hospitality and interest in my project. Thanks also to a wonderful cohort—Reina A. Prado, Jaime Cardenas, Miroslava Chavez, Maythee Rojas, and Natalia Molina—for making my trip to Washington, D.C., an intellectually inspiring experience and to Estevan Rael y Galvez for his friendship, encouragement, and wisdom.

Other colleagues have been generous with their time in commenting on early drafts, sharing ideas and resources, and encouraging me to complete the book. These include, Zaragosa Vargas, George Lipsitz,

Ricky T. Rodriguez, Anna Sandoval, Linda Maram, Richard Flacks, Dionne Espinoza, George Sánchez, David Montgomery, Dana Frank, Anthea Hartig, Elliott Young, Elizabeth Jameson, Katherine Morrissey, Mike Willard, Amalia Cabezas, Howard Schor, Steve Pitti, Antonia Castañeda, Frank Barajas, Carlos Cortes, Kenneth Burt, Pedro Castillo, Samuel Regalado, Chris Friday, Guadalupe San Miguel Jr., Luis Arroyo, Albert Camarillo, Ramón Gutiérrez, Karen Mary Davalos, Horacio N. Roque Ramírez, and Ernesto Chavez. Vicki Ruiz offered insightful and detailed comments on several chapters, allayed my fears of being a first-time book author, and encouraged me to complete the book because, as she reminded me, it no longer belonged to me but to the people I interviewed. Special thanks to Gabriela Arredondo for her friendship and advice on the ins and outs of academia. I am especially grateful to Matt Garcia, who early on nurtured my work, shared sources, made sure our kids played and partners met, and provided feedback on the manuscript.

I am also grateful to those institutions that provided financial support. A postdoctoral fellowship from the Chicano Studies Research Center at the University of California, Los Angeles, allowed me to finish writing the manuscript. Special thanks to Chon Noriega, Lisa Catanzarite, Shirley Hune, Carlos Haro Erica Bochanty, Wendy Belcher, Reynaldo Macias, Isabel Castro-Melendez, and Jacqueline Archuleta. I also received financial assistance through the Washington State University Academic Achievement Career Development Award in Support of Diversity, College of Liberal Arts Completion Grant, UC MEXUS Dissertation Fellowship, and UC Regent's Dissertation Fellowship.

At the University of Illinois Press, I thank Joan Catapano for her guidance in shepherding this manuscript through the publishing process. Special thanks to Cathy Sunshine, who helped tremendously with copyediting and brought "sunshine" to my prose. I thank the two anonymous reviewers for their extensive comments and for helping me sharpen the analysis.

I have had the privilege of working with a number of supportive colleagues in the Department of Comparative Ethnic Studies at WSU. Many thanks to Yolanda Flores Neimann, Alex Kuo, Rory Ong, John Streamas, Matthew Guterl, Carmen Lugo-Lugo, C. Richard King, David Leonard, Sheli Fowler, and Lisa Guerrero. Linda Trinh Vo and Bill Ross have been great colleagues and friends who helped my family adjust to Pullman and continue to be great hosts during our California visits. Special thanks to E. San Juan Jr. and Delia Aguilar for their mentorship and support. Linda Heidenreich has been a great friend and collaborator on all things *Raza* at WSU. Outside of my department I received support and encouragement from Chicano/a-Latino/a Faculty and Staff Association, WSU colleagues, including Brian McNeill, Alex Hammond, Marian Sciachitano, Victor Villanueva, Susan Armitage, Laurie Mercier, Noel Sturgeon, and T. V. Reed. I also learned much from an excellent group of undergraduate and graduate students, including Francisco Tamayo, Maria Cuevas, Marta Maria Maldonado, Jennifer Mata, José Anazagasty, Alma Montes de Oca, Tomas Madrigal, Carlos Adams, Majel Boxer, Petra Guerra, and Tony Zaragosa. Special thanks to Cecilia Martinez, who assisted me with newspaper research.

Inspiration for this project began with my family's experience in the lemon industry, and without their support I could not have completed this book. My grandfather, Antonio Herrera, first shared with me his stories of living and working at Limoneira Ranch during the 1930s before returning to Mexico. He encouraged me to read books and nicknamed me "el profesor" at a young age to ensure that I would become one. I hope I fulfilled his wish. *Muchas gracias a mis padres for su apoyo;* Jose and Rosa Alamillo first taught me the value of hard work and how to make "lemonade" from the bitter "lemons" in life. Many thanks to my big brothers, Steve, Ralph, and Esaul, and big sister, Yolanda. My little sister, Angie, has been incredibly supportive of my career and makes me proud of her dedication to educational equity issues. Thanks also to Leti, Maria, Valerie, Brandon, Amanda, Joey, Armando, Jesse, and tia Aurelia and tio Miguel and their kids, Erica, Liz, Eliseo, Cesar, Mike and *compadre* Rick. The late Richard Neville taught me the importance of being a dedicated teacher and mentor. I would like to thank Libia S. Gil and Rick Hanks, Anica, Solana, Kolina and Jeff, and Kamala for their warm support, babysitting, and hospitality during our many visits.

My beloved partner, Leilani, first encouraged me to enroll in graduate school and since then has tolerated my absences, pressing deadlines, conference trips, and all-night writing bouts. Most of all, I am thankful for her love and companionship during our many years together in California and now Washington State, and even through hard times she continued to be a source of strength and inspiration. Our journey into parenthood with the arrival of Lorenzo, Maya, and Danilo has made me realize how blessed I am to have this *familia*.

MAKING LEMONADE
OUT OF LEMONS

Introduction

Growing up on a southern California lemon ranch near the Pacific Coast, I spent my boyhood in a world bounded by vast orchards with rows upon rows of lemon trees. I remember the sweet fragrance of lemon blossoms in springtime and the sour taste of freshly picked fruit. Wedged between the cities of Ventura and Santa Paula north of Los Angeles, the Limoneira Ranch was owned and operated by the Limoneira Company. A member of Sunkist Growers, Inc., Limoneira is still considered the largest lemon ranch in the country and continues today to depend on Mexican immigrant labor.

We lived in what was essentially a company town. The families on the ranch lived in company-owned houses, bought their groceries on credit from the company store, used company-built recreational facilities, and answered to a ranch supervisor who policed the groves and the resident workforce. When the temperature dropped, the ranch foreman would sound the loud horn in the middle of the chilly night, summoning workers to light the smudge pots to save the fruit. The pots produced sooty black smoke that smelled like crude oil, and my father would return home covered in dark soot. My mother packed lemons at the packinghouse. During the peak season she worked day and night, while in the low season she had to clean houses to make ends meet. These "lemon" jobs were marked by low wages, dangerous working conditions, and strict forms of company surveillance.

Despite their lack of autonomy in the workplace, pickers and packers forged community ties that stretched beyond the lemon ranches. Leisure activities were the main arena where Mexicans could exert a measure of control over their lives. These included weekend dance parties, baseball games, picnics, patriotic festivals, church events, weddings, baptisms, and wakes. Coming together for these occasions and leisure pursuits, Mexican workers forged bonds of community solidarity and created sweet memories from the often bitter circumstances they had been dealt in life.

Across southern California, thousands of Mexican families, like my own family, labored in citrus orchards and packinghouses and lived in citrus communities. I found this out when I attended the 1994 reunion of citrus workers at the Joe Dominguez American Legion Post Hall in Corona, a Riverside County town once known as the Lemon Capital of the World because of its multimillion-dollar lemon industry. Because of economic hardship, citrus workers were forced to end their schooling early and thus could not attend high school reunions. So in 1992, they began a reunion of former pickers and packers.

I was introduced to these reunions by the organizers, Rudy Ramos and Onias Acevedo, whom I first met at a local Mexican bakery. The reunions became an important social space for longtime city residents to share photos and memories of the old days. Many of the reunion participants shared their stories with me in separately scheduled interviews, in both Spanish and English, and willingly suggested other names to contact. Many remembered the Cinco de Mayo festivals, the street dances, the baseball games, and silent movies at the Chapultepec Theater. Others recalled less happy times: lighting smudge pots on freezing nights and enduring segregation in schools, movie theaters, parks, and pools. Despite these common experiences, men and women did not always remember events in precisely the same ways. And there were silent moments during which I was able to bring up the strike that divided the community. In coming together half a century later, these participants sought not only to highlight their contribution to the lemon industry but also to re-create a sense of community largely lost amid the rapid population growth and suburbanization of Corona in recent years.

Besides the reunions, I contacted individuals with the help of Frances Martínez, who provided me with a long list of women to interview, mostly former packers and Cinco de Mayo queens, and directed me to the Corona Senior Center's women's sewing circle. Many of these women invited me to their homes to share their family pictures and memories of work and play. Frances also advised me to work with the Corona Public Library's Heritage Room, whose staff showed genuine interest in documenting Mexican American contributions to the city and in expanding their oral history, photo, and archival collections. Frances expressed concern that the city's history would privilege the efforts of Anglo citrus growers at the expense of Mexican workers who helped the city become the Lemon Capital of the World. The Heritage Room staff supported my efforts in conducting oral history interviews and allowed me to peruse their extensive citrus company records.

This book was inspired by many of these oral histories, especially those that looked beyond the workplace. In spite of the hardships of life in this single-industry town, Mexican men and women challenged, transformed, and expanded the arena of leisure for their own purposes. Leisure spaces included saloons, pool halls, baseball clubs, churches, Cinco de Mayo festivals, and movie theaters. Employers, city officials, and social reformers all made concerted efforts to control the lives of working men and women in the community, including how and where they spent their leisure time. Despite these efforts, Mexican immigrants and Mexican Americans used certain leisure activities to build ethnic and worker solidarity and forge relations with employers, city officials, and Anglo residents to achieve greater power in the community. These gains were modest at best, limited by the economic power of the citrus industry and the intransigence of city officials as well as by racial, ethnic, class, religious, and gender divisions within the community. Nonetheless, Mexican American groups blossomed into a political force. They laid the groundwork for civil rights struggles and electoral campaigns in the post–World War II era that achieved some notable successes, including the desegregation of recreational facilities and the election of Mexican American candidates to local political office.

Historians have cited the real estate, motion picture, oil, and automobile industries as the pillars of southern California's economic development before World War II.[1] The citrus industry, however, also played an important role in the region's economy and culture. Carey McWilliams, a lawyer, activist, and journalist, first recognized the significance of citrus to southern California in his classic 1946 study, *Southern California: An Island on the Land*.[2] Since then, scholars have expanded upon and revised some of McWilliams's observations. Gilbert González, in his 1994 study *Labor and Community: Mexican Citrus Worker Villages in a Southern California County, 1900–1950*, examined the work, community, and unionization experiences of Mexican citrus workers in Orange County's orange industry.[3] A year later a new group of scholars published important essays on "citriculture" in southern California.[4] More recently, Matt Garcia's *A World of Its Own: Race, Labor, and Citrus in the Making of*

Greater Los Angeles (2001) examined the citrus suburbs in Greater Los Angeles. These important studies have inaugurated a "new" citrus history that has deepened and enriched our understanding of the role of citrus in the making of California.[5]

Building on these earlier works, this book explores several new directions. First, it focuses on lemons, whereas most studies to date have been concerned with the orange-producing districts.[6] Valencia oranges were grown in coastal areas, principally in Orange County and parts of Los Angeles, Santa Barbara, San Diego, and Ventura counties, while Washington navels occupied the foothills along the San Gabriel and San Bernardino mountains and around the inland cities of Riverside, Redlands, and San Bernardino. Lemons, particularly of the Eureka and Lisbon varieties, were less resistant than oranges to cold weather, so lemon orchards were concentrated on gently sloping land in Santa Barbara and Ventura counties and alongside the Santa Ana Mountains. Located in a frost-free belt on the southeastern side of the Santa Ana Mountains, the town of Corona became a center of lemon fruit production and lemon by-products manufacture.

Second, this book focuses on a geographic area that has received relatively little scholarly attention. Past studies have examined the working-class suburbs, citrus-belt towns, and smaller cities in Los Angeles, Orange, Santa Barbara, and Ventura counties, where many Mexican Americans lived and worked. But inland southern California, a vast region of twenty-eight thousand square miles that includes Riverside and San Bernardino counties, remains understudied. This area has changed rapidly in recent years, with a booming multiethnic population, new freeways, and endless tract housing built over what used to be citrus orchard land. But its roots are in the citrus industry and the experiences of a mainly Mexican workforce.[7]

Third, previous works have provided an overview of dispersed citrus *colonias* within counties, valleys, and regions. In contrast, this book is a detailed community study of a single industry town. Lemons dominated Corona in much the same way that certain other industries dominated towns in other parts of the country—from the cigar factories that created Ybor City, Florida, to the cotton mills that built Dalton, Georgia, to the gold mines that enriched Cripple Creek, Colorado, and the copper mines that formed Anaconda and Butte, Montana. Grounding this study at the grassroots provides a unique opportunity to examine leisure practices over time and across space and to understand why and how workers used leisure pursuits for affirmation of as well as for resistance to the established social order.[8]

In the last few decades, U.S. historians have produced important studies of the American working class that extend beyond the workplace. Important works by Roy Rosenzweig, Kathy Peiss, George Lipsitz, Robin D. G. Kelley, Mary Murphy, Nan Enstad, and Susan Lee Johnson closely examine the realm of leisure to understand the complexity of working-class culture. These works have revised our understanding of saloons, patriotic celebrations, amusement parks, dance halls, and movie theaters, casting them as alternative spaces of autonomy and community rather than as mere recreation venues. Working men and women arguably had more control over leisure than any other aspect of their lives, and they sometimes challenged the powerful in their determination to reclaim and transform their leisure activities. Such local struggles over leisure also took place in single-industry towns such as Corona, California.[9]

Leisure activities were and continue to be a central element in the lives of Mexican immigrants and Mexican Americans in the United States. As historians Vicki Ruiz, Douglas Monroy, and George Sánchez have shown, among Mexican immigrants and Mexican Americans in Los Angeles, encounters with American popular culture and commercialized leisure did not lead to assimilation but allowed for the negotiation of cultural identities in the face of working-class realities.[10] Similarly, this book explores Mexicans' leisurely pursuits but in a single community. Unlike Los Angeles, the semirural town of Corona depended on a small elite group of citrus growers whose control extended beyond the workplace into the daily lives of Mexican working men and women. Nonetheless, Mexican working men and women drew upon cultural resources at their disposal—pool halls, sporting events, church-related events, and patriotic festivals, among others—to build ethnic solidarity, critique social inequities, mobilize oppositional resistance, and to some extent improve the conditions of their lives.

The pursuit of leisure did not always lead to resistance but sometimes reinforced conservative norms and contributed to gender inequalities in the home and community. Some leisure practices did not necessarily improve the position of the entire Mexican community, nor were they intended to do so. The underside of certain male leisure spaces, principally saloons, pool halls, and gambling joints, led to alcoholism, dwindled family earnings, and violent assaults against men and women. Historian Peter Way, for example, has cautioned historians about romanticizing working-class culture and overlooking the "rough" edges of male leisure behavior that intensified male privilege over women and undermined working-class unity.[11]

~ (Another aim of this book is to examine the role of gender in shaping work, leisure, and politics.) Feminist scholars have reminded us that working-class formation is also a gendered process, not simply because men and women experience the worlds of work, home, and leisure differently, but because gender ideologies are embedded in institutional and everyday practices. A key area of inquiry is exploring how femininity and masculinity are socially constructed. In Corona, the leisure practices of Mexican American men and women were played out in the field of gender relations in which notions of masculinity and femininity were reproduced and challenged. Mexican men forged a rough masculine culture in homosocial settings such as saloons, pool halls, and sporting events that often conflicted and overlapped with more respectable male cultural forms promoted by company officials, social reformers, and temperance groups. Mexican women, whose leisure opportunities were limited to heterosocial spaces (churches, movie theaters, festivals), challenged and reproduced traditional feminine ideals promoted by husbands, churches, companies, and reformers.[12]

This book also touches on the changing relations between Mexican immigrants and Italian immigrants, mostly from Sicily, and their children. Italians and Mexicans in the United States have typically been studied in isolation from each other, even though these groups have often lived in multiethnic neighborhoods.[13] In Corona's citrus industry, native Anglos made up the majority of owners and managers, Italians were incorporated in the packinghouse labor force, and Mexicans were relegated to field orchard work. Although Italian immigrants encountered prejudice and discrimination, they were structurally positioned as "white" in the U.S. racialized social system. By the 1930s, Corona's Italian Americans had gained greater economic and residential mobility, whereas Mexican Americans still faced economic and political roadblocks and were relegated to the nonwhite racial status of "Mexican."[14]

Part I of this book traces the development of Corona's citrus industry and its dependence on Mexican and Italian immigrant labor, whose contributions enabled the industry's tremendous growth during the first half of the twentieth century. Chapter I sets the context by sketching the political and economic development of Corona from a fledgling fruit colony in the late nineteenth century into a thriving citrus hub. By World War I, the town was the largest producer and shipper of lemon fruit in the state. Unlike larger fruit-growing communities, Corona was essentially a single-industry town in which a small group of Anglo citrus growers exercised undue political influence on city politics, civic affairs, and public spaces. Chapter 2 describes the migration and work experiences of the Mexican men and women who worked in Corona's citrus industry and lived in citrus ranches or in city barrio neighborhoods. It also offers a glimpse of the experiences of Italian immigrants, many of whom lived next door to Mexicans, worked with them in the citrus packinghouses, and sent their children to the same schools.

Part 2 examines workers' attempts to create autonomous leisure spaces despite the limited recreational choices available and the efforts of employers, temperance crusaders, social reformers, and municipal authorities to control all aspects of workers' lives. Chapter 3 focuses on the leisurely pursuits of Mexican men in pool halls, saloons, underground bootlegging operations, and gambling joints. Chapter 4 charts the activities of Mexican women, who gathered in churches, at movie theaters, and Cinco de Mayo festivals. Chapter 5 examines the creation of a Mexican American sporting culture centered on baseball that helped to strengthen community ties and create an activist, albeit male-dominated, culture.

Part 3 shows how Mexican American men and women transformed two relatively autonomous leisure spaces—baseball clubs and Cinco de Mayo festivals—into venues for incipient political activism aimed at improving conditions in the Mexican community. Chapter 6 describes the fledgling 1940–41 unionization campaign led by the Congress of Industrial Organizations (CIO) and Mexican labor organizers, including some baseball players who transferred their teamwork skills from the playing field to the picket lines. The growers' repressive tactics, the police arrests, and the inherent structural weakness of an all-male union leadership contributed to the labor movement's eventual defeat.

Finally, chapter 7 looks at the emerging civil rights battles waged by Mexican Americans in Corona during and after World War II. Los Amigos Club and the Joe Dominguez American Legion Post mobilized support for the desegregation of schools, theaters, and swimming pools; contested negative media images; and registered voters. Mexican American women led by Frances Martínez occupied informal leadership roles in these campaigns, challenging patriarchal authority within organizations and the larger community. The Good Neighbor Policy and Cinco de Mayo festivals played a central role in this process. The festival leadership appropriated the discourse of the Good Neighbor Policy to legitimate their demands at the local level, and thus the fiesta became a springboard for Mexican Americans to gain local political representation and access to community resources.

PART ONE

Corona's Citrus Industry and Immigrant Labor

1 Lemon Capital of the World

When Corona, California, celebrated its fiftieth anniversary in 1936, the opening event of the five-day celebration was a lavish pageant portraying the town's history from the time of its founding. Performed by four hundred schoolchildren on the high school athletic field for an audience of thousands, *The Golden Circle* began with children costumed as Luiseño Indians performing the "Eagle Dance." This was followed by depictions of Franciscan padres, dancing señoritas, and a Spanish soldier, Don Leandro Serrano, described as "the first white settler in the region." The next episodes showed the founding of the citrus industry: boys dressed as "sterling pioneers from Iowa" crossed the stage in covered wagons with spades and plows, while girls dressed as water sprites helped plant the first citrus trees. The drama heightened as insects, cold winds, and hungry gophers attempted to destroy the orchards. In the final scene, "fruit girls" representing the bountiful harvest formed an immense golden circle around the cast.[1]

The play was written and produced by local historian and citrus grower Janet Williams Gould, who was inspired by the popularity of the pageant based on Helen Hunt Jackson's epic romance novel *Ramona*. Nicknamed the "Corona Duchess," Gould often lectured on California's Spanish past "wearing a mantilla from distant Seville, earrings from Madrid and a black lace gown." Similarly romantic in approach, *The Golden Circle* both explained and elided the stark racial, gender, and class hierarchies that underlay the "colorful" history of Corona. It showcased exotic Indian dancers, Californio rancheros, stereotypically docile Anglo women, and of course the manly, risk-taking Anglo "founding fathers" from Iowa who planted the first citrus trees. Notably absent from this narrative were the immigrant groups, principally Mexicans and Italians, who provided the labor and most of the expertise on which the citrus industry was built. *The Golden Circle* starkly symbolized which groups belonged inside the Circle City and which were kept outside, relegated to the fringes of history.[2]

On the last day of the Corona celebration, May 5, Mexican Americans staged a Cinco de Mayo fiesta to commemorate the Mexican army's victory over invading French troops in the 1862 Battle of Puebla. The citrus industry newspaper, *California Citrograph,* described the event as a "concluding tribute to the citrus industry" in which "the Spanish-speaking residents, mostly workers in the citrus industry, in parade pageant and address paid homage to production of fruit from which their livelihood is gained." Although Mexican Americans were willing to participate in the city's anniversary celebration, they wished to do so on their own terms. This public celebration sought to establish a counternarrative to *The Golden Circle* by making their presence visible and implicitly questioning and challenging their social position within American society. For Corona's Mexican population, this patriotic holiday offered the occasion to reflect on their own culture and history and the many obstacles they would have to overcome to be accepted as full citizens.[3]

The European American colonists who laid claim to the "golden circle" of Corona contributed to its transformation from a fledgling fruit colony to the so-called Lemon Capital of the World, led by a small but powerful group of citrus growers who wielded enormous economic and political power in local and state affairs. Growers attempted to reshape and redefine labor-management relations by implementing a corporate welfare system to retain workers, foster loyalty, and prevent labor strife. A key paternalistic institution was the citrus ranch system that resembled "industrial plantations" devised to keep the Mexican immigrant labor force under control. This confining situation set the stage for the exodus of workers to the Corona barrio and their efforts to reclaim leisure as an element of labor organizing and community mobilization.

Founding a Citrus Colony

Land speculators descended on southern California during the 1870s hoping to make fortunes on the region's land boom. Even before they

visited the Golden State, wealthy investors in the Midwest and on the
East Coast were selling the idea of "colony settlement" to interested
parties. The colony system involved cooperative enterprises in which
wealthy eastern and midwestern investors would jointly purchase a
large tract, subdivide it among themselves, and build an agriculture
economy to subsidize township schools, churches, and a civic infra-
structure. These colonists, according to Carey McWilliams, "came from
the same locality, had much the same background, and had worked
together in planning the colony before they arrived in Southern California. As a consequence, the colony settlements, out of which the towns
in the citrus belt developed, had a homogenous character which they
have retained through the years." Colonists openly expressed their
racial preferences for Anglo settlers: one promotional item boasted of
"persons skilled in a great variety of agricultural pursuits; families from
the states and the industrial classes from Europe."[4]

One of the most prosperous citrus colonies was Riverside, located
in the inland valley. Before Riverside's founding in 1870, Cahuilla Indians had long inhabited this area, followed by a group of Mexicans from
New Mexico who formed La Placita and Agua Mansa (collectively
referred to as San Salvador) in the 1840s along the Santa Ana River. Don
Juan Bandini, owner of the Jurupa Rancho, donated a tract of land for
New Mexico settlers in return for protective services against horse
thieves. The Salvadoreños endured floods, droughts, a smallpox epidemic, battle for water and grazing rights, and a lengthy court battle for
their land against successive Anglo claimants. Although they won the
court battle, Salvadoreños lost the larger political and economic battle
against Anglo politicians and land speculators who fenced off their land
under the 1872 No Fence Law. San Salvador residents were conse-
quently displaced and forced to enter the citrus labor force.[5]

Following the U.S.-Mexican War of 1846–48, the thirty-two hundred acres of the Jurupa Rancho was subdivided into smaller land plots
and sold off to prospective orange growers such as John Wesley North.
A retired judge and real estate investor from Knoxville, Tennessee,
North recruited a group of Anglo upper-class businessmen to join him
in 1870 to form the Southern California Colony Association of Jurupa.
Judge North advertised his vision: "We wish to form a colony of intelligent, industrious and enterprising people, so that each one's industry
will help to promote his neighbor's interests as well as his own." Their
first action was to change the town to "Riverside," after the Santa Ana
River that flowed nearby. Several years later an eccentric Anglo woman,
Eliza Tibbets, who claimed that she looked like Queen Victoria, planted

the city's first navel orange trees with seeds imported from Bahia, Brazil. After winning several first prizes at citrus fairs and gaining national recognition in the late 1870s, the seedless navel orange variety was given a patriotic brand name—the Washington Navel. The navel's popularity and lucrative profits spurred citrus production in the belt that stretched from the subtropical coastal regions of Santa Barbara to San Diego, moving eastward toward the desert inland valleys in Riverside and San Bernardino counties.[6]

Hoping to build on the success of Riverside, businessmen from Iowa organized a land company in 1886 to build a fruit colony named "South Riverside" (later changed to Corona). Robert B. Taylor left Sioux City, Iowa, for southern California and decided to stay when he discovered the lucrative potential of land with fertile soil and an abundant water supply. "On going to visit the land," Taylor wrote, "I was captivated by the beauty of the site, the rich soil, and the prospects of obtaining water for the tract from Temescal Valley." Immediately afterward Taylor told his engineer, "I am going to buy the land, and will go east to organize a company." With backing from retired Iowa investors Adolph Rimpau, George Joy, A. S. Garretson, and Samuel Merrill, Taylor formed the South Riverside Land and Water Company and purchased 11,510 acres of Rancho La Sierra, owned by heirs of Don Bernardo Yorba, and 5,000 acres of Rancho El Temescal, formerly occupied by the Serrano family.[7]

South Riverside colonists made their racial preferences known. One colonist bragged: "This colony is a representative American settlement. It is not composed of foreigners, but of an intelligent, thrifty and cultured class of people." Unlike residents of other southern California citrus towns that depended on Chinese immigrant workers, South Riversiders exhibited racial animosity and mobilized white supremacist sentiments against Chinese "heathens." The anti-Chinese movement that spread across California and the American West reached southern California's citrus belt, where Anglo workers viewed the Chinese as competitors, unassimilable, and a racial problem, even though large-scale citrus growers needed them as low-wage labor. In Riverside, the Chinese continued to work in the groves, laundries, and restaurants, despite being ejected from downtown and facing harassment and exclusion legislation. Conversely, in South Riverside, with an incipient citrus industry, anti-Chinese sentiment brought together different segments of the Anglo population to "keep the heathen out." In 1888, for example, the *South Riverside Bee* reported that a Chinese laundry opened in a downtown building owned by a Riverside contractor. In response, one resident proposed to launch an anti-Chinese boycott "to prevent a Chinatown being established within our midst." Another angry resident retorted, "It would be far preferable to boycott the odorous heathens entirely. Money paid to a Chinaman is as good as wasted. . . . Let every dollar, if possible, be paid to Anglo labor and the development of the country encouraged." In their opposition to the Chinese presence, South Riversiders proclaimed a "white" racial identity and sought to create a community that reflected their deeply rooted Protestant Christian mores and temperance beliefs.[8]

Despite South Riverside's rapid growth, the town remained under the shadow of Riverside, so residents began to push for a new name for their "pretty colony." In June 1896 residents considered such names as "Circle City," "Montello," "Rondel," and "Superior." At first "the majority could not agree upon a name," reported the *South Riverside Bee*, but "when Corona was proposed it seemed to unite a great many people." Barron James Hickey, an international traveler and novelist who married the daughter of J. H. Flager, a Standard Oil magnate, proposed the Spanish word *corona*, which means "crown" or "garland." By a vote of 120 to 13, "Corona" won over "Circle City." The Spanish name evoked not only the region's romanticized Spanish past but also the shape of a citrus fruit and the town's unique circular design.[9]

Building a Lemon Town

The Corona vicinity proved to be an ideal location for lemon growing. Encircled on the south side by the Santa Ana Canyon, on the north by the Santa Ana River, and on the east by the Temescal Canyon, Corona is located in what geologists call a "frost-free" belt, where heavy winds and cool breezes from the west temper the summer heat and surrounding hills protect crops from ocean fog during the winter. Compared with oranges, lemons are less resistant to cold weather, especially when temperatures drop below thirty degrees Fahrenheit. Cold spells can reduce profits, or, as a veteran lemon salesperson put it, "the price of lemons follows the movement of the thermometer upward." Between December 1912 and January 1913, a devastating freeze struck the citrus belt, reaching two degrees below zero in some areas and causing severe crop damage and catastrophic losses. In the aftermath of the "big freeze," the secretary for the Queen Colony Fruit Exchange wrote, "As conditions commenced to readjust themselves and the results of the freeze could be sized up somewhere near accurately Corona found herself occupying a most enviable position in comparison with most of the less fortunate fruit sections." While most citrus districts curtailed shipments to less

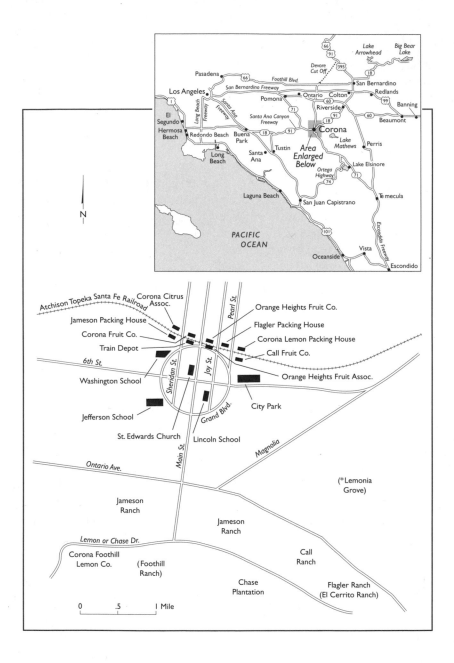

Big Bear
Lake
Lake
Arrowhead
66
91
Devore
Cut Off
395
Foothill Blvd.
Pasadena
66
San Bernardino
18
San Bernardino Freeway
Redlands
Los Angeles
Ontario
Colton
99
Banning
Pomona
60
El
71
Riverside
60
Beaumont
Segundo
Santa Ana Canyon
91
Hermosa
Freeway
18
Beach
Buena
Redondo Beach
18
91
Corona
Park
Lake
Perris
Long
Santa
Mathews
Beach
Ana
Tustin
Area
Enlarged
Lake Elsinore
Below
71
Ortega
Highway
74
Temecula
Laguna Beach
San Juan Capistrano
PACIFIC
OCEAN
101
Vista
Oceanside
Escondido

N

Atchison Topeka Santa Fe Railroad   Corona Citrus Assoc.   Orange Heights Fruit Co.
Pearl St.
Jameson Packing House   Flagler Packing House
Corona Fruit Co.   Corona Lemon Packing House
Train Depot   Call Fruit Co.
6th St.   Orange Heights Fruit Assoc.
Sheridan St.
Joy St.
Washington School
Jefferson School   City Park
Grand Blvd.
St. Edwards Church   Lincoln School
Main St.
Magnolia
Ontario Ave.
(*Lemonia
Grove)
Jameson
Ranch
Jameson
Ranch
Lemon or Chase Dr.
Call
Corona Foothill   Ranch
Lemon Co.   (Foothill
Ranch)
Chase   Flagler Ranch
Plantation   (El Cerrito Ranch)

0   .5   1 Mile

than 14 percent of the normal quantity, Corona's fruit shipments remained at around 75 percent.[10]

While the region's subtropical climate favored the growth of Corona's citrus fruit industry, an efficient railroad system opened the gates to national markets. On June 30, 1887, the Atchison, Topeka and Santa Fe Railroad extended its line from Riverside to Corona. Soon thereafter, a Victorian-style depot was built north of Grand Boulevard and west of Main Street to provide passenger train service and carloads of fruit shipments to eastern markets. The first shipment in 1892 contained fruit wrapped in newspapers, with different sizes packed in one box. Early shipments suffered a loss due to spoiled fruit; it was not until the refrigerated boxcar was introduced in the mid-1890s that this problem was solved, saving the industry millions of dollars. By 1916, Corona was shipping more than four thousand carloads a year, becoming the leading shipper of lemon fruit.[11]

Although citrus growers had improved their shipping methods, they still faced new problems: destructive insects, rising shipping rates, the threat of overproduction, and marketing difficulties. While some of these issues brought citrus growers together to find common solutions, lemon growers also organized separately into clubs and advisory groups, claiming that unlike oranges, the lemon business was in its infancy and faced greater challenges in production, distribution, and marketing. By 1897 lemon shipments still languished below orange fruit shipments, thus prompting lemon growers to form the Lemon Growers Advisory Board within the Southern California Fruit Exchange (renamed the California Fruit Growers Exchange in 1905). According to the sales agent for the exchange, T. H. Powell, "The selling of lemons required special attention because the creation of a market was much more difficult than with oranges."[12]

American consumers considered California lemons, in comparison to oranges, a poor-quality fruit. With the introduction of the Eureka and Lisbon varieties in the 1880s, California lemons struggled to capture eastern markets. By the turn of the century, California lemons were still considered too big, carelessly bruised, and hastily packed. For this reason, they sold for less than one dollar a box in American fruit markets, whereas a box of Italian lemons sold for five to six dollars. Italian lemons commanded premium prices due to centuries of experience and monopoly of the fruit markets of New York City. The poor quality of California lemons was attributed to deficient curing methods.[13]

Eventually growers discovered that lemons, unlike oranges, had to be handled like "golden eggs." In 1891, G. W. Garcelon of Riverside developed an effective curing method that required lemons to be picked at intervals while still green and stored in cool, dry temperatures for four to five months or until they matured. In 1927 Italian lemon imports decreased to an all-time low of 734,000 boxes compared to 2.975 million in 1914, thus allowing California to capture a larger share of the U.S. lemon market. A 1956 *Saturday Evening Post* article declared lemons "California's Yellow Gold." It noted that the state was producing 32 million grocery-sized cartons per year—95 percent of the total national crop—with earnings reaching $60 million. Corona played a central role in making California the largest producer of "yellow gold" in the country.[14]

In order to produce superior-quality lemons that would satisfy the consumer, lemon growers needed to share information and educate themselves about new experiments and improved methods. At the recommendation of the exchange, managers of lemon associations formed the Lemon Men's Club (all-Anglo and all-male) with a five-dollar membership fee and a special levy of fifty cents per car of lemons shipped by its members. One grower described the Lemon Men's Club as "the oldest, most conservative and dignified of all the service organizations connected with the citrus industry in Southern California."[15]

Every year a lemon district hosted the Lemon Men's Club field day, which featured tours of packinghouses and groves, grower presentations on various topics related to lemons and labor issues, and a keynote speaker during lunch or dinner. The field day concluded with musical entertainment, a sporting event, or leisurely activity. The concluding feature at the 1921 Ontario Field Day meeting, for example, was a "classic" baseball game between the inland lemon growers and the coastal lemon growers in which the latter group won by one run. The following year, Corona growers hosted the meeting on the Jameson Ranch property. The daughters, mothers, and wives of the Corona men served a "delightful luncheon" with after-dinner entertainment provided by "a pretty Corona miss, who in Spanish costume, mantilla and all, served the guests with cigars, cigarettes and matches after the dinner."[16]

After Robert Taylor resigned as head of the South Riverside Land and Water Company, W. H. Jameson took over as company president to further develop the fruit colony. At the urging of his father-in-law, George Joy, Jameson left St. Louis in 1887 for California, accompanied by his wife, Hetty Joy Jameson, and young son, Joy Jameson. Following the unexpected death of his father in 1912, Joy Jameson took over the Jameson Ranch Company until 1955, managing more than six hundred acres of citrus plantings and a modern packinghouse that packed and shipped citrus fruit through the Sunkist brand. Considered "one of the large lemon growers of Southern California," Jameson served as president of the Queen Colony Fruit Exchange, the Lemon Men's Club, the Exchange Lemon Products Company, the Temescal Water Company, the First National Bank of Corona, and the Corona Chamber of Commerce and as director of the California Fruit Growers Exchange (CFGE). Apart from business and civic affairs, Jameson was active in the First Baptist Church, giving generously of his time and money and preaching the gospel to local Mexican and Italian populations.[17]

The Jameson Company and other California citrus growers faced problems shipping their fruit through agents who charged exorbitant prices, so they decided to pool and sell their fruit through the largest marketing cooperative in the world—the CFGE, forerunner of today's Sunkist Growers, Inc. The CFGE appointed its own fruit agents to represent its member-growers in eastern markets. This was an attempt to reduce risk, stabilize production, and increase profits in an unstable fruit industry where speculative buyers, overproduction, and overseas competition were constant threats. Apart from acting as a clearinghouse for individual growers, this agricultural cooperative, according to one researcher, "typified contemporary American business" and "followed the trend of consolidation, in size and control if not in ownership. Its aims, unstated of course, remained frankly monopolistic in the sense that it worked to control the price of citrus fruits throughout America."[18]

The cooperative marketing movement had spread to Corona with the creation of the Queen Colony Fruit Exchange. Before 1893, Corona growers hand-washed and packed their fruit at the Santa Fe Railroad depot and shipped it through the Riverside Fruit Exchange. A year later, the Queen Colony Fruit Exchange built the city's first packinghouse and then shipped its fruit under the Sunkist brand. The Queen Colony exchange acted as Corona's district exchange or local Sunkist representative that organized the shipment and marketing of the fruit worldwide. By 1905 the Queen Colony exchange represented the largest citrus companies in the city: Orange Heights Fruit Association, Corona Foothill Lemon Company, Corona Citrus Association, W. H. Jameson Company, and A. F. Call Association. "Suffice it to say," according to the *California Citrograph*, "the citrus industry and [Queen Colony] Exchange in Corona are practically synonymous."[19]

Despite improvements associated with cooperative marketing, California lemon profits remained stagnant until higher tariffs were erected against imports. At the turn of the century Sicily held a stranglehold on the world lemon market, resulting in fierce competition with California fruit. Italian imports accounted for 41.3 percent of U.S. lemon consumption in 1898. Through the Lemon Men's Club and the Citrus Protective League, California growers successfully lobbied Congress to impose protective tariffs against lemon imports.[20]

Protective tariffs made it possible for California lemon growers to gain a large share of the U.S. lemon market. California had supplied only 18 percent of U.S. lemon consumption in 1900, but this rose to 45 percent in 1910. By 1929 California supplied more than 80 percent of total U.S. lemon consumption, while less than 20 percent came from Italy. When President Herbert Hoover appointed California's most prominent lemon grower, Charles C. Teague, to the Federal Farm Board, the tariff on lemons increased to an all-time high of two and a half cents a pound under the 1930 Hawley-Smoot Tariff Act. This legislative victory prompted Teague to boast that "California's gain has been Italy's loss."[21]

While protective tariffs propelled California's lemon industry ahead, consumer demand for lemons remained low compared with the demand for oranges. Cool summers in the East and Midwest caused lemon prices to drop dramatically. With the exception of lemonade in hot weather, there was no day-to-day use for lemons, so growers developed by-products from surplus lemons to increase year-round consumption and lessen the impact of unfavorable weather. G. H. Powell, a former U.S. Department of Agriculture scientist and head of the Citrus Protective League, visited Sicily in 1908 to study by-product manufacturing, which involved converting lower-grade lemon fruit into citric acid, oil, food flavoring, and other products. The high profits generated from these lemon by-products won over Powell and other lemon growers. One of them, Joy Jameson, argued for a by-product plant to control shipments and stabilize a quirky fruit market. In June 1915 seventeen lemon growers met to form the Exchange By-Products Company; in 1921 they changed the name to Exchange Lemon Products Company to differentiate it from the orange by-products plant in Ontario. The founders converted a rickety Corona packinghouse owned by the Flagler Fruit Company into a technologically efficient processing plant handling more than six hundred tons of surplus lemons daily and generating more than $5.5 million in cash revenues per year. This figure increased dramatically in 1921 when Congress, citing high Italian government subsidies to the Italian lemon industry, imposed a twenty-cent tariff on Italian citric acid. According to the secretary of the Queen Colony Fruit Exchange, "Having this plant here should prove a valuable asset to both the growers and the city. Far too many low grade lemons were shipped out this season, returning nothing and only doing their share to ruin the market for the better class of stock, and a plant that can take care of cull and standard lemons and return a profit will certainly be a boom [*sic*] to the entire industry." In 1958 the name of the Corona plant changed to Lemon Products Division of Sunkist Growers, Inc., following the official merger with the fruit marketing cooperative.[22]

As the world's only completely integrated lemon processing plant, the Exchange Lemon Products Company helped Corona gain the title of "Lemon Capital of the World." In fostering the lemon by-products industry," the *Corona Independent* boasted, the "'Queen Colony' made its crowning bid for recognition as the most far-sighted of the citrus districts." Growers were encouraged to turn their culls into money by shipping their damaged or poor-quality fruit to the Corona plant. "The lemon industry will not be a complete industry until the entire production of the lemon tree is put to economic use," declared one exchange official. Joy Jameson explained: "By eliminating an increasing percentage of the low grade lemons from the market at a substantial return to the grower, I believe that the lemon product industry has achieved an important and almost indispensable position in the marketing of the California lemon crop." By 1934 lemon growers sent an average of 20 percent surplus to the by-products plant.[23]

Increased demand and the increasing cost of raw materials forced the plant to experiment with new by-products. In the early 1920s Stanford University graduate and biochemist Dr. Eloise Jameson, sister of Joy Jameson, helped develop and patent citrus pectin extracted from the white part of the lemon peel. It became widely used as a jelling agent for jams, jellies, and candies. In later years a wide variety of lemon juice products replaced the heavy manufacture of citric acid. In the mid-1940s, for example, the exchange introduced a frozen lemonade concentrate, Sunkist Lemonade. By the 1950s the Corona plant generated phenomenal sales in frozen lemonade (reaching more than seven million cases in 1953), giving Corona a new unofficial title, Lemonade Capital of the World.[24]

The by-products plant became the largest employer in town with more than two hundred permanent employees on its payroll, reaching one thousand employees in 1953 but dwindling to five hundred in the 1960s. The plant employed predominantly Anglo skilled professionals, including chemists, engineers, technicians, operators, and maintenance employees. Corona residents relied on the plant's whistle "to awaken them . . . to get them to work on time . . . or simply to check on their timepieces for accuracy." The plant whistle could be heard all over town, perhaps symbolizing the imposition of industrial time on the lives of laboring men and women.[25]

Apart from keeping lemon imports down and finding new uses for lemons, citrus growers faced the almost insurmountable task of increasing consumer demand for lemon products. Unlike sweet oranges, which are consumed day after day in large quantities, lemons proved difficult to sell to the ordinary consumer. Beyond making cold lemonade on hot summer days, new uses for lemons had to be invented; accordingly, ways were found to use lemons as a hair rinse, a food flavoring, a beauty product, and as remedies for scurvy and rheumatism. For this reason orange and lemon advertising were kept separate. Most lemon advertising was featured in magazines, newspapers, outdoor posters, streetcar cards, and fair exhibitions. One 1915 advertising campaign proposed "86 Ways to Use Lemons," and a *Saturday Evening Post* ad featured women wrapped in Sunkist Lemons. Another ad in *Ladies Home Journal*, titled "Why 1,000,000 Women Prefer California Lemons," promoted the use of lemons for mouth-watering pies and other dishes. Since 1907, the CFGE has used its trademark name, Sunkist, to sell citrus fruit, and the brand has become a household word. The Sunkist name, of course, suggested that the fruit has been "kissed" by California sunshine.[26]

Southern California growers sought to distinguish their fruit through colorful citrus crate labels that featured the brand name, the name of the individual grower or association, and the town or ranch where the fruit originated. Citrus fruit labels attached to the front side of rectangular boxes proved to be an effective modern advertising technique that began in the 1880s and lasted until the 1950s, when cardboard cartons replaced wooden boxes. The content and imagery of citrus labels also revealed degrading racial and gender stereotypes of Asian Americans, American Indians, African Americans, and Mexican Americans. For example, sleepy-eyed sombrero-wearing, peonlike Mexican male figures adorned the Santa Rosa, Troubadour, La Fiesta, and El Verrano labels. Other labels (Spanish Girl, La Paloma, Adios, Señorita, and La Reina brands) depicted dancing señoritas wearing low-cut dresses or short skirts and sporting wide lipstick smiles who resembled the stereotypical spicy, hot-blooded, untamable Latin temptress. Packed with racial, gender, and sexual meanings, citrus labels reinforced the paternalistic notion that Mexican men and women were in need of governance and management because of their supposed docile, childlike, and emotional attributes.[27]

Controlling Corona

The citrus industry's domination extended into the local community. The city's largest citrus concerns, Jameson Company and Corona Foothill Lemon Company, wielded strong influence in city politics and used their political clout to, among other things, keep competitors out of Corona. One local historian described how citrus growers kept seats on the Corona City Council, Chamber of Commerce, Planning Commission, School Board, and County Board of Supervisors filled with their representatives. This made it very difficult for "industries larger than 200 employees to come into the city to offer competition for the cheap unskilled Mexican American labor." A former Foothill packinghouse foreman, Mike Lunetta, reasoned that growers "tried to keep industry out because they paid more money, and they wanted them out because they brought unions." Following the lead of business promoters and manufacturing concerns in Los Angeles, Corona growers were intent on keeping Corona an "open shop" town.[28]

Citrus growers also delayed industrial development by controlling the city's water system. Formed in October 1897 to supply water for the city, the Corona City Water Company, according to one historian, "remained captive of the [citrus grower–dominated] Temescal Water Company, being controlled and owned by it . . . with 745 shares of capital stock." The Corona City Water Company remained under citrus grower control until voters approved a $4.2 million bond in 1964 so that the city could purchase the water company. This lack of competition for the lemon industry reinforced the dependence of the immigrant workforce on the town's growers and the jobs and services they provided.[29]

Jameson family members flexed their political muscles in city and county government. W. H. Jameson's brother, T. C. Jameson was elected to the board of supervisors for Riverside County in 1923 and for more than a decade was "very instrumental in furthering many of the really progressive movements of the county." T. C. Jameson helped build the Corona Public Library and a county hospital in Arlington and founded the Corona chapter of the Rotary Club. Following a family tradition, Joy Jameson's son, Charles Jameson, served as city councilman and mayor for Corona in the late 1950s and early 1960s and, because of his family connections, became the Republican Party nominee for U.S. Congress in 1960.[30]

Corona growers staffed the board of the city's chamber of commerce. First organized in 1915, the Corona Chamber of Commerce promoted the city's citrus industry through advertising and exhibit entries and by sponsoring talks on citrus-related topics. Every year the chamber was responsible for selecting and submitting Corona fruit exhibits for lemon competition at the National Orange Show in San Bernardino. The chamber also launched publicity campaigns to boost the city and attract potential citrus grove owners—for example, the 1923 campaign that targeted Los Angeles residents by exhibiting Corona fruit and city booklets in store windows. A Los Angeles resident became so enthralled with the city that he "wanted to know where Corona was and [what] opportunities [were] there," and after visiting the area he purchased a ten-acre orange grove and became a Sunkist grower. The directors elected Joy Jameson as president of the Chamber of Commerce in 1928 because of "his loyalty to the city." Upon his death in 1955, Joy Jameson was remembered as "a man of wide interests, including the fields of religion, education, agriculture and business, . . . [and] a constructive force for the welfare of this community."[31]

During the 1920s Corona growers founded and belonged to all-Anglo male lodges and fraternal organizations and country clubs. Chief among these were the Corona Rotary Club and Lions Club, dedicated to community service and civic projects including raising funds for a city park and recreational facilities. A popular gathering place for Corona growers was the Parkridge Country Club, located on a hill northeast of town, that catered to an all-Anglo male patronage. This exclusive resort first opened its doors in 1925 and was built in Spanish colonial revival style with a prominent tower and front arcades. It featured a hotel, an indoor spa, a clubhouse, a shooting range, an airfield for private planes, and the "finest championship golf course in the West." After careful inspection by the "bankers, business and the most conservative" and being "aware of the benefits that have accrued to our citrus belt through the world-wide reputation of [Riverside] Glenwood Mission Inn," Parkridge received the full endorsement of the Corona Chamber of Commerce because of "what this splendid enterprise means for the future of our Citrus Belt community."[32]

The exclusive resort lasted until August 1927, when the owner Dan Gilkey sold it to African American businessmen from Los Angeles. This transaction triggered a burning white cross in the front lawn of the Parkridge Country Club. The Ku Klux Klan appeared ready to wage a "race war" if the owner did not reconsider. Anglo club members responded by taking Gilkey to court to prevent "the club from falling into the hands of the negroes" and leaving "a black spot on Corona's forward progress." A legal fund was set up, according to the *Corona Inde-*

pendent. "Many responded last night and many more visited the First National Bank of Corona this morning where contributions of members and citizens may be received to aid in the fight of keeping the white spot white." The Ku Klux Klan used the cross burning to keep African Americans out of town and keep Mexicans in their place.[33]

At the onset of World War I a severe labor shortage, higher manufacturing wages in urban areas, and sporadic waves of labor unrest forced citrus growers to reconsider a new approach toward labor relations. "Substantial modifications had to be made in the industry's labor system," noted historian Cletus Daniel; "the alternative system that gained the widest support among employers was, at least to the extent that it contained distinct elements of paternalism, similar to those being developed in the manufacturing sector by pioneering welfare capitalists." Relaxed immigration restrictions and the importation of Mexican labor were part of the solution, but, according to one citrus official, "there is another side to the labor question that must be considered before we can expect to have a permanent labor supply, and that is the condition under which the laborer must live." Growers' concern for workers' living environment was also crucial toward maintaining an efficient and reliable labor force.[34]

Employers throughout the industrial world sought to use paternalist strategies to build worker loyalty and blunt labor unionism. Although widespread, welfare capitalism or corporate paternalism assumed multiple forms and varied according to industry type, the current labor situation, and local material and cultural contexts.[35] A highly personal style of management characterized the citrus industry's early history until the end of World War I when the CFGE institutionalized a system of welfare capitalism or corporate paternalism. The CFGE formed the Industrial Relations Department (IRD) in 1920 to study and resolve "labor problems" of the industry, especially in regard to "stabilizing employment and increasing the efficiency of labor." The general manager appointed George Hodgkin as IRD director due to his labor management experience with the Goodyear Tire and Rubber Company. The IRD resembled the Committee on Industrial Relations, established by the Hawaiian Sugar Planters' Association in the aftermath of the 1909 sugarcane strike and renamed the Social Welfare Department in 1919, to deal with matters of worker housing, sanitation, recreation, and medical care.[36]

The IRD offered permanent workers regardless of skill an array of welfare benefits that ranged from housing, recreation, medical care, elementary schools, and company store credit. The IRD publicized these nonwage incentives through speaking engagements at the California Citrus Institute and detailed articles in the *California Citrograph*, hoping the message would percolate down to packinghouse associations and citrus ranches. These benefits varied greatly and were implemented in a piecemeal fashion depending on the citrus-belt community, company size and number of employees, and the managerial philosophies of citrus growers. The expanded scope of these benefits thus required the cooperation of community centers, school districts, city nurses, women's club members, Americanization teachers, and settlement houses.

The CFGE housing program was one of the most popular because, according to the *California Citrograph*, "good housing pays." Entire housing tracts were built near packinghouses or on ranch property and varied from bunkhouses and dormitories to adobe or wood-built homes and small concrete cottages. The IRD supplied architectural plans, building materials, and floor plans; profiled "model" housing programs in *California Citrograph;* and worked closely with the California Commission of Immigration and Housing (CCIH) on developing housing projects for packinghouse associations in the San Gabriel and Pomona valleys. Some growers shook their heads, unconvinced "that [housing] would pay." A. D. Shamel, author of several *Citrograph* articles on employee housing, pointed out that "the employees work better than before. They stay on the job. They are satisfied and their families grow up under decent moral and physical surroundings and become useful and substantial citizens." Central to the housing schemes was the idea that disease-ridden, unsanitary dwellings would not only hurt job productivity but inhibited employees' ability to become disciplined workers and "better citizens."[37]

A central feature of citrus industry paternalism was the promotion of an idealized vision of "nuclear family," which prescribed that men become wage earners and heads of household and that women devote themselves to the household, taking care of their husbands and children. Such a strategy reinforced patriarchy and hegemonic heterosexual relations in the home.[38] Compared to married heads of households, single males lacked responsibility because they tended to drink, gamble, and engage in illicit sex. According to one ranch manager, "It was not long before we realized that unattached men of this [Mexican] nationality are not very dependable workmen." Corona growers believed that male employees needed to be domesticated, so they were required to be married to be eligible for a company home. As Joy Jameson described his ranch, "our regular ranch labor is mostly housed at two ranch headquarters and most of the regular help are married men. The houses for the ranch employees are all well constructed, equipped with modern plumbing, city water, electric lights and one group of houses is provided with gas for cooking and heating purposes." Jameson Company's "ideal of domesticity" prescribed for women a key role in forming nuclear-type families and ensuring a new generation of healthy semiskilled workers. As discussed in later chapters, a strict gender division extended into company recreation; males were offered baseball, sports clubs, and musical bands, whereas women received classes in child-rearing practices, health and sanitary activities, home economics, sewing, and gardening.[39]

Citrus growers built and operated citrus ranches with employee housing, schools, stores, and recreational facilities. Improvement and expansion of housing alone were not enough. "A Mexican cannot be satisfied merely by a good place to sleep," explained George Hodgkin. They "must have an outlet [that] would . . . express itself in the ordinary forms of social relaxation, recreation, entertainment, and perhaps in education." He advised ranch owners to provide garden plots, a local society, baseball teams, musical bands, a community center, and English instruction classes "to increase the physical and mental capacity of the workers for doing more work." Although they varied in size, demographics, management, and locality, the citrus ranches all followed strict codes of racial and gender segregation. As one citrus industry official admitted, "On large ranches . . . employees frequently live on the ranch, a separate camp or living quarters being provided for each nationality. The married men with families are given individual cottages while the single men live in dormitories."[40]

In the Corona area these ranches included Jameson Ranch, Call Ranch, El Cerrito Ranch, Chase Plantation, and Foothill Ranch. The first ranch to maintain a resident workforce was Chase Plantation, which resembled an "industrial plantation" in more than name only. Built in 1900 by Riverside citrus tycoon Ethan Allen Chase, the 1,300-acre ranch was the first large settlement of Mexican immigrants in the Corona area. The Chase Plantation consisted of 750 acres of citrus fruit, of which 500 were devoted to oranges and 250 to lemons. By calling his ranch a plantation Chase invoked the Southern plantation system, but instead of black slaves he relied on Mexican "help." Chase wrote in his diary: "I have bought the two arroyos running from Colton Avenue to the canal containing six acres and bought chiefly so we could locate our Mexican help down by the canal, out of the way, we will build adobe homes, pipe water from [the] Riverside domestic system to the place and make a respectable Mexican settlement." The "Mexican settlement" consisted of thirty-six adobe houses for families, each with one ten-by-ten-foot room and a six-by-ten-foot screened porch area. A dormitory for single Anglo men contained thirteen rooms and a clubroom, while six Victorian-style homes, each with a vegetable garden, were reserved for Anglo supervisors. The plantation's architectural design and spatial hierarchy suggested a kind of feudal relationship between Mexican workers and their Anglo supervisor.[41]

Archibald Shamel, a U.S. pomologist, praised the Chase Plantation in the pages of the *California Citrograph* for "providing comfortable adobe homes" for its Mexican workers "coming here from the state of Michoacan, in Central Mexico"; they "are good workers, faithful to any trust that may be reposed in them, and anxious to make their families happy and comfortable." Although housing on the Chase Plantation may have been an improvement over rural living conditions in Mexico, it was considered below minimum standards for the Anglo middle class. City nurse Mathilda Jacobson visited the "Mexican quarters" in the summer of 1919 and reported: "Here, conditions are not so favorable. The old barracks, which are all filled with Mexican families[,] may be good enough for Mexicans (in Mexico) but they should not be tolerated here."[42]

The absence of a city housing commission and the lack of political will on the part of the grower-controlled city council forced Jacobson to appeal to the leading state agency on housing and immigration, the CCIH, for assistance. Formed in 1913 in response to the labor upheavals and rising immigration that followed the opening of the Panama Canal, the CCIH investigated labor camp conditions throughout the state, but the commission's weak enforcement powers and the thinly veiled racism of Progressive politicians left labor camp conditions in the hands of growers. Leo Mott, chief labor camp inspector for the Los Angeles district office, responded to Jacobson's request by recommending a local solution. "I told Miss Jacobson that this was a condition to be remedied by the local authorities . . . but she stated that nothing in the way of enforcement could be expected from [city officials] on account of local politics." The failure of city and state officials left it up to Mexican residents to improve living conditions for themselves.[43]

The Foothill Ranch was another citrus plantation complete with a headquarters complex, a company store, company housing, stores, schools, and recreational facilities built and operated by the Corona Foothill Lemon Company, which was founded in 1911 by former Iowa native Samuel B. Hampton, who remained president until 1918 when he fell victim to the flu epidemic. Upon his father's death, son Robert

Lester Hampton took over ranch operations and remained company president until 1966 when his nephew, Edward Willits, took over. This sixteen-hundred-acre ranch was considered one of the largest citrus ranches in southern California, second only to the Limoneira Ranch near Santa Paula. Foothill held majority stock in the Temescal Water Company, which controlled water rights in the Corona vicinity.[44]

During the 1920s Foothill instituted welfare capitalist measures to recruit and keep workers on the premises and cultivate worker loyalty. Foothill built housing tracts for Mexican employees in four labor camps and two bunkhouses scattered throughout the ranch property. These "modern" single-family homes were built with concrete on a standard quarter-acre lot, with two bedrooms, a kitchen, and a living room. The largest of these was "Wash Camp," named after the Wash River that ran alongside the six rows of houses. Foothill's welfare offerings extended into the next two decades with a community center that offered an Americanization class, schooling for elementary-age children, and a baseball diamond, garden plots, and park for recreational use.[45]

Lester Hampton lived with his wife, Jessimine, in a small bungalow on the ranch property to closely manage daily operations and keep close surveillance on ranch employees. "The Ranch's remarkable staying power in a changing, modern world," according to *The Press-Enterprise*, "has to do with people—those who run and work on the ranch and their predecessors . . . from top management personnel to field workers."[46] Foothill's highly personal management style displayed elements of "familiar paternalism" characterized by personalized paternalist relationships, a family labor system, and subaltern forms of labor resistance. During an interview with Foothill president, Edward Willits, he discussed how three to four generations of the same Mexican family remained working for Foothill. The main reason, Willits admitted, was that "we were generally more paternalistic" than other citrus ranches. "Foothill has had the reputation of paying the highest wages and best housing around, certainly more comfortable, and a company store, a big store that stored beans. It was very helpful when there were tough times and [Mexicans] had immigration problems." Workers were not passive; instead, they actively negotiated their loyalty to the company within the physical and social constraints of the citrus plantation system.[47]

The Foothill Company offered its employee-residents generous credit at the commissary or company store. Built in 1927, the small store began as a general store stocking shelves with canned food, fruits and vegetables, picking gloves, and other job-related equipment. During the 1940s, the store expanded to include a meat market, dry goods, and a clothing line, resembling a "real department store." While these amenities seemed to offer workers' families many benefits, especially those who did not own an automobile, they also served as instruments of labor control. An employee number assigned to each family allowed them to purchase produce, meats, canned food, beans, rice, and other groceries on credit; two weeks later the amount was deducted from their paychecks. This kept many workers indebted and unable to accumulate enough savings to move out. "A lot of people took out too much and did not have anything left," remembered one former resident. "Every two weeks they would deduct from the paycheck and my brothers would never get any money, instead they would get pink slipped." Because families could easily find themselves in a web of chronic indebtedness, residents used store credit judiciously or relied on the extended family network for small loans. Many preferred instead to shop for groceries in the town's business district.[48]

Before Corona was founded as a fruit colony during the 1880s "great boom," the inland valley was populated by Indian tribes who faced successive waves of foreign invaders, arriving first from the South and then from the East. When Anglo colonists entered southern California, they brought with them Christian temperance values, white supremacist beliefs, and Victorian ideals of manhood. The group of Iowa businessmen, portrayed as "sterling pioneers from Iowa" in the *Golden Circle* play, were not poor migrants. "The colony was never a poor colony," Janet Williams Gould admitted in a 1961 newspaper interview, "though the pioneers encountered many difficulties in establishing the town. Well-to-do men took up the options on the land . . . the community was not colonized by poor immigrants as in the case of some sections of the United States. All have been business men of some means."[49]

Unlike Los Angeles and San Francisco, all of which had diversified economies, Corona was founded as a one-industry town. Lemons, and to a lesser extent oranges and grapefruit, were Corona's reason for being. Corona's interior valley district and Santa Paula coastal district were the two largest lemon-producing sections of southern California. Lemons dominated the local economies of both citrus towns, but Corona claimed the world's only lemon by-products plant. In 1915 Corona boasted more than five thousand acres of citrus plantings, divided among seven ranches and fourteen packinghouses, and shipped upwards of 1,500 carloads of fruit. The same year the world's only lemon by-products plant opened in Corona to process surplus lemons. By 1946 fruit carloads reached 11,168, the third largest in Corona's history. As a result of these developments, Corona became the leading shipper and producer of lemon fruit in the state, boosting itself as the Lemon Capital of the World.[50]

Corona growers belonged to the all-Anglo male business club, the Lemon Men's Club, to share industry secrets, tour different lemon-growing districts, and promote the lemon business to governments from the local to federal levels. Club members strived to fulfill the ideals of the "self-made man" who, according to Michael Kimmel, displayed self-control, economic autonomy, and individual achievement in the business world. Through their field day meetings they displayed their knowledge of the citrus business, savored delicious luncheons prepared by the wives of local growers, and for entertainment listened to musical performances or showed off their athletic prowess at baseball games. These get-togethers mirrored racial and gender relations within the citrus industry, in which Anglo women were relegated to subordinate roles and nonwhites were rendered invisible.[51]

Corona growers exercised undue influence in city government, schools, and churches, making city residents politically and economically dependent upon the citrus industry. A primary objective for growers was to prevent manufacturing companies from setting up shop and bringing higher wages and labor unions to the city. Like single-industry towns elsewhere, Corona was run by owners of the largest citrus interests, the Jameson Company and the Foothill Lemon Company. "These citrus families have formed a tight social group with a very distinct WASP characteristic," wrote one local historian. "They control the money in town and thus have been able to influence the development of the city."[52]

Citrus growers fashioned paternalistic strategies to keep labor unions at bay and win worker loyalty. With the assistance of the IRD, Corona growers built single-family homes for married male workers and offered a wide variety of social and cultural activities to educate, entertain, and distract workers during their leisure hours. Although these paternalistic measures varied in size and degree, depending on management styles and local conditions, they nonetheless permeated all levels of the citrus industry. A more personalized form of corporate paternalism emerged in citrus ranches such as the Foothill Ranch, in which management attempted to reform workers' everyday habits, control relations between men and women, and promote racial and class harmony.

The profitable Corona citrus industry relied on immigrant workers, mainly from Mexico and Sicily, who were recruited and incorporated into a labor market stratified by race and gender. Without the invaluable contributions of immigrant laborers, the town's citrus industry would not have experienced such tremendous growth during the first half of the twentieth century. In spite of the citrus industry's dominance in this racially segregated city and countryside, Mexicans created their own separate worlds in the Corona barrio.

2 Red, White, and Greening of Corona

In the early morning of July 19, 1915, Carmelita Toledo and Antonio Corselli secretly drove to the city of Riverside, California, to get married at the county courthouse. A native of Michoacán, Mexico, Toledo had arrived in 1911 with her family and settled in Corona's north-side barrio, two doors down from the house at 140 Merrill Street where Antonio Corselli lived with his brother, Mimi, and father, Nicolas. Recruited in 1903 from Palermo, Sicily, for their lemon-packing expertise, the Corsellis were the first Sicilian family to settle in the city and worked in the bustling packinghouse district. After a short honeymoon, the newlywed couple returned to Corona's barrio and to their work at the Jameson Company, where they first met.[1]

Seven years later a newspaper article reported that Carmelita had filed for divorce on the grounds of "extreme cruelty" and pleaded to the court for "judgment granting her custody of her four-year-old son [Joe] who [was] one of three children, and her maiden name." Court transcripts revealed more details about their turbulent marriage. Carmelita alleged that Antonio "violently struck her in the face with his fist, pinched and twisted her arms and ran her out of the house and in a loud and boisterous manner cursed and called her a *'dammed cholo'* and numerous other vile names." She added that Antonio would spend more time in the city's pool halls than with his family and "would only ridicule the people of her race and curse and swear at her." Although he admitted having been "guilty of extreme cruelty at times," he denied all allegations and instead filed a cross-complaint accusing Carmelita of "absconding and eloping in company with one Pete Aguilar" and "kidnapping and abducting their child and [being] a fugitive from justice." Since she was not a U.S. citizen or legal resident, Carmelita failed to appear in court for fear of deportation, so the judge ruled in favor of Antonio, granting him custody of the three children and the home property. It is unclear whether Carmelita ever reappeared with their son Joe in Corona or returned to fight for custody. The 1930 census records, however, do reveal that Antonio remarried an Anglo woman and lived in the same residence with his two sons from his previous marriage and a new daughter and stepson.[2]

This story of interethnic marriage that ended in a bitter divorce reveals much about the broader forces that brought Italian and Mexican immigrants together in highly personal relationships as both neighbors and coworkers in the city of Corona. In the first two decades of the twentieth century, immigrants from Mexico and Sicily arrived in Corona seeking relief from economic and political disruption in their homelands and a chance to better their lives. Husbands and wives such as Carmelita and Antonio often worked for the same citrus company, but women stayed home to raise children, making them dependent on husbands' wages. But when these wages were spent in pool halls and saloons, it contributed to domestic conflicts. For Carmelita at least, violence against women was linked to the predominantly male leisure culture in town. Ultimately, these new immigrants who sought economic stability and full acceptance were pulled apart by shifting institutional and ideological forces—demographic changes, intensified racialization, and economic marginalization. As later chapters will show, these forces restricted the opportunities of Mexican immigrants to gain upward social mobility, unlike Italians whose "white" privilege contributed toward a higher economic and residential mobility.

In their quest for economic stability during the first three decades of the twentieth century, Mexican and Italian immigrants searched for the best agricultural jobs they could find. Upon finding stable work in Corona's citrus industry, some settled into company homes in outlying citrus ranches, and others moved into the Mexican barrio and the Italian neighborhood, on the north side of town. The culture of segregation that characterized this town limited employment opportunities outside agriculture and constrained public spaces for community organizing, yet the citrus grower elite did not exercise absolute power over immigrant lives. Mexican and Italian immigrants relied on family, kinship,

and neighborhood ties to fashion a vibrant community life and managed
to turn segregation into a form of congregation whereby they developed
their own separate institutions, organizations, and leisure activities.

changed segregation

Leaving the Homeland

During the latter part of the nineteenth century, U.S. financial capital
subjected Mexico to economic domination and produced a migratory
surplus population that first moved into cities and then headed northward, crossing over into the United States. One of the first disruptions
was the displacement of thousands of *arrieros* (muleteers) who could no
longer compete with an extensive railroad network. Such was the case
for Julio Cruz, a professional muleteer who routinely left his wife and
three sons behind in Puruandiro, Michoacán, and traveled long dis-
tances across the countryside selling wheat, corn, and other merchan-
dise and bringing news and information to isolated villages. As railroad
transportation gradually made travel by mule packs obsolete, Cruz left
Mexico in 1905 to take his chances at finding work across the border in
the expanding industries of the Southwest.[3]

Upon arrival Cruz immediately entered the world of the common
laborer—mostly unskilled, continually mobile, underpaid male workers
of rural origin who constituted a significant, yet often overlooked and
exploited, sector of the American labor force. Between 1905 and 1909
Cruz traveled back and forth across the border without inspection from
immigration authorities, living for three months in Mexico and then
returning to pick lemons in Corona, California, for the remaining
months of the year. However, when Julio Cruz's wife died unexpectedly,
he returned home to bury her and decided to bring his sons to the United
States. In 1910, all three sons arrived safely in Los Angeles, then traveled
by car to the city of Corona. The youngest son, Luis Cruz, was surprised
to find so many familiar faces from his hometown in Mexico. "I found
out that a lot of old friends came from Michoacán to Corona. They
would write to each other and say hey, life is good here, and they would
come over. My dad would bring his *compadres* from the Rio Lerma area
. . . they all knew each other." These established social networks from
the same Mexican village served an important function, helping new-
comers find job connections, housing, and a home-cooked meal.[5]

Mexican immigrants relied on an extended social network that
comprised cousins, aunts, uncles, and *comadres* and *compadres* (or co-
parents) and served as the basis of support during economic hard times.

*Borders are never regulated * now (running) do not have actual border.*

Through *compadrazgo*, a system of godparentage that extended beyond immediate kin, men and women found jobs within the citrus industry and strengthened their community ties. Families and friends who originated in the same area of Mexico reunited in southern California's citrus belt towns and in some cases solidified their ties by marrying off their sons and daughters.[6]

These early Mexican immigrants who arrived in Corona were mostly single or married men, often termed "solos," who traveled back and forth without the presence of women or heterosexual family. They created a "fraternal culture" that facilitated male friendships that in turn helped them adjust to new surroundings.[7] In most cases, however, men were not alone but journeyed with other male members of their extended families; if this was not an option, they created fictive kin networks that reinforced ties to a common town, region, or state of origin. Typically understood as "genderless beings," immigrant solos lived in all-male bunkhouses, dormitories, or other makeshift housing arrangements. The absence of women tested traditional masculine roles, since some solos necessarily performed "women's work" such as cooking meals and washing clothes.[8]

Single mothers or women unaccompanied by a man who endured the long journey often encountered suspicious immigration agents but ultimately found a way to cross the border. In 1926, Juanita Ramírez found her mother crying with excitement as she read a letter from her father telling her to make plans to leave Yuerecauro, Michoacán, with their three children for the move to Corona. Ramírez recounted the humiliating experience of medical inspection at the border inspection station. "We were separated from my mother and told to undress by male [immigration] officials and passed through some foul-smelling showers." In order to screen out potential carriers of diseases, officials forced immigrants to strip naked for inspection and delousing before they were allowed to cross the border. In the words of Ramírez, "We were showered with disinfected water to kill any germs in our body or lice in our hair. . . . My mother [was] crying with embarrassment."[9]

With war breaking out in Europe, agricultural employers faced severe labor shortage that led to a wartime emergency program to recruit workers from Mexico and a successful campaign to weaken the provisions (literacy test and eight-dollar head tax) of the 1917 Immigration Act.[10] According to the U.S. census, the Mexican population of the United States (those who were Mexican-born and those who were natives of the United States with Mexican-born parents) rose from

382,000 in 1910 to 730,400 by 1920. Succeeding immigration quota restrictions in 1921 and 1924 did little to impede the outflow of workers from Mexico. Between 1920 and 1930, the number of people counted by the U.S. census as "Mexican" reached almost 1.5 million; this new racial category created by the Census Bureau also included people born in the United States to Mexican parents. The number of Mexicans in Corona followed a similar trajectory. In 1900, Mexican-born residents made up a mere 79 of the city's total population of 1,434. Ten years later, the census revealed 427 Mexicans out of 3,540 city residents. Not until the 1920s did the numbers increase significantly, from 1,281 in 1920 to 2,456 in 1930, and 2,824 in 1940.[11]

Like their Mexican counterparts, Italian immigrants used labor migration as a survival strategy, first taking part in seasonal migration within the country and later to the United States. During the latter part of the nineteenth century and early part of the twentieth century, rural peasants from Sicily and southern Italy were leaving their rural villages to escape poverty, hunger, and political corruption caused by economic dislocation in the southern countryside. Nicolas Corselli, father of Antonio whose marriage to Carmelita ended in a bitter divorce, was one of these peasants living under intolerable economic conditions in the Sicilian countryside. After the United States cut off imports of Italian citrus fruit, the Sicilian lemon industry, considered the world's leading lemon producer at the turn of the century, suffered a jarring blow. Sicily's ruined export economy convinced Corselli to consider an offer made by a California citrus recruiter, and in 1901 Corselli left Palermo to work in the Arlington Heights Citrus Company packinghouse in Casa Blanca, near Riverside; he then moved to Corona to work for the Jameson Company packinghouse. Soon thereafter, Corselli began recruiting other *paesani* (countrymen) to join him, telling them that "things are better in Corona than they are in Sicily."[12]

California was one of the main destinations for Italian immigrants, where an expanding agricultural and fishing industry and a more tolerable racial climate opened more opportunities to achieve "success in the sun."[13] California's Italian population remained small until the early 1900s, when the population experienced its fastest growth. By 1920, California's foreign-born Italian population (86,610) roughly equaled the foreign-born Mexican population (88,502). But the Immigration Act of 1924 restricted immigration from southern and eastern Europe, halting the growth of the Italian foreign-born population, while Mexican immigration continued unabated. Compared to other California cities,

Corona's Italian population, mostly from Sicily, remained relatively small. There were 140 Italian-born residents in 1910, 170 in 1920, 227 in 1930, and 917 in 1940.[14]

Women left behind in Sicily struggled to feed their families until they could garner enough savings to make the long journey overseas. In 1911, Carmela Danieri packed up her most prized belongings and her two daughters and boarded a ship for the two-week voyage to Ellis Island. While she went through customs, someone stole her luggage; she could not get any assistance since she did not speak English. However, she managed to board a passenger train to Los Angeles and upon arrival reunited with her husband after two years of separation. Soon thereafter Carmela joined other Italian women in Corona's packinghouse, grading and packing citrus fruit for piece-rate wages and working alongside relatives.[15]

Working at Homes, Groves, and Packinghouses

Corona growers possessed great wealth but had very little experience in the production of lemon fruit, so they began recruiting male pruners and female packers from southern Italy, mainly from the island of Sicily. Sicilians were highly regarded as skilled lemon experts, with "knowledge handed down from their fathers." As one Corona grower explained, "The Italians were brought over to teach the Chinese how to pack lemons in the field . . . [and] almost all of the early Italian immigrants were thorough professionals in the packing business." One of the first recruits was John Triolo, hired in 1898 by the Flager Fruit Packing Company and described as "an enterprising, broad gauged, sociable gentleman."[16]

Italian immigrants were preferred over Asian workers due to their "white manhood." As one Corona citrus grower observed, "A Jap came here [to Corona] from L.A. and rented a building on West 6th Street to start a pool hall and an employment agency. He never got his stuff unloaded at the depot. Corona was a white man's town. The first foreigner to come to Corona was an Italian, [and] no objection was made to him. He at least was a white man." In January 1905 a group of Japanese pickers were attacked by a white mob, thrown into wagons, and transported back to Riverside. Energized by an anti-Japanese movement that pressured legislators to halt Japanese immigration and take away their land and citizenship rights, and fearing the rising power of Japanese contractors, Anglo Coronans demanded the immediate expulsion of the "Japanese race." Corona's Italian immigrants benefited from a "white" color status that put them socially above Asian immigrants.[17]

With the expulsion of Asian workers from the orchards, Corona growers increasingly turned to Mexican immigrant men to fill the lowest-paying and most physically demanding field jobs in the citrus industry. In the words of the secretary of the Queen Colony Fruit Exchange, "[We] need this Exchange to sign a contract with the United States Immigration Service, covering the importation of Mexicans for use in our [citrus] groves." Mexican immigrant men rarely were promoted into supervisory positions but remained classified as unskilled suitable only for "field labor" or "ranch labor." The term "ranch laborer" was widely used among citrus growers to refer to arduous jobs inside the orchards that included picking, irrigation, fumigation, and smudging. By contrast, citrus officials situated native Anglos and Italians as a skilled labor force mainly concentrated in packinghouse-related jobs such as grading, sorting, and transporting fruit.[18]

Scholars have documented the highly racialized division of labor in California's agricultural system and the racial ideologies that constructed Mexican immigrant men as cheap, docile, tractable, and biologically and culturally predisposed for "stoop" labor.[19] Citrus growers reproduced and mobilized these racialized constructions to ensure a plentiful labor supply and justify Mexicans' subordinate position within the industry.[20] Speaking before the Lemon Men's Club, George P. Clements, head of the Los Angeles Chamber of Commerce, explained why "the Mexican peon" was best suited for picking work over Asian and Anglo laborers. "He is the result of years of servitude, has always looked upon his employer as his *padron*. . . . He is strictly honest, thoroughly responsible and considerate of his employer's property." Clements urged lemon growers to establish a kind of patron-peon relationship with their Mexican male employees to ensure a reliable workforce entirely under growers' control.[21]

The formation of Corona's citrus labor force began in the early 1900s with the employment of Mexican male immigrants in the orchard fields. By 1920, according to city census figures, more than 80 percent of Mexicans in Corona were "ranch laborers," followed by 2.8 percent who were "teamsters/truck drivers," and 2.5 percent who were "railroad yard laborers." The majority of ranch laborers were pickers, but when there was not enough fruit on the trees to pick, they planted new trees, dug ditches, and fumigated and irrigated the orchards. In terms of wages, ranch pickers were paid less than packinghouse association pickers. According to the U.S. Immigration Department, Mexican pickers employed by the packinghouse association earned $2.25 to $2.50 for a nine-hour day and only worked on a seasonal basis, whereas ranch pickers earned from $1.50 to $1.80 for a ten-hour day and worked on a year-round basis.[22]

During the 1920s citrus employers sensed that recruiting family men both restricted the mobility of labor and ensured a new generation of workers. Growers' policies encouraged families to introduce their children to citrus packing at a young age, scrutinize their children's work behavior, and train them to become disciplined and obedient workers. In picking work, for example, fathers and sons often worked together to increase family earnings. On weekends, after school, and during school vacations young boys between eight and fifteen years old—dubbed *ratas*—accompanied their fathers' crews into the groves. Without work permits or job protections, *ratas* worked under their fathers' picking numbers, helping fill the fathers' field boxes to augment the day's wages.[23]

As young boys reached adulthood, they received their own picking number and crew assignment, and if married and still living on ranch property, they obtained their own company home. Joining a picking crew meant becoming an independent wage earner. Each picking crew, or *cuadrilla*, was composed of twenty-five to thirty-five men. The crews assembled early in the morning either at the main ranch headquarters or in front of the packinghouse, waiting for the bus to transport them to the assigned groves. On rainy and foggy mornings, workers often had to wait three to four hours until the dew evaporated from the fruit. During this "wet time" workers were not compensated for waiting, and in later years this became a main grievance among citrus pickers who attempted to organize a union. Workers returned ten hours later with huge calluses and sometimes even dislocated shoulders. Only veteran pickers who displayed loyalty to the company were promoted as crew leaders.[24]

Being careful not to bruise the fruit, pickers injured themselves instead. Natividad Cortez recalled the unbearable conditions in the hot climate of the Inland Empire. "Since the trees had thick thorns we had to wear long-sleeve shirts and denim pants, along with gloves, a fruit sack and a gallon of water." Picking work required great physical strength as well as a significant level of skill and knowledge of the precise size of fruit to be plucked. Orchard workers also experienced frost-bitten hands, gas poisoning from chemicals and pesticides, sprained backs and broken arms from ladder falls, and a host of other injuries.[25]

Smudging was one of the work activities that generated the most complaints. When the temperature fell below thirty-three degrees Fahrenheit, the ranch foreman would summon all resident workers in the middle of the night to light up smudge pots one by one. The work-

Smudging

ers inhaled sooty black smoke and returned home with black faces and the clinging odor of crude oil. Frances Martínez remembered the harsh, freezing nights at the Foothill Ranch when her husband had to go smudging in the middle of the night. "They would come and bang and bang like the police from door to door to wake you up. . . . You hear about the haciendas in Mexico—well this is no different." Smudging revealed a patron-peon relationship commonplace in Mexican haciendas and citrus plantations in California.[26]

The California Fruit Growers Exchange Field Department implemented a bonus system for pickers to increase output with minimal injuries to the fruit. Before a bonus of ten cents per box was paid, workers had to pick a minimum of forty field boxes with less than 1 percent of defective fruit.[27] At times *cuadrillus* competed against each other to demonstrate which crew was physically strongest and most productive, thus increasing the overall output of each crew. During the remaining months of the peak season (January to March) workers teamed up, selected a set of six or seven trees, and produced at least ten to fifteen boxes per set, with each worker taking credit for half the boxes filled. This method, according to Santos Garcia, was known in Spanish as *vamos a hacer una vaca* (let's make a cow). "In order not to walk with the ladder, water, and half a bag of lemons, we paired up and helped each other out." Although this method fostered teamwork and mutual solidarity among workers, it also acquiesced to the company's incentive system.[28]

Inside the all-male orchard terrain, pickers built a masculine work culture by vesting their pride and honor in hard physical labor and ability to endure dangerous working conditions. The masculine "picking culture" was not only expressed in a shared language filled with storytelling, proverbs, gossip, or vulgar jokes but also in physical gestures, incessant horseplay, and illicit behavior. Frank Salgado related a common expression used in the orchards: "When I showed up to help my dad after school, he would holler '*Hay ropa pendida*' [laundry is hanging on the clothesline], which meant watch your mouth, my kid is around. You know how men are when they work together." This warning to refrain from foul language in the presence of young boys or women used a specific idiom, incomprehensible to outsiders.[29]

Pickers engaged in illicit activities—drinking, gambling, and fighting—that were tolerated by management, but when these activities threatened job performance violators were readily dismissed. According to a ranch supervisor, "When the orchards were wet [pickers] played some kind of Mexican poker. I didn't understand it, but they had a big time with it." Not all male pickers took part in this popular pastime. Reynaldo Aparicio was typical of citrus pickers who started working at a young age, dreamed of better job opportunities, and therefore chose to use the wet time for better purposes. Aparicio explained: "Whenever it was too wet to pick a lot of the guys would play cards. But I would stay in the car and read." Aparicio and other young pickers faced a manly workplace culture that prized physical prowess, foul language, and rough behavior as expressions of the pickers' independent will in the face of the harsh demands imposed on them.[30]

Pickers developed a "rough" masculine culture typically found in workplaces where dangerous and physically arduous work is mainly performed by unskilled male laborers. One ranch foreman's daughter related an incident in which her father broke up a knife fight between two pickers. "After disarming two Mexican pickers, taking their switchblade knives from them, he realized there might be a time when he wouldn't be able to convince them to give up and go home without their knives [so] he asked to be made Deputy Sheriff, and for years he wore a badge pinned inside his jacket." Although this characterization verges on ethnic stereotypes of Mexican men as knife-wielding bandits, it reveals the tightly controlled and exploitative work environment that dominated their existence. In other cases, workers directed their anger toward supervisors by cursing, quitting, or engaging in a physical confrontation.[31]

Mexican women's work inside the home was crucial for the survival of pickers and entire families. As husbands carried heavy fruit sacks on their shoulders six days a week for ten hours at a time, wives shouldered the burden of childbearing, child rearing, cleaning, healing, and keeping house as well as putting food on the table and clean clothes on children's backs. Before sunrise, the men woke up to the sound of rolling pins pounding the *masa* (corn dough) on the table and the smell of fresh corn tortillas on the *comal* (flat cooking pan). "I remember getting up to go work with my dad and it was still dark," recalled one grateful son, "yet my mom was already up making tortillas and beans and she made the best burritos for our lunch." The daily ritual of cooking and packing a lunch for their husbands and sons was no minor undertaking for women who lived on citrus ranches. Women's household chores and caring for the family performed in private spaces took up most of the day and often went unrecognized by the larger community.[32]

Women's unpaid work extended beyond the house to front and back yards where they planted vegetables, fruit trees, and herbs to nourish and heal family members. Women who lived at citrus ranches used gardens as a survival strategy, however, to lessen their dependence on the company store, selling fruit and vegetables to make some extra money. At the Foothill Ranch, each household received a small garden plot for flowers and vegetables. Ruth Cortez, for example, spent many afternoons in the garden sowing, weeding, irrigating, and harvesting crops. "The [company] gave us all a plot of land for vegetable gardens, and provided the water to irrigate. We had so many vegetables and all the families who wanted a plot had one. We had better vegetables than the [Foothill] store." The garden not only allowed women to make a little extra money but also provided them with a social and cultural space for forming new friendships and save a little extra money. Even so, the hand of company management was never far off. As Cortez recalled, "We grew the most beautiful banana squashes. But one day my big squash was missing. Later I found out it was one of the bosses. He took it and [they] divided [it] among themselves."[33]

To complement family incomes women did laundry, ironing, cleaning, and cooking for wealthy Anglo families. As an underregulated, underpaid, and physically and emotionally draining occupation, domestic work was one of the few jobs available for Mexican immigrant women. At the young age of fifteen, Juanita Ramírez worked for the Willits and Jameson families as a housekeeper, sweeping and scrubbing floors, dusting furniture, washing clothes, and attending to the children's needs. As a live-in caretaker for more than ten years, Martínez faced low wages, arduous chores, and emotionally draining work. Although she received "free room and board," the duties of "emotional labors" were taxing, especially when her female employer passed away, leaving two children to be cared for around the clock. Guadalupe Delgadillo was typical of many live-out house cleaners who labored in Anglo homes after school and on weekends. After performing a dizzying array of tasks, her employer still questioned her work ethic. Delgadillo recounted: "I was on my hands and knees waxing the floor when I heard one of the white ladies tell another lady, 'Don't you think the women down south [in Mexico] work a lot harder than they do here [in the United States]?'" Deeply offended by this remark, Delgadillo quit immediately and later found a job as a packer in the Orange Heights Association packinghouse.[34]

Women packinghouse workers played a central role in the successful development of California's citrus industry.[35] According to a 1939 survey of citrus packinghouses conducted by the Women's Bureau of the U.S. Department of Labor, more than 65 percent of 7,400 employees in California's citrus packinghouses were women. According to 1920 census figures, a majority of Corona's packinghouse workforce consisted of

Anglo women (225) and Italian women (50), and Mexican-origin women (27). A decade later the number of Mexican women doubled to 47, and by 1940 it peaked to more than 150. Women were highly concentrated in the grading, sorting, and packing job categories, whereas box-making, loading, maintenance, office work, and supervisory positions were reserved for men. Full-time packers worked long hours during peak months, and "seasonal" employees worked part-time throughout the year and were often unemployed during slow periods. In terms of wages, women packers earned an average of $1.50 to $2.00 per day in piece-rate wages. Women graders earned an hourly wage but did not exceed $2.50 per day.[36]

Once the fruit was unloaded onto conveyer belts and cleaned up by washing machines, female graders separated different sizes and grades of fruit, which were then mechanically stamped with the brand. Then, female packers—using eye-hand coordination, speedy and agile fingers, and sharp eyesight—carefully wrapped the fruit with tissue and placed it inside a standard box ready for shipment. Despite the long hours and low pay, women remained in the same job because of the close friendships they developed over time. As Teresa Enríquez tells us, "We used to work next to each other and be talking away. Sometimes we could not talk [because] the fruit was coming so fast that we would lose concentration." Through informal socializing and lunch room rituals, packers helped developed a "work culture" that sometimes crossed ethnic lines and made possible collective forms of resistance.[37] women were close

Hoping to build a loyal workforce, company management promoted the work culture of women by sponsoring picnics, birthdays, and Christmas parties. Additionally, packinghouse supervisors selected the fastest female packers to participate in competitive packing contests at the National Orange Show in San Bernardino. Although supervisors intended to show off their "prized packers" to rival packinghouses, women packers participated for their own reasons. At fourteen years old in 1929, Alice Rodríguez quit junior high school and got a job at the Foothill packinghouse with the help of her older sister, who trained her and watched over her. After six years, Alice packed faster than her sister and was soon competing at the National Orange Show. "I won first prize for the fastest one and neatest packer," Alice proudly recalled. Apart from gaining enormous respect from coworkers, winning first prize was also an acknowledgment of her determination and hard work. The company also benefited from these packing contests by increasing productivity.[38]

Conflict also developed among the packinghouse workforce. "At the conveyor belt we made friends," remarked one ex-packer. "But you also had women with lots of *chisme* [gossip] and those that kept a grudge." Women's friendships went sour when hurtful gossip spread across the packinghouse floor like wildfire. Interethnic rivalries also emerged between Mexican and Italian women. "There was one Italian woman with dark and curly hair who thought she was really something," recalled Frances Martínez. "She said that Mexicans were really dark. . . . I turned around and told her that she looked more African than Italian . . . [and] she was stunned that I understood Italian [language]." Resentment against Italian packers also emerged because of perceived favoritism from Italian supervisors.[39]

Making New Homes

Mexican immigrant solos arriving to the Corona area during the first two decades of the twentieth century settled into company bunkhouses in one of the five citrus ranches (Jameson Ranch, Chase Plantation, Foothill Ranch, El Cerrito Ranch, and Call Estate Ranch). According to inspection reports of labor camps, there were eight bunkhouses with more than one hundred Mexican male occupants scattered throughout Corona's citrus ranches. Each wooden bunkhouse contained three to four large rooms with bunk beds, a toilet and shower, and minimal facilities for cooking. These all-male bunkhouses, often termed "Mexican solo camps," were physically separated from "Mexican family camps." Compared to the heterosexual nuclear family, solos were viewed as dysfunctional and potentially dangerous. As one ranch manager put it, "Much cannot be said for the single men who have no local family ties. It is to this class that the lawless, inefficient, and unreliable usually belong."[40]

Although immigrant solos traveled, worked, and lived alone, they also sometimes brought their children. Such was the case for Julio Cruz, who brought his two boys after he lost his wife and lived in bunkhouses for several years. Some men paid local women to do their laundry and frequented restaurant-bars in town for hot meals. Immigrant solos also rented rooms in downtown rooming houses or stayed with relatives. Immigrant solos performed the bulk of picking work until they earned enough to bring their wives and children and settle into a company home.[41]

Mexican families had few housing options upon their arrival, so a company home proved to be a mixed blessing. Company housing at the

Chase Plantation offered Esperanza Olvera and her family a chance to remain together, even though it lacked basic amenities. She recalls: "There were adobe homes in two rows, separated by a wall, with only one big bedroom and a small kitchen. In the middle, there were big washbasins to wash the clothes." Olvera complained about the small amount of water supplied by the company, and with no transportation available she had to walk a half-mile to the nearest arroyo to fetch buckets of water. There was also very little privacy for women because, according to Olvera, "One communal shower room had to be shared by all the women." In the face of harsh living conditions and constant surveillance by company management, women managed to keep their families together and survive until they could find better job opportunities and move into town.[42]

Many preferred to rent or buy a home in the Corona barrio because of a lesser degree of company intervention. The Mexican barrio was made up of a cluster of neighborhoods in the northeast and northwest quadrants inside the circle and several smaller ones outside the circle. The earliest settlement, "La Sección," sprang up in the early 1900s near the Santa Fe Railroad yard, where many unattached railroad workers lived in boxcars along Blaine and Harrison streets. Another small neighborhood evolved along Quarry Street, sandwiched between the city park on the south and the Pacific Electric Railroad tracks on the north. Residents commonly referred to this neighborhood as "La Garra" because of the outdoor clotheslines that dotted the yards of homes. On the eastern side of the circle, a cluster of single-family homes on Buena Vista Street made up "El Jardin," named for the beautiful flower gardens that flanked each home. In the 1920s, two larger neighborhoods emerged in the northwest and northeast quadrants, bounded by the packinghouses on the north, a small Italian neighborhood on the northwest, St. Edward's Catholic Church on West Sixth Street, the city park on the east side, and in the center the North Main Street business district.[43]

Very few families could afford to purchase their own homes, so they rented from individual homeowners or purchased lots and over time built their own homes. Once Luis Cruz and his sons opened a bakery and small grocery store on North Main Street, they saved enough money to purchase their own home on Ramona Street and move out of Foothill Ranch. Juan Villa and his wife, Guadalupe Zamora Villa, who came to Corona in 1910 from Mexico with three of their nine children, had to wait seven years to purchase a lot on which to build their own adobe home. Using stone masonry skills he acquired in Mexico, Villa built a two-story structure in 1917 with adobe slabs, bricks, and local rough-hewn granite stones for the arched windows and doorways, giving the house a hacienda-style appearance.[44]

Building an adobe home was an extended family affair, relying on siblings, cousins, uncles, and *compadres.* House construction was not limited to males only, however. When their father became ill and could not build a home on an empty lot he purchased, Mary and Virginia Govea decided to build the home themselves. On days off from their packinghouse jobs, the Govea sisters learned carpentry and adobe construction and after six months built an adobe home. Surprised at their accomplishments, one neighbor marveled, "How they can do all the work they get done and still have time for their many friends is an art all their own." The Govea daughters, described as "feminine and dainty" and "fashion plates," defied traditional feminine roles by learning a predominantly male occupation while still caring for their ailing father.[45]

Housing reformers encouraged Mexican residents to own their own homes but for different reasons. In 1919 the city's leading housing reformer and city nurse, Mathilda Jacobson, mounted a public campaign to improve living conditions in the barrio after discovering "absolutely filthy" homes occupied by Mexican renters. According to Jacobson, "The sooner some definite steps were taken to improve the living conditions of Mexicans now living here the sooner will they become better citizens and the sooner will the source of the flies be done away with." Jacobson's attempt to better housing conditions was part of a Progressive reform movement to promote middle-class standards and American citizenship. Mexican immigrant views of homeownership, however, often clashed with these Anglo middle-class notions; immigrants chose instead to build adobe homes like the ones they left behind in Mexico.[46]

Reformers' push for housing reform and Mexicans' pursuit of homeownership ran up against racial restrictions. Mexicans were restricted from renting or buying homes south of Sixth Street for fear of depreciating property values and racial mixing. Anglo homeowners placed racial restrictions in land deeds or displayed overt resistance to keep Mexican residents out of the south side of town. Onias Acevedo remembered when he became a real estate agent discovering property deeds and home sale listings with explicit instructions of "Do Not Show to Mexicans." Racial restrictive covenants were informed by eugenics scholars and public health officials who viewed Mexican households as overcrowded, disease prone, and unhygienic. Real estate agents and lending institutions and realtors found ways to circumvent the law in order to maintain control over the local housing market and preserve property values as well as to maintain a homogenous "Anglo" identity.[47]

Turning Segregation into Congregation

The Mexican barrio was surrounded by Grand Avenue circling around the north side and Sixth Street running east to west and cutting through the heart of the city, literally and metaphorically dividing residents according to race and nationality. In later years Mexican American veterans who had lived north of Sixth Street referred to this racial divide as the "38th parallel" in reference to the dividing line between North and South Korea. In the words of one barrio resident, "The only reason we would go south [of Sixth Street] was to pick fruit in the groves." After a long workday in the fields, Mexican men returned in a shuttle bus operated by the packinghouse association that dropped them off in the north side of town. Mexican women walked several blocks to pack citrus fruit in one of the nine packinghouses lined up on both sides of the Santa Fe railroad tracks.[48]

To justify segregation of Mexican residents, Corona reformers pointed to the dilapidated conditions of homes, buildings, and parks in the "cholo district." One newspaper editorial titled "What's the Matter with Corona?" opined that "the two parks on the Mexican side of town . . . might better be planted in potatoes, so little can a Mexican appreciate a park." The editorial described the poor conditions of "shacks" and "shanties" and blamed the city "for not imposing the proper building restrictions in the beginning," thus causing an "eyesore and shame for all Coronans." The writer appealed to city officials for stricter housing regulations, but to no avail.[49]

City officials did not intend to improve Mexicans' economic lot and living conditions but rather to castigate them as "dirty" and prone to carrying communicable diseases—with the ultimate aim of preserving a cheap labor supply for the citrus industry and maintaining racial segregation in the movie theaters, public schools, parks, and recreational spaces. The "culture of segregation" in Corona resembled southern Texas communities where segregationist practices were based on germ theories of hygiene and cleanliness. Herbert Priestley, a former superintendent of Corona city schools (1910–11) and University of California professor of Mexican history, was invited to speak to Corona Rotary members on "Mexican affairs" and observed that "Mexico, as backward as the republic seems to the American mind, is one country where it is no uncommon thing to see a policeman stop and arrest a man on the street and order him to report at the sanitary station for a bath." Professor Priestley and other so-called experts on the "Mexican Problem" maintained that Mexicans and Mexican immigrants were incapable of "good health, good morals or educational advancement" without supervision of American health officials, social reformers, and Protestant missionaries.[50]

The practice of segregation extended to Corona's public school system through gerrymandering school zone boundaries. Like elsewhere throughout the Midwest and Southwest, Corona's Mexican children were denied entrance into "American" schools and sent instead to "Mexican schools" with inferior classroom facilities, low academic tracking, and a curriculum that emphasized Americanization and vocational training. In 1926 school board trustees debated and voted in favor of changing zoning boundaries to force Mexican children to attend Washington Elementary School and Anglo children attend either Jefferson or Lincoln Elementary School. Being familiar with the "Southerner's problem with the negro," one school board member became convinced that the "Mexican problem [in] the schools can be much improved and segregation will go a long way toward making the Corona schools fit places for white boys and girls to attend." Even though they were closer to Lincoln Elementary School or Jefferson Elementary School, Mexican children from citrus ranches were bused to Washington Elementary School. Children from Italian homes and two black families who lived on the north side also attended Washington Elementary School.[51]

Corona's Mexican population experienced covert and overt forms of racial discrimination in city parks, swimming pools, movie houses, and shops. In 1925 the city opened a swimming pool ("municipal plunge") in the park on East Sixth Street to provide residents with relief from the hot summer heat of the inland desert. Mexican swimmers, however, were deterred from using the pool by a sign that read, "For the White Race Only." Mexicans, Italians, and other "foreigners" were allowed to swim only on Mondays. Ralph Covington, who worked as a towel boy, remembered the Jim Crow-style conditions. "The city park had two wading ponds, a clean one for whites and another for minorities and dogs . . . [and] the minority pool wasn't clean at all." Racial exclusion at municipal pools was based on heightened race-based sanitation fears reinforced by public health reports and the routine practice of changing the "dirty" pool water on Tuesdays so whites could swim in "clean" water.[52]

Even Anglo-owned shops in the south-side business district made Mexican patrons feel unwelcome. "I can remember the scared feeling

I would get when we went south on Main Street to the Harris Department Store," said Juanita Ramírez. "I always felt that we did not belong, like we were going into alien territory. We had the uncomfortable feeling that clerks were looking down their noses at us because we were Mexicans." These alienating experiences were reason enough to shop in Mexican-owned stores where the language and culture were familiar.[53]

Given their limited freedom in this citrus-controlled town, Mexicans opened small businesses where customers could interact and create their own spaces to congregate without fear of discrimination.[54] During the 1920s a small business district emerged on North Main Street to cater to the needs of an expanding Mexican population. The 1927 Corona city directory listed more than twenty-one Mexican-owned businesses including dry goods stores, a tortilla factory, a meat market, a bakery, barbershops, pool halls, restaurant-bars, and a silent movie theater. Julio Cruz opened the first Mexican grocery store in 1915 at North Main Street, providing customers with a wide selection of canned products, meats, and baked goods. The two Cruz brothers remembered how their father purchased a horse and wagon to deliver groceries to ranch residents who lived in outlying areas of town especially those with no access to a company store. Cruz offered store credit to loyal customers, but unlike company store debt their job was not in jeopardy if they could not pay. In addition to offering goods and services, the Cruz store functioned as a social center where residents from town and outlying ranches could meet family and friends, exchange news and information, and listen to the latest gossip.[55]

Mexican women played an important role in the daily operation of family-owned businesses and occasionally became their own boss. Out of the twenty-one Mexican-owned businesses listed in the 1927 city directory, only one, a dry goods store, was female-owned. Delfina Canchola, a widow and a native of Michoacán, operated a dry goods store at 507 North Main Street. The Canchola store served as a meeting center for El Club Zaragoza, the leading organizational force behind Cinco de Mayo celebrations.[56]

Mexican consumers also sought pleasure in commercial places along North Main Street. In 1926 Julio Cruz and Sons opened a silent movie theater, El Teatro Chapultepec, next door to the grocery. The theater featured Hollywood's top silent films, vaudeville shows, *revistas* (variety reviews), and musical performances. Male customers in search of alcoholic drinks, card games, or rounds of pool usually frequented the Commercial Hotel saloon, Jesus Abalos pool hall, or Frank

Leonti pool hall. These leisure outlets offered Mexican male residents relief from the rigors of daily labors and presented more opportunities for entertainment and socializing. However, strict gender norms prohibited women from patronizing these male-centered establishments. As discussed in chapter 3, the world of saloons and pool halls was primarily a masculine domain.[57]

Apart from business ventures, Mexican immigrants organized mutual aid societies, volunteer organizations, recreation clubs, and a Spanish-language supplement printed in the *Corona Independent*. Members of Corona's *mutualistas* (mutual aid and benefit organizations)—La Alianza Hispano Americana, Asociación de Trabajadores Mexicanos Unidos, Leñadores del Pacífico, and José Maria Pino Suarez Pregresista Logia—expressed a Mexicanist orientation and practiced what Emilio Zamora termed "ethic of mutuality" based on fraternalism, reciprocity, and altruism. Another popular club, El Deportivo Mexicano de Corona, organized amateur boxing matches, baseball games, and recreational activities for Mexican youth. The leadership and membership of these groups was predominantly male, with the exception of El Club Zaragoza, which were founded by Delfina Canchola and included women in its membership roster. A short-lived Spanish-language newspaper, *Revista de Corona*, kept barrio residents informed of local and national news, entertainment, and sporting events. Corona high school graduate and *Corona Independent* reporter Leon Heredia started the weekly newspaper in 1929 after convincing his employer of the growing Mexican business clientele and potential readership among the second generation. In a 1929 editorial, Heredia praised community club efforts for making "La Colonia Mexicana de Corona a model community in which everyone helps out each other."[58]

Italian Neighbors

Corona's Italian immigrant community emerged in the early 1900s when citrus companies visited Palermo to recruit experienced lemon fruit pruners and packers whose old-country skills would help boost Corona's lemon industry. The early Sicilian immigrants settled along Belle Street in the northwest quadrant of the circular boulevard. As more immigrants from southern Italy arrived in later years, the community expanded into Washburn Street. Compared to Italian settlements in larger cities, Corona's "Little Italy" was a small, close-knit neighborhood anchored by strong family and kinship ties that extended back to the same villages.[59]

The concentration of Italian immigrants into a small area, however, was not due to cultural ties but also the result of residential segregation imposed by real estate officials and homeowners who refused to rent or sell to "Mexicans" and "foreigners." "Because of racial views of that time it was very difficult for anyone but Anglos to buy any property above Sixth Street," explained Mike Lunetta, a packinghouse foreman for the Corona Foothill Lemon Company. In addition, there were a few cases of discrimination in the movie theaters. "We had segregation in the theaters," remembered ninety-five-year-old Domenica Danieri. "The center section was saved for white people and the two narrow sections were reserved for Italians and Mexicans." Italians were pilloried with such derogatory terms as "dagos," "wops," and "guineas" that made them "in-between" European immigrants. Despite the group's racial undesirability and "foreignness," however, Italians benefited more systematically from the privileges of "whiteness." Compared to the structural location and racialization experiences of Corona's Mexican population, Italians monopolized packinghouse supervisory jobs and moved out of segregated neighborhoods and schools more readily.[60]

For more than three decades, Italians and Mexicans shared the same neighborhood, where religion, language, commercial relations, schooling, and marriages helped bridge the cultural gap. Both groups shared certain aspects of folk Catholic religion and attended the same Catholic parish, St. Edward's Catholic Church. In addition, the Spanish and Italian languages share the same Latin root, and similarities between the Mexican dialect of Spanish and the Sicilian dialect of Italian facilitated individual and group interactions in churches, schools, and neighborhood stores. As mentioned earlier, Washington Elementary School, designated primarily as the "Mexican school" regardless of residence, also enrolled Italian and a few black children, thus allowing interethnic friendships to develop. The use of Spanish and Italian languages, however, was discouraged in public schools.[61]

Despite moments of interethnic solidarity and shared community experiences, larger structural and ideological forces compelled Italians and Mexicans to reevaluate their relationships with each other and with the dominant Anglo society. The first sign of strained relations appeared as the Mexican immigrant population nationwide more than tripled in size during the mid-1920s and fears mounted about the so-called "Mexican problem"—a catchall phrase referring to Mexican immigrants' perceived poor health, substandard housing and living conditions, criminal behavior, and educational deficiency. Emory Bogardus, a student of sociology at the University of Southern California, emphasized, "The Italian in Los Angeles plainly does not constitute as large a problem as does the Mexican, from the standpoint of numbers, the economic situation, and his life in general."[62]

The effects of racialization extended well beyond racial categorization and filtered into institutional practices that shaped and constrained the educational experiences of Mexican and Italian children. In the beginning of the 1934 school year, Italian community leaders met with school board officials to allow their children to enroll at the Lincoln or Jefferson schools. Former Washington student John Guirbino wrote in his autobiography about the integration of Italian children into "white" schools. "I guess the city trustees and school board decided not to contest this mass [Italian] exodus. None of us were hassled for being out of the [school] zone as indicated by our home addresses." Guirbino remembered the excitement in the Italian community. "Hey, we did it! We were integrated!! . . . Going to a school where the children were 'white' was a new and enjoyable experience. . . . I was able to make the Honor Roll while at Lincoln." While Italian children reaped the benefits and rewards of better academically equipped elementary schools, Mexican children remained in vocational training classes at Washington Elementary School, thereby reproducing the racial and class status of the Mexican community.[63]

Mexican immigrant men and women traded their pueblo homes of western Mexico for company homes in Corona's citrus ranches and family-built homes in the north-side barrio in order to gain economic and social stability for their families. Male workers performed the repetitive, backbreaking work of picking fruit, sometimes waiting three to four hours without pay as the dew evaporated from the fruit trees. Mexican women's work included not only childbirth, child rearing, cooking, and doing laundry for their families but also working in packinghouses and in Anglo family homes. Immigrant women experienced sexual, racial, and economic subordination within the household, the workplace, and the community but still managed to squeeze by with help from an extensive social network made up of family, friends, and coworkers. These social networks, which first developed in Mexico and carried over into the United States, opened new opportunities for employment and marriage prospects necessary for building families and communities in a new environment.

Immigrant solos roomed with other men in bunkhouses provided by the citrus companies, rented rooms in downtown boardinghouses, or stayed with family relatives if available. Some men paid local women to do their laundry and frequented restaurant-bars for hot meals. At work, pickers developed a rough camaraderie that created male companionship but also led to fighting and "antisocial" behavior. As chapter 3 shows, a small business district emerged on North Main Street to meet the needs of Mexican immigrant solos. The most popular included saloons, pool halls, barbershops, restaurant-bars, brothels, shoeshine stands, and boardinghouses.

Mexican immigrants who settled into company homes in one of the five citrus ranches faced a paternalistic institution devised to keep them under control. Those who could rent or own a home in the Corona barrio also faced a system of dependencies that limited employment opportunities outside agriculture and constrained public spaces for community gatherings. A strict segregated residential pattern divided Mexicans on the northern semicircle and Anglo Americans on the southern semicircle of Corona. Mexicans were also denied access to public parks, theaters, businesses, swimming pools, and other recreational areas. This culture of segregation, reinforced by a public health racial discourse that viewed Mexicans immigrants with suspicion, enabled residents to build their own businesses and community institutions. Most of all, Mexicans created spaces of congregation so that they could hone their ethnic identity, which became a valuable resource in an alienating environment. Ultimately, ranch and barrio residents alike did not allow segregationist practices in a grower-controlled town to exercise absolute power over their lives.

Like other multiethnic settlements in southern California, Corona embraced transplanted native Anglos from the Midwest, Mexican immigrants, and southern Italian immigrants, mostly from Sicily. At first, Mexicans and Italians in Corona shared cultural and language similarities and a sense of racial exclusion from public spaces that produced a mutual sense of empathy, which in turn sometimes translated into individual acts of interethnic solidarity. A Mexican "race problem" emerged in the public imagination during the late 1920s and early 1930s, while Italian immigrants were moving up the occupational ladder, sending their children to predominantly Anglo elementary schools, and moving across town to become "white" homeowners. Their ability to do so—while Mexicans could not—reflected the different racialized views that Anglo American society held about the two groups. Another major rift occurred during the 1941 strike in which both groups clashed along racial and class lines.

Mexican and Italian women workers at the Jameson Company packinghouse, circa 1920s. Courtesy of Corona Public Library.

Mexican pickers and Anglo foremen at the Foothill Ranch, circa 1920s. Courtesy of Corona Public Library.

Mexican men celebrating Mexican Independence Day, 1917. Courtesy of Corona Public Library; donated by Manuel Cruz.

Interior view of Abalos Pool Hall, circa 1920s. Courtesy of Corona Public Library; donated by Ray Delgadillo.

St. Edward's Catholic Church, 1924. Courtesy of Corona Public Library; donated by Frances Martínez.

Moviegoers inside El Teatro Chapultepec, circa 1920s. Courtesy of Corona Public Library; donated by Frances Martínez.

Cinco de Mayo street dance on North Main Street, circa 1920s. Courtesy of Corona Public Library; donated by Frances Martínez.

Cinco de Mayo parade on Sixth Street, circa 1920s. Courtesy of Corona Public Library; donated by Frances Martínez.

Mexican women working the food booths during Foothill Ranch's Cinco de Mayo fiesta. Courtesy of Corona Public Library; donated by Carl Hercklerath.

Mexican girls in their "Sunday best" in front of St. Edward's Catholic Church. Courtesy of Corona Public Library; donated by Frances Martínez.

Corona Athletics baseball player in front of Santa Fe Depot, 1937. Courtesy of Corona Public Library.

Las Debs de Corona softball team, 1947. Courtesy of Corona Public Library.

CIO-led picket line in front of the Jameson Company packinghouse, 1941. Courtesy of Corona Public Library.

Members of Los Amigos Club, 1943. Courtesy of Corona Public Library; donated by Frances Martínez.

Frances Martínez between Lalo Guerrero, Donald McGaffin, and Danny Thomas at a St. Edward's Catholic Church fund-raiser, circa 1940s. Courtesy of Corona Public Library; donated by Frances Martínez.

PART TWO

Creating Leisure Spaces

3 Saloons, Pool Halls, and Bootlegging

Margarita Villa was abruptly awoken in the middle of the night when she heard her ex-boyfriend Juan Placensia calling her name outside her house. Placensia had been drinking and playing pool all day. He left North Main Street and headed toward the Villa home on Ramona Street. As Placensia attempted to enter the Villa home, "He was prevented by the girl and her mother, who were holding the door when the Mexican [man] started shooting through it." Placensia fired three shots and one hit Margarita on the left arm. Placensia was subsequently arrested, taken to jail and charged with assault with a deadly weapon. Margarita and her mother were lucky to have survived this violent episode. Fights, quarrels, and murders occasionally erupted around the North Main Street vice district where saloons, pool halls, brothels, and gambling dens catered to a predominantly Mexican male population, single or married. Drinking, gambling, fighting, and other forms of leisure contributed to a rough style of working-class masculinity that produced both constructive and destructive effects on the community.[1]

Saloons, pool halls, and bootlegging served as centers of the Mexican male leisure culture. Mexican men, single or married, drank collectively with other men, gambled their earnings in poker and pool games, and sought sexual services from prostitutes. Women participated in the trade as petty sellers, lookouts, and go-betweens and, privately, as consumers in underground saloons. These forms of antisocial behaviors ran into conflict with the city's dry law and with temperance forces, employers, and police officials, who sought to socially control the Mexican population through strict law enforcement and punishment of violators. Despite efforts to curb alcohol drinking and smuggling, however, Mexican immigrants continued to resist the state prohibition law. In so doing, they fashioned their own version of working-class masculine identity that celebrated male fraternity, rough behavior, and, eventually, incipient worker resistance and workplace organizing. This rough masculine culture, fueled by economic exploitation and social marginalization, reinforced gender inequality in the home and community.

Mexican Solos and Working-Class Masculinity

Because of the preponderance of Mexican solos (unmarried or married with wives in Mexico) in Corona's labor camps and lodging houses, a gender imbalance emerged during the first two decades of the twentieth century. The 1910 city census listed 271 Mexican men and 156 Mexican women. A decade later the census revealed a similar disparity, with 740 Mexican males and 541 Mexican females. Census enumerators used the terms "lodgers," "boarders," and "roomers" to identify their living conditions in labor camps, boardinghouses, and family homes. The unequal sex ratios that led to excessive drinking, gambling, fighting, and visiting houses of prostitution contributed to the formation of the Mexican working-class masculine identity.[2]

While these leisure activities helped to bring workers together to offset their loneliness and bolster their spirits, they also produced social instability in the community. Arguments over card games, bets, and women that occurred in saloons frequently turned into violent confrontations with deadly consequences for both men and women. As Peter Way has shown, the vice, intemperance, and rough culture among antebellum canal workers "pulled at the seams of group unity . . . often turning shanty communities into warring camps." For Mexican solos, too, the consumption of alcohol, combined with the presence of knives and handguns, often led to squabbling and fights, thus increasing levels of violence in the city.[3]

These forms of antisocial behaviors elicited the concern of employers due to their potential to disrupt work habits and reduce job productivity. As discussed in chapter 2, orchard workers developed a masculine picking culture expressed in rituals of jokes, horseplay, gambling, and other forms of illicit behavior. These kinds of behavior, according to one citrus ranch manager, were not confined to the workplace. "Most of them [solos] worked well when they did work, but all too many of them made Sunday last an extra day or two." Workers' consumption of inordinate amounts of liquor during nonwork hours reinforced the view that solos were unreliable, transient, and prone to vice and lawlessness.[4]

The rough leisure world of Mexican solos reinforced gender inequality and often led to violence against women in the household and community. Public displays of working-class masculinity were not only a defensive reaction to class and racial oppression but also asserted power and privilege over women. Newspaper reports and court records revealed alcohol-related conflicts between boyfriends and girlfriends, husbands and wives, and boozing men who harassed women in private and public spheres. The rough style of working-class masculinity and its attendant forms of antisocial behavior raised the ire of prohibitionists and antisaloon zealots who saw the drink and its effects on the laboring classes as a threat to the social order.[5]

Saloons and Pool Halls

From its inception, Corona and other colony settlements in southern California were founded as temperance communities. During the late nineteenth century, a large wave of native-born Anglo Protestants left their small Midwest towns for sunny southern California. By 1910 Anglo Protestants eclipsed native inhabitants and foreign-born populations to become a demographic majority in Los Angeles, unlike San Francisco where 85 percent were foreign-born and non-Protestant. These transplanted midwesterners sought to counter the demoralizing effects of saloons, pool halls, movie theaters, and gambling houses on the city's youths and on its foreign-born population by founding more schools, churches, and religious organizations. The Reverend Dana Bartlett, a proponent of the social gospel and a settlement house worker, preached about how unattached single migrant men living in lodging houses easily fell into corruption. "He wanders to and fro on the streets, drawn tonight into a cheap theater, tomorrow night into a dance hall, after that into the brightly lighted saloon. . . . For the sake of the . . . young man, close the saloon!" The plight of the fallen young man disappearing into the clutches of saloonkeepers became a pressing concern for moral reform groups.[6]

The neighborhood saloon from 1890 to 1920 has been described as a refuge for the working man and the quintessential poor man's club.[7] As

Roy Rosenzweig has suggested, the saloon "offered a space in which [male] immigrants could preserve an alternative, reciprocal value system." Although some women ran saloons and some became regular customers, the majority of bartenders and bar-goers were adult males; thus, the saloon became an exclusive masculine space. Saloons offered camaraderie, fraternity, and companionship for working-class men and opportunities to develop homosocial relationships over time, express uninhibited emotions with other men (especially if under the influence of alcohol), and reaffirm their masculine identity. Within the walls of this homosocial environment, group solidarity was reinforced by ritual drinking practices in these all-male hangouts; it also created problems for the community and threatened marital relations.[8]

The masculine pleasures inside the saloon came under attack by the two leading organizations, the Women's Christian Temperance Union (WCTU) and the Anti-Saloon League (ASL). Founded in 1893 in Ohio, the ASL under the leadership of E. S. Chapman launched a campaign against more than 12,600 licensed saloons in California. In Los Angeles, the ASL joined forces with the ministerial union to persuade the city council to pass an ordinance limiting the number of saloons to 200, requiring them to close on Sundays, and establishing a saloon district within the working-class immigrant neighborhood of Macy Street, located near Chinatown and La Placita. Unlike San Franciscans who defeated prohibitionist ordinances, Los Angeles residents voted in 1917 for the abolition of saloons in the city, stipulating that distilled liquors be available for medicinal purposes only.[9]

Industrial and agricultural employers sided with the ASL and forbade their employees from patronizing saloons. Henry E. Huntington, president of the Pacific Electric Company, kept his Mexican track workers out of saloons for fear they would not return on Monday morning. Citrus officials also complained that drinking alcohol interfered with worker productivity. Writing in the *California Citrograph*, A. D. Shamel claimed that "the chief enemy of the Mexican laborer is whiskey. The only Mexican disturbances or quarrels the writer is familiar with were brought about by some outsider surreptitiously bringing American whiskey into the Mexican quarters." Apart from reduced levels of job productivity, employers grew concerned that Mexican workers would associate with other workers in saloons and make plans to resist or organize a union.[10]

The racial stereotype of Mexicans as deviant drinkers was perpetuated by university academics. A Los Angeles investigator claimed, "The excessive use of liquor is the Mexican's greatest moral problem. This is not only destructive of their morals and a leading cause of their criminality but also produces the irregularity, uncertainty and inefficiency which are the chief objections to Mexican labor." University of Southern California sociologist Emory Bogardus, a purported academic expert on all things Mexican, sounded the alarm on the Mexican's liquor problem. "Saloons and access to liquor have demoralized the Mexican more than has any other factor. The Mexican laborer is often shiftless and thriftless."[11]

Corona's North Main Street, not unlike the Macy Street district in Los Angeles, catered to foreign-born immigrant groups, principally Mexican males who flocked to downtown to mingle freely with friends and spend their meager earnings at restaurants, pool halls, barbershops, and saloons. Of the city's four saloons, the most popular was Pete's Saloon, owned and operated by a French merchant, Pete Provensal, who proclaimed to offer a "good quality of beer and whiskey." Another popular saloon was located in the New Mexican settlement of San Salvador, located along Santa Ana River near Riverside. Built in the 1890s by Juan Trujillo, La Placita Cantina, according to one former resident, "continued its alcoholic beverage business while bootleggers operated more or less openly in the river bottom area." Saloonkeepers such as Trujillo played a pivotal role in the lives of working-class men by offering a free lunch, acting as job placement officers and money lenders, and most of all upholding the code of reciprocity by treating customers to a free drink on the house.[12]

The Corona campaign against the saloon began in the 1890s and gathered strength in the 1908 city election when prohibition forces declared victory and passed a new city ordinance to close the saloons. Before the election, antisaloon zealots wrote to the newspaper with disgust about the town's negative reputation. "The pool rooms and saloons are about the first thing the stranger sees when entering out town. What an impression!" Another resident framed the election as "the great struggle of Home vs. the Saloon" and advised voters to help "Corona emancipate itself on the side of right, decency and order." An irate resident labeled the prohibition movement a "ghastly farce" because "more liquor is drank in Corona today than when licensed saloons were allowed."[13]

Antidrink crusaders also preached against the evils of card-playing and gambling. In 1912 the city council imposed a heavy fine of ten dollars for playing poker, throwing dice, or wagering on sporting events.

The police chief recounted about a raid on a gambling joint: "The players were entirely surprised. There were 21 of them, all Mexicans seated around a table, one with a sack of silver in front of him and one shuffling cards." The officer then proceeded to "relieve the men of their shooting irons and other deadly weapons of which there was a good-sized collection." During the court hearing, one man claimed that they were not gambling with money but raffling off a revolver. Showing no sympathy, the judge gave each man the option of a ten-dollar fine or five days in jail.[14]

The closing of saloons did not end drinking, gambling, and other forms of illicit activity but shifted them into pool rooms, underground saloons (blind pigs), and informal private settings. One business owner blamed the city for its lack of enforcement and allowing booze to be sold from blind pigs. A resident claimed that "one night as many as 100 shots were fired." The city mayor agreed that "[North Main Street] has been giving Corona a black eye for a long time." In response, the Corona City Council appointed a special night policeman to patrol Main Street in search of violators. When interviewed about the violators, the city marshal bluntly stated that "Mexicans and booze can't mix. A white man can drink where a Mexican cannot. The latter becomes crazed when intoxicated and is much more apt to be troublesome than a white man." The marshal's statement revealed the manifest hypocrisy of antisaloon zealots and prohibitionists as well as existing racial ideologies that viewed Mexicans as culturally inferior and lacking in self-control.[15]

To rid the town of this black eye, city marshal Grant Alexander called for strict antigun legislation because "the Mexicans seem to think for them not to carry a gun on their hip at a dance would take away all of their pleasure." In summer 1913 the marshal led a major crackdown on unlawful activity and arrested more than fifty violators; he claimed to have reduced gunshots from one hundred to twenty-five per night. Tensions reached a boiling point in December 1913 when a Mexican was suspected of shooting and killing the city marshal. The *Corona Independent* reported on the event: "All Corona was horrified to learn at an early hour Monday morning that the marshal Alexander had been shot and killed by a Mexican when he attempted to restore order in the shack in which some foreigners lived." One Anglo resident expressed his indignation to the editor: "Since the outrageous and utterly cold blooded murder of our city marshal, it appears to me that the time has come . . . that we [Anglos] meet in a body and consider segregating these foreigners in some part of town outside of the circle." One Italian resident, John Beschi, defended his Mexican neighbors by stating, "Americans who thought all the Mexicans should be run out of town are making a mistake, as not all of them are bad. In every country there are good and bad men." Although they did not expel Mexicans outside the circle, the city council allocated a five-hundred-dollar reward for the capture of the alleged killer.[16]

Following the murder of the city marshal, a *Corona Independent* editorial proposed legislation against Mexicans carrying guns. "Corona should have some legislation on this subject as she already has enough advertising of an uncomplimentary nature. If the Mexicans do not value the lives of each other, the Corona citizens do value the reputation of their town." By June 1914 the city council passed the alien gun law ordinance that imposed a stiff penalty of fifty dollars for carrying a gun. While some knowingly violated the alien gun law, others did so unwittingly. Because Corona was a dangerous place, Mexicans carried guns to protect themselves and their families; a pistol was often the only form of defense against outside attackers and assailants. Veterans of the Mexican army who fought during the Mexican Revolution were accustomed to carrying firearms, sometimes showing them off as a symbol of resistance and masculine honor. It is possible that many Mexican army veterans resided in Corona and were employed in the citrus industry. Despite the alien gun law, Mexicans continued to use their firearms not only for safety reasons but also to affirm their masculine and national identity by shooting to the sky during Mexican Independence Day celebrations.[17]

The relative absence of women during the 1910s led Mexican solos to seek prostitutes to fulfill their sexual needs. The second floor of the Emerson Hotel was known as a house of prostitution with small rooms and a rickety staircase that led to a back door in the rear of the building. According to one newspaper report, a Mexican proprietor was arrested in his restaurant along with two Mexican women "who [were] alleged to have been used as 'bait' for peso-laden hombres." Two days later the women were released. "The proprietor was advised to search for a more suitable climate in which to conduct his disorderly houses." Single women who could not find wage work often entered the underworld of prostitution in the city's red-light district. These women were labeled as "bad women" by members of the Mexican community and Anglo temperance advocates. Mexican males, single or married, who sought sexual services did not receive the same punishment from local authorities. When Anna Picoli was arrested for "disorderly conduct" with J. Vasquez in the Mirabella rooming house, it was Picoli who received a one-hundred-dollar fine and "in plain English [was] told to get out of town and stay out." The only punishment Vasquez received came from his wife. As Vasquez walked out of jail, the police officer commented that "the look on his wife's face bode ill for brother Vasquez when he reached home."[18]

The mix of extramarital relationships, excessive drinking and gambling, and availability of deadly weapons could easily lead to male-on-male fighting and violence against women. The scarcity of women often led single Mexican males to fight for the same woman. For example, Heracio Viramontez, "crazed by jealously over affections to the same Mexican girl," shot and killed Angel Ortiz, then fled to Mexico. In another incident, an unidentified woman was dragged into the lemon groves by four Mexican men who assaulted her "with knives [and] then decided to allow her to escape." Other women were not as lucky. In a rage of jealousy, Francisco Perez shot his former wife after she refused to return to him and leave her new job at the local restaurant where she was dating the boss. The intensely masculine work and leisure culture that reinforced notions about male control of female sexuality helped shaped men's violence against women.[19]

Wives also complained of husbands' irresponsibility and blamed alcohol as the cause of their domestic conflicts. Luisa Vasquez took her husband Natividad to court for "his drinking and neglecting his work and family." A social worker testified that he failed to provide food, clothing, shelter, and medical attention to their five children. Luisa told the judge, "When he is sober and not under the influence of liquor he is a good man, we are a happy family, but it seems to be the liquor. When he earns a check he often gives it to the family and then he will earn another and drink that one up, and then trouble begins." The judge ruled in favor of Luisa and ordered Natividad to quit drinking and provide for his children. The vulnerability of married women's position within the household and dependence on husbands' wages did not mean they were powerless; rather, they drew upon a network of support and used the courts to get husbands to fulfill their familial responsibilities.[20]

With the closing of saloons, Mexican immigrants regrouped in pool halls, also known as poolrooms. Similar to saloons, pool halls were an exclusively masculine space in which groups of men would get together, discuss the latest news, and gamble at a game of poker or pool. Although drinking often accompanied these activities, especially before prohibition, the main leisure activity was gambling in a poker game or round of pool or betting on sporting games. Women and young children typically were denied entry into the poolrooms.[21]

For Mexican immigrants, especially solos, drinking provided a means to meet male and female companions and recoup and reclaim their bodies from alienating workplaces and racially charged climates. For unemployed Mexican men, moreover, the pool hall functioned as a job bureau, providing job information or attracting job recruiters seeking workers. On rainy days, Corona's citrus orchard workers gathered at pool halls. Two of the most popular pool halls in Corona were Feliz Pool Hall, owned by Samuel Feliz, and Abalos Pool Hall, owned by Jesus Abalos. Ray Delgadillo remembered as a young child visiting his father's barbershop located inside the Abalos Pool Hall. "My dad had his barbershop in the pool hall. I guess that is where many men used to go and while they waited to get a haircut they played pool. That was the main recreation area for Corona at that time. As a matter of fact Jesus Abalos owned the building and lived in the back of the building quarters. There were also shower stalls where you could take a shower for a quarter. They had two or three shower stalls and you got a bar of soap and towel so you could take a shower."[22]

One of the main leisure activities for adult men at the Abalos Pool Hall was gambling. A researcher observing the leisure activities of a Mexican colony in Orange County stated, "When they have money they congregate in poolrooms and restaurants and drink and play cards until a late hour." Although as a young kid he was not allowed to enter the pool hall, Ray Delgadillo recalled, "They had a big poker table and the owner would run the poker games. . . . It seemed like the same men were there almost every day. They were really gambling." The police attempted to enforce the city's antigambling ordinance with little success. There was typically a lookout person outside the pool hall to warn the gamblers.[23]

Because they attracted gambling, drinking, and prostitution, pool halls became an easy target for police and social reformers. Critics objected not so much to pool playing itself but to its association with vice and criminality. One researcher observed the wagering and idleness of a Mexican pool hall clientele in Belvedere. "There is nothing to be said in favor of the typical pool hall crowd. They are slouching, cigarette smoking fellows who comment on the girls who go past and make remarks. These boys are usually out of work. Perhaps they leave home in the morning with the implication that they will be looking for work." These young Mexican Americans used the pool hall as a daytime diversion, and according to the researcher, "Their day is spent in this lazy fashion and their plans are here made for the evening's activities. Perhaps they will consist of more pool hall; perhaps they will necessitate a disturbance call for the police." Another researcher studying recreation among Mexican immigrants in the Imperial Valley referred to pool halls as the "bane of our society," citing the numerous arrests of young boys for gambling. "No chain is stronger than its weakest link and the good citizens of our community should recognize the menace which comes from this kind of commercial amusement."[24]

The Corona City Council debated whether to close down pool halls on Sundays. Sunday closures of sport and leisure entertainment were part of a series of "blue laws" passed in towns throughout America with the aim of making Sunday a church-going day. During the 1910s debate emerged within the city council about passing an ordinance to close poolrooms, shooting galleries, and moving picture theaters on Sundays. W. H. Jameson, the citrus tycoon who was also a founder of the local First Baptist Church, urged council members on May 12, 1914, to pass a strict ordinance to close down pool halls, bowling alleys, and shooting galleries on Sundays. This ordinance, which had the support of the Methodist church and the WCTU, would, according to Jameson, "prove beneficial for the communities." The ordinance finally passed on February 23, 1916, and stipulated the Sunday closure of poolrooms. A year later, however, calls to completely close down pool halls grew louder when Mexican agricultural workers engaged in a series of work stoppages and strikes to demand higher wages and better working conditions.[25]

In a town where spaces for organization were limited and citrus companies held extensive political and economic sway, the pool hall took on a more political cast. In 1917 a Spanish-language flyer appeared in the pool halls. Addressed to the "working class in general," it urged workers to "develop a strong movement to protest the bad conditions and low salaries that are developing this season." Pool halls served as a central gathering place where citrus pickers could discuss grievances and strategize work actions. This is probably where discussions about unequal pay rates by different growers began and ended in a consensus to stage a work stoppage.[26]

At the height of the First World War organized labor unleashed a massive strike wave that crippled entire industries and towns. Of the more radical unions, the Industrial Workers of the World (IWW) stood for building One Big Union across racial and ethnic lines and organizing agricultural laborers. In the aftermath of free speech fights and a violent confrontation in Wheatland, California, the IWW attempted to organize workers in the citrus-growing districts of southern California. On the morning of March 2, 1917, Mexican pickers threw down their clippers and fruit sacks, refusing to work until they received a higher wage. Striking pickers demanded that all growers follow the lead of the Jameson Company, which had recently begun paying two dollars a day. The

Corona Independent reported, "It seems that the W. H. Jameson interests only began paying their Mexican help the $2 rate some two or three weeks ago, and it was the raise . . . which is said to have inspired the Mexican uprising on the [other] ranches yesterday to demand the $2 a day wage." Rather than conceding to worker demands, Corona growers decided to hire Anglo labor. A newspaper editor reasoned that "even with the Mexicans at $1.80 per day they are more expensive than white men at a higher and fairer rate. If not to the fruit companies direct, then to the tax payers of the city both direct and indirect. . . . Because of [the Mexicans'] low standard of living, frequent quarrels and indulgence in all the known vices, the tax payers of the city are forced to maintain extra police help." By conflating Mexican immigrants' low standard of living with their "quarrels and vices"—rather than acknowledging the role of low wages in keeping living standards miserable—the town's Anglo establishment defined Mexicans as outside the domain of whiteness and middle class life, and thus undeserving of upward mobility through higher pay.[27]

Concerned that the strike would spread to other citrus-growing districts, growers enlisted private security and undercover agents to conduct espionage and surveillance activities on pool halls and other settings where clandestine worker organizing was believed to take place. According to a police informant, "There were over forty laborers from Corona in Fullerton Wednesday night when a large meeting of Mexicans was held inside a pool hall, the purpose being to organize a union whereby more definite results might be obtained in securing shorter hours with more pay." A second strategy was to use the *Corona Independent* to discourage Mexican workers in their efforts to organize a union. In an editorial one Corona grower declared, "Should any internal outbreaks occur in any of the fruit picking centers more than likely there will be a concerted action on the part of all southern California to quietly take all who could not show naturalization papers and set them well over on the other side of the border where they will be privileged to live a life best suited to them."[28] Apart from using the local newspaper to instill fear of deportation among their Mexican employees, Corona citrus growers affiliated with the Queen Colony Fruit Exchange held special closed sessions on the "question of labor troubles amongst the pickers." The first motion was for members to "arrive at some maximum scale of wages for pickers if possible." A second motion was passed to collect data on pickers currently employed and on the different nationalities employed. The collection of employee data was intended for a mass meeting in Los Angeles of representatives from different district exchanges to discuss the recurring labor troubles.[29]

During the industry-wide meeting, a resolution was adopted to seek assistance from the State Employment Bureau office in Los Angeles. Sunkist growers spent considerable energy in bringing every member grower on board and setting standard wage rates as well as threatening unpatriotic and troublesome agitators with deportation. Although it is not clear how the strike ended, local growers evidently mounted a strong campaign to discredit the strikers and drive out the agitators. Despite repressive measures, however, Mexican citrus workers continued to engage in spontaneous walkouts and slowdowns and refused to work for certain growers when other regions promised them better picking wages.[30]

To ensure worker loyalty and support the war effort, the federal government promoted 100 percent Americanism campaigns throughout the country. Americanization fervor also reached Corona. Awaiting the arrival of returning soldiers at the Santa Fe Depot on Sunday afternoon, September 29, 1918, the audience was instructed to stand and salute the American flag and sing "The Star-Spangled Banner." All followed suit with the exception of an unidentified Mexican man, described as "too ignorant [to] know what was expected of him." According to the *Corona Independent*, "It seemed that one young Mexican in particular, who kept his hat on was requested to remove it. He refused to do so, and after the third or fourth request, his hat was taken from his head and handed to him. He replaced it and started to walk away when one of the soldiers who was standing on the platform was called down to take care of the fellow." A fight ensued until the man was subdued by ten soldiers, who then proceeded to teach him a lesson. As the newspaper reported, "The Mexican was taken to the platform and compelled to kneel and kiss the flag." The man resisted, and before he kissed the flag, "he cried out in his own language, most of the spectators not knowing what he had said." Then, he was abruptly arrested and taken to jail and given a sixty-day jail sentence. This incident revealed the ways in which Anglo Coronans defined Mexican immigrants as racially inferior and as foreigners with illegitimate claims to American society. If they displayed resistance to Americanization, they were subjected to heightened forms of racial hostility.[31]

Making Corona "Dry"

The early settlers of Corona, many originating from dry midwestern towns, viewed drinking and saloons as threatening to their Victorian manhood ideals of self-discipline, order, frugality, and Christian values.

At the colony's founding, Robert B. Taylor expressed his contempt for the presence of saloons when he recalled a confrontation with a saloon keeper: "When our camp was located at the Harrington ranch, a party from San Bernardino came there and started a saloon under a large live oak. I asked him not to sell my men enough drinks to make them drunk, as he had been doing, but he said he would sell them so long as they had money to pay. [Later] we three went to the saloon and tore down the tent and broke the bottles and totally wrecked the outfit." During the first meeting of the WCTU held at the Methodist church, the organization's president spoke on the campaign to ban alcohol from public spaces because "[we] believe we can see the dawning of the time which shall bring emancipation from this terrible curse [of alcohol]. The crusade against the saloon was directly supported by evangelical Protestant churches that urged its congregations to vote against the saloon and uphold Christian values in the home and community."[32]

The closing of saloons and the regulation of pool halls did little to reduce public drinking and its disruptive effects on work habits, family life, and social order. Between 1913 and 1919, temperance forces redirected their efforts at the alcohol problem by pushing for a ban on the manufacturing and sale of liquor. Despite some success at local and state levels, the ASL, the WCTU, and other dry forces sought a prohibition amendment to the United States Constitution. By 1917 the U.S. Congress received the necessary two-thirds votes and three-fourths of the states approved the Eighteenth Amendment. The bill, officially titled the National Prohibition Act but popularly know as the Volstead Act, was ratified in January 1919 and became effective a year later.[33]

Unrestricted immigration, with more than six million immigrants entering the United States between 1910 and 1919, combined with the suppression of radicals and the patriotic fervor that accompanied the First World War and led to a speedy adoption of national prohibition. After three failed attempts (1914, 1916, 1920) to pass a statewide prohibition bill, California dry forces were successful in passing the 1922 Wright Act, also known as the Little Volstead Act. WCTU delegates at their 1922 Los Angeles County convention passed resolutions supporting the prohibition bill, including one favoring the deportation of undocumented Mexican immigrants. The resolution stated that "many of our bootleggers are aliens, therefore we favor deportation of these enemies of our government when they are convicted of selling liquor in violation of our laws." A member of the WCTU Corona chapter warned Corona voters about becoming a "wide open town" where "the saloon is allowed to run unrestricted, where gambling place[s] know no laws, and where pool halls and picture shows run seven days and seven nights each week." The WCTU appealed to the anti-immigrant and antivice sentiments of voters to make Los Angeles and Corona "dry towns."[34]

Corona dry forces enlisted the support of the Women's Improvement Club (WIC), considered the most progressive women's club in the city. Formed in 1899, the club founded the city park, plunge, and library; promoted city beautification projects; and participated in civic affairs. Hetty Joy Jameson, one of the club's early presidents and wife of W. H. Jameson, donated the site for the clubhouse. In the 1922 election, the WIC passed a resolution in support of prohibition, "That this club is in sympathy with temperance work and that it stands [for] any measures that will rid our community permanently of the open saloon." The club also founded the Corona Settlement House to conduct its Americanization efforts on the Mexican population, principally the women and children.[35]

The prohibition movement enlisted the support of Mexican Protestant churches that viewed alcohol and saloons as leading to moral and social degeneracy. Mexican Protestant denominations proselytized about the evils of alcohol through testimonies and conversion stories of the Mexican Protestant faithful. Once a Mexican man accepts the gospel, according to one Mexican Baptist minister, "He is a changed man. He no longer squanders his pay in drink and gambling and therefore is now able to dress better and to provide more adequately for the care of his family." In Corona, one Mexican Baptist minister spread the gospel to the Mexican population. When the First Baptist Church erected the Mexican Mission church building on North Main Street, the Baptist minister walked along streets encouraging pool hall patrons to attend religious services. The newspaper praised the missionary work in that part of town. "A regular [Mexican] pastor in charge of the Mission is taking a commendable part in bringing up the standard of that foreign population to that of Corona's ideal." As chapter 4 shows, the Mexican Baptist Mission competed with St. Edward's Catholic Church for the religious faith of the Mexican population.[36]

At first the citrus industry grew concerned that the antisaloon movement would eliminate one of its chief customers—saloonkeepers who used lemons for mixed alcohol drinks—but then used prohibition to its advantage by promoting lemon juice drinks as an alternative to alcohol. Concerned about negative publicity, the Sunkist advertising office eliminated mixed-drink recipes using alcohol, and the company cut its supply of lemons and oranges to saloons. "Now of course this outlet [saloons] is wiped out," wrote Don Francisco, director of Sunkist advertising. "But people are going to drink something. They are going to spend that liquor money for something. And that something might very logically be lemonade." Prohibition presented a new opportunity to sell lemonade as a substitute for alcoholic drinks, as reflected in one Sunkist slogan, "Good-bye to liquor, here's to lemonade."[37]

Corona temperance forces also attempted to stop Italians from producing and selling wine. Prohibition forces persuaded city council members to pass a "bone-dry" ordinance that prohibited the manufacture of wine and set a $100 fine for violators. One city councilman cited the city's bad publicity as the reason for his support. He remarked, "The city is getting a large amount of fine advertising as a result of the frequent murders and shooting scrapes among the undesirable Mexican element harbored here. . . . What the Mexicans fail to do to advertise the city, the Italians who operate 'blind pigs' further keep us in the limelight." In response, leaders of the Italian community complained to the city council that wine was part of their culture and dietary habit. In 1918 Tom Danieri, convicted and fined $150 for violating the ordinance, challenged the city in court, and after several appeals the ordinance was upheld in higher courts. "It is not that the people of this city have any grievance against these particular people," remarked one city councilperson in defense of the ordinance. "The Italians are known to be a law-abiding, hard-working class of people and while they, themselves feel it is working a hardship on them, they should realize that there are other classes who would abuse the privilege and to favor one and deny the other would be out of the question." Despite the city's antiwine ordinance, Corona Italians continued to produce wine and sell it for profit on the underground market.[38]

La Bootlegada

Despite the temperance efforts to redirect immigrants away from saloons and pool halls that caused so much drinking and vice, Mexicans forged an alternative culture in which bootlegging operations figured prominently as symbols of resistance and community. As one local historian wrote, "In Corona at the time, homemade beer and wine were known to flow fairly freely in spite of the WCTU and the drys who favored the Volstead Act, making alcohol beverages illegal." Whereas Italians cornered the market on the manufacturing and selling of wine,

Mexicans took over the bootleg whiskey trade. Alcohol smuggling became a way for Mexican men in Corona to offset the low wages earned in the citrus industry and to challenge racial discrimination in the community that restricted their ability to provide for their families.[39]

Despite the moral and religious arguments marshaled against it, contraband liquor provided economic opportunities for some Mexican Americans who saw the lucrative potential of *la bootlegada*. Smuggling liquor, however, was risky business, as operators faced the possibility of arrest and lengthy jail sentences. Mexican bootleggers set up stills up and down the coast and in eastern desert areas. Mike Rodríguez related his father's bootlegging experience during an interview. "During Prohibition my father made distilled liquor called *mula* in New Mexico and Arizona and later in Barstow, California. He boiled raisins, prunes, and potatoes, put the mixture in a large crock with sugar, let [it] cool some and added yeast and let it sit and ferment. After it fermented, he distilled it to make the *mula*. He and a friend sometimes sold it for one dollar per gallon. It was strong clear alcohol; gave quite a kick. That's why it was called *mula*, the Spanish word for mule." It cost five hundred dollars to start up an illegal still that could produce fifty to one hundred gallons of liquor daily. Each gallon sold for a dollar, so the still fairly quickly paid for itself.[40]

Corona's Mexican bootleggers attempted to stay one step ahead of the police as they tried to make money from the illicit bootleg trade to supplement low agricultural wages. Having worked as a citrus picker for several Corona growers, Refugio Lopez entered the bootlegging business with the help of his brother and friends. Court transcripts offer an insight into the motivations of Lopez and other bootleggers convicted under the Wright Act. Lopez justified "breaking the law" because he had to support his wife and four sons, one of whom suffered from a life-threatening illness. He stated that he "was not in the habit of drinking and had never been drunk." When two unidentified men asked him where they could get a drink he told them he would get them a drink of whiskey but that he had no intention of selling to them and would not take their money. After the men received the alcohol, dry agents arrested Lopez and he remained in jail, unable to make bail, until his court date. The judge granted his appeal and suspended his jail sentence, since a "nominal fee would work a real hardship upon the dependent family."[41]

Bootlegging was more than an economic strategy; it also represented a way for men to construct a masculine identity and culture within the family and community. Men demonstrated their physical strength, courage, and virility through gambling, drinking, carrying a gun, and other male leisure activities. Take, for example, Juan Salvador Villaseñor's "manly" confrontations with police and other bootleggers that earned him a reputation among his male friends as "the man who couldn't die." After a series of encounters with police and company bosses, Juan Salvador promised himself that he would "never work for another son-of-a-bitch gringo bastard again." As a result of these frequent conflicts, he attained a mythic status among barrio residents. One resident even compared him to the Mexican revolution leader Francisco Villa, considered "a man among men." For others, Juan Salvador represented social mobility. "The people stared at Juan as he drove into the barrio of Corona in his big new green Dodge convertible. He looked [like] a king, the mayor of Corona, as he nodded hello to them and went slowly down the street."[42]

Alcohol smuggling opened new opportunities for Mexican women to supplement meager family incomes. The role of women in Prohibition-era bootlegging is less understood, however, since both popular culture and historiography have typically ignored female bootleggers. Women often served as small-time dealers or go-betweens, linking sellers and buyers, and used their homes as blind pig operations. Blind pigs, or underground saloons, were unlicensed informal spaces, often hidden in home basements, that allowed immigrant groups to maintain a drinking subculture in opposition to the intrusive reformers and police surveillance. Los Angeles barber Felipe Montes told Manuel Gamio how he set up his bootlegging operation with the help of his wife. "When I'm not here my wife takes charge of waiting on them [customers] and also when I am very busy." The presence of "kitchen bootlegging" caught the attention of the newspaper editor who wrote, "The liquor business is said to be passing from the saloon to the kitchen [where] the bootleg stuff is produced in small quantities." Corona's most prominent female bootlegger, Carmen Ayala, driven to bootlegging by financial circumstances, faced arrest and six months in the county jail. After she pleaded guilty, the judge denied her parole because "she refused to disclose her supply of liquor to the officers."[43]

Mexican bootleggers used the proximity of the U.S.-Mexico border to evade enforcement officials and smuggle liquor into the United States. "As [the Mexican] enters the United States alone, he tends to become a social problem," declared one California commentator, who added that "he commonly acquires venereal disease, gets into brawls, as a concomitant of imbibing bootleg whiskey, and sometimes joins ultraracial labor movements." Enforcement was made more difficult with the large number of American tourists descending on border towns in search of alcoholic beverages, gambling casinos, dance halls, brothels, and other sinful pleasures not available in their dry hometowns. Francisco Gómez related his bootlegging experience to anthropologist Manuel Gamio. "A short time after Prohibition was established and smuggling liquor became a touchy business, I took charge of getting forty cases of tequila and other liquors each week to a colonel and captain at Fort Bliss [El Paso]." After several violent confrontations with police, Gómez returned to Ciudad Juárez to hide out for several months. Because Mexico acted as a safe haven for "booze smugglers," the only way to stop the flow of illegal liquor, according to a State Law Enforcement League official, "was to close the Mexican border." Even the U.S. Border Patrol had a difficult task in halting bootlegging activities. One U.S. border patrolman referred to the border areas as "rivers of liquor flowing north" and recounted how the same methods were used for "catching illegal aliens and booze smugglers." New evidence from recently classified U.S. Border Patrol documents revealed that the U.S. Border Patrol was more concerned about stopping bootlegging activities than the illegal crossing of Mexican nationals.[44]

Sensational newspaper stories about the latest liquor raids in the Corona barrio contributed to the erroneous idea that Mexicans were more criminally inclined than the general population. The *Corona Independent* ran the headline "Mexicans Cause Most Trouble to Law Officers" to alarm readers of the "predominance of foreigners in the lawlessness of the county despite their minority in numbers." The article cited liquor violations and driving while drunk as the chief offenses among Mexican defendants. In Riverside County alone, Mexicans made up four-fifths of the total prison population arrested for liquor-related violations. According to a crime survey of eight southern California counties from October 1926 to October 1927, of 2,974 Mexicans booked for various crimes, 751 were for Wright Act violations, of which 69 were in Riverside County. According to one Prohibition historian, "A double standard attitude existed toward minorities whereby one eye was closed more often with non-minorities. Whites were not as apt to be arrested, not as apt to be prosecuted, and certainly not as apt to serve jail time."[45]

One of Corona's sensational liquor raids occurred on Saturday night, July 27, 1929, when federal authorities confiscated more than five hundred gallons of wine and whiskey from four homes and arrested seven Mexican and two Italian violators. Federal agents recruited two Anglo teenage boys to buy bootleg liquor. The boys testified against Italian and Mexican bootleggers who allegedly supplied the liquor. When questioned about the identity of offenders, one of the Anglo boys responded, "I believe they were Mexicans. I know they were dark, but I am not certain whether they were Mexicans or Italians." The other Anglo teenager testified that "you can get all you want in this part of town. . . . I can take you to a dozen bootleggers." The teenagers' testimony, reprinted in the local newspaper, set off angry editorials by Anglo parents. One parent clamored, "It must stop this time! We hope to make the others see they can't trifle with the law and laugh at the courts. When these defendants are through, they'll not have any contempt for American laws!" Another parent demanded that the police "put a clamp on the booze traffic in this foreign settlement, [and that] bootleggers should be given higher sentences. They are not out of jail one day, until they are right back in the bootlegging business." During the trial, which lasted several months, angry Anglo citizens packed the courtroom demanding harsher penalties for suspected Mexican and Italian violators for selling liquor to minors. The jury found the defendants guilty and imposed high fines and lengthy jail sentences. The defendants pleaded for mercy and leniency "because they were fathers of large families" and stated emphatically that they were "through with liquor."[46]

Apart from apprehending bootleggers, police authorities faced another enemy—fruit thieves. During the late 1920s Corona citrus growers claimed that "two-footed orchard pests" were "looting the groves," resulting in the loss of thousands of dollars. To stop the "fruit raiding," growers deputized foremen as police officers, hired "special police" on motorcycle to patrol the groves day and night, required fruit buyers to show receipts, and enlisted the help of the Corona police to inspect vehicles. One newspaper editorial praised the police for keeping close scrutiny on both fruit and liquor smugglers. "For the purpose of detecting fruit thieves the officers are stopping night motorists as they drive along the highways if their cars have any bulky packages or give any evidence of having any stolen fruit but likewise booze which householders have secured by making trips to their favorite bootleggers."[47]

Despite severe jail sentences and excessive fines for liquor violators, Mexican and Italian bootleggers continued to thrive by establishing connections with wealthy clients and sympathetic officials willing to overlook the trade. Corona resident Frances Martínez remembered how some Italians got advance notice before raids. "One day all of a sudden we saw cars running out of the Italian colony and [then] we saw a bunch of federal policemen come out. They found out that [Italian] was a bootlegger but when they got there nothing was there because he got a tip that they were coming. Some guys tipped off the bootleggers. The

Italians were well connected because the chief of police was a drunk himself." Mexican bootleggers also had police and firemen "on the take" and cultivated a network of support from hotel owners, pool hall regulars, and other businesses interested in satisfying their customers.[48]

Despite the passing of prohibition statutes, Mexicans enjoyed a steady flow of smuggled liquor as they engaged in a constant battle with reformers and police over the control of their livelihood and daily lives. Police authorities faced an immense task trying to stem the flow of liquor in southern California, which stretched 539 miles along the coastline and 500 miles along the U.S.-Mexico border. According to the *New York Times*, "alcohol is cheap and plentiful, hijacking is a favorite outdoor sport, gang murders are becoming episodical, and the police, fettered by political interferences, espionage and other harassments, seem to be helpless." Nearly a decade after the adoption of national prohibition, middle-class Americans, troubled by lack of enforcement, crowded jail cells, bootlegging "gang" violence, and corruption, began to oppose prohibition. On December 5, 1933, the Eighteenth Amendment was finally repealed, bringing back legal drinking, albeit with some regulations, to American life.[49]

For the first two decades of the twentieth century the Mexican population in Corona was overwhelmingly male. Inside the citrus orchards, pickers constructed a masculine work culture exemplified by rough behavior, vulgar jokes, incessant horseplay, and fighting with coworkers and bosses. This combative work culture extended into the community, where many nonwork hours were spent in the city's North Main Street commercial district, where saloons, pool halls, gambling establishments, and other forms of entertainment appealed to male tastes. Women were typically discouraged from entering these male domains unless they offered themselves as sexual partners in back rooms or other spaces hidden from public view.

These all-male establishments provided welcome relief from long work hours in the hot sun and lonely nights of longing for the comforts of Mexico. It was in these spaces where gender was constructed. Mexican solos developed a rough masculine culture expressed in brawls, scrapes, excessive drinking, and sexual control of women. The rowdy behavior they displayed while asserting their masculine autonomy and pride also served to reinforce unequal gender relations, leading to corrosive effects on family and community unity. Paradoxically, these same forms of male bonding could be mobilized during labor conflicts. Free of employer surveillance, workers voiced grievances and plotted labor actions. During World War I, workers launched work stoppages and spontaneous strikes in an attempt to gain higher wages, though an organized labor movement did not emerge in Corona until the late 1930s. These politicized spaces came under attack by employers, reformers, and city leaders attempting to abolish or regulate them.

Alarmed at the social and economic effects of excessive drinking and related antisocial behaviors, Corona temperance forces sought to pass antialcohol ordinances to socially control the immigrant laborers within the city's borders. These transplanted midwesterners sought to build a Christian city without slums, vice, and saloons. Corona drys blamed Mexican immigrants for committing crime, violence, gambling, and prostitution in the city's central amusement district. Ideas about Mexican criminality were reinforced by academics, arrest records, government reports, and newspaper headlines that portrayed Mexicans as lawless, pistol-wielding, immoral drunkards. Temperance crusaders accomplished their goal of closing down saloons, regulating pool halls, passing ordinances against guns and gambling, and making Corona dry.

During the Prohibition era, Mexican immigrant men and women resisted the Wright Act by manufacturing homemade whiskey, transporting barrels of liquor, acting as lookouts, and consuming alcohol in hidden spaces. Mexican bootleggers offered an important cultural symbol of resistance by undermining the city's dry law and defying the authority of temperance forces and police officials who called for strict enforcement and punishment of violators. Women played a key role in masterminding the trading and manufacturing of bootleg liquor. *La bootlegada* became another way for Mexican men and women to earn extra money and reclaim a sense of cultural autonomy in the face of racial antagonism and economic exploitation. As bootleggers gained some degree of autonomy, they were swiftly marked as undesirables and as a racial threat to the American nation. Italians were also subjected to police arrests and harassment for violating the city's antiwine ordinance, but they still continued to reap profits from selling wine.

As more families moved into Corona during the 1920s, men were stirred toward more wholesome amusements such as the baseball and sports clubs that emerged as a popular form of recreation during the Great Depression. Having been excluded from male-dominated saloons and pool halls, women flocked to churches, movie theaters, outdoor dances, and other forms of commercial leisure integrated by gender. As chapter 4 shows, Mexican women fashioned their own notions of womanhood through their leisurely pursuits and cultural work that often ran in opposition to the traditional roles of femininity.

4 Churches, Movie Theaters, and Cinco de Mayo Fiestas

After her mother's death in an accident in Durango, Mexico, one-year-old Frances Martínez came to Corona with her aunt and uncles. Her strict and deeply religious aunt sent Frances to St. Mary's Parochial School in Los Angeles until the eighth grade. There Frances lived in a rooming house with female students from different ethnic backgrounds, learned English, and excelled in music and dance. She remembered "hanging around La Placita and riding red streetcars all over East L.A." But when Frances returned to Corona to complete high school, she had to live with an aunt who "stuck with the old, old ways." The aunt and uncles would not allow her to date; indeed, Frances recalls, "she wanted to send me back to Mexico to get married, but I refused." Frances's independent spirit routinely drew her into conflict with her family. "When I went to dances, my aunt went along and if a boy danced two dances with me, my aunt made me sit down." After graduating from high school in 1932, Frances defied her aunt's wishes and eloped with a former boxer from New Mexico. When asked in an interview whether it was her husband's idea to elope, Frances responded candidly, "He did not take me. I took myself."[1]

Frances was one of many young Mexican women who negotiated their way into an American culture whose feminine ideals sometimes clashed with ideals of Mexican womanhood and the middle-class ideology of domesticity promoted by citrus companies and social reformers. At a time when Anglo women were broadening their social roles, Mexican women were expected to exemplify "Mexican womanhood," defined by virginity until marriage, piety, and submissiveness, and to fulfill their domestic roles as mothers and wives, placing husbands and children before themselves. Whenever Mexican women entered the public sphere, they were supposed to be chaperoned or escorted by husbands, brothers, or sons. While some subscribed to these gender conventions, others challenged familial expectations and traditional notions of femininity imposed by middle-class reformers and employers. During the 1920s and 1930s, the leisurely pursuits of Mexican women in Corona included church-related activities, movie theaters, and Cinco de Mayo festivals.

Mexican Women and Ideology of Domesticity

As discussed in chapter 1, citrus companies implemented a series of paternalist measures in the 1920s to attract and stabilize the Mexican labor force. The cornerstone of these new company policies was the promotion of "domestic ideology" to regulate and reorganize gender relations in ranch communities. The company believed that married employees, unlike unreliable rowdy solos, with a company home would become more firmly wedded to the job and serve to counter drinking, gambling, and other vices. More importantly, the company understood that married men were less likely to risk their family's livelihood by engaging in labor activism. Male employees were required to be married to be eligible for a two-bedroom home, employee saving programs, Christmas bonuses, and other welfare benefits. During the 1920s, very few ranch wives and daughters worked outside the home for wages. According to the company, a woman's place was in the home caring for her husband and children and ensuring a new generation of workers.[2]

The Corona Foothill Lemon Company promoted its own brand of domesticity through a series of welfare programs aimed at Mexican wives, mothers, and daughters. In 1933, the company built a community center in the largest Mexican labor camp to offer Americanization, English-language, child-rearing, health and sanitation, and home economics classes. The idea for a community center began with Jessimine Hampton, wife of the company president and a graduate of Claremont University, who realized that "since the [Mexican] women did not speak English, I had to have classes for them." Home economics classes, according to the company, were intended to "teach foreign girls the real art of cooking since many marry very young and become home makers, [and] there is no better service to them than [that] they could become efficient cooks and housekeepers." The company also donated a small garden plot for each household, promoting gardening as an extension of women's domestic role. By participating in company welfare programs, women established female networks of support and allowed them to appropriate the company's ideology of domesticity to demand resources and defend their own interests.[3]

The Corona Settlement House, along with Washington Elementary School and the El Nido Maternity Home, also committed themselves to domesticating Mexican immigrant women in the community. The Americanization programs, scholars have noted, included efforts to reeducate Mexican immigrant women to conform to American middle-class domesticity.[4] At Washington Elementary School, home economics teachers held classes in sewing, cooking, and house decorating, all aimed at "acquainting Mexican girls with the ideal home." The Corona Settlement House, located in the Corona barrio, also catered to the needs of Mexican women and families. It was founded in 1912 as part of Associated Charities by the Women's Improvement Club (WIC), which financed and operated the settlement house. The meeting minutes revealed that apart from providing clothing, free meals, and other char-itable assistance, settlement workers also offered Bible study, sewing classes, housekeeping, and English classes. One settlement worker described the popularity of the sewing classes: "The [Settlement] House has organized a well-attended sewing class for Mexican girls from eight to 14 years of age. . . . They are all eager to learn and delight at being taught the art of sewing on the machine." Another volunteer described how the Corona Settlement House helped rescue "wayward girls" in need. "The Settlement House is a gathering place for children who have no place to keep warm. Mothers have been permitted to call the deten-tion home on our phone for word of their lost children."[5]

Well-baby clinics and maternity programs also promoted an ideol-ogy of domesticity. After delivering more than two hundred Mexican babies in Corona's outlying ranches, Dr. Henry Herman opened El Nido ("the nest") Maternity Home in 1933. Dr. Herman, a native of Germany and a Seventh-day Adventist missionary who lived in Argentina for nine years, opened the three-bed maternity home to attend to the med-ical needs of expectant Mexican women instead of "wandering the countryside delivering babies in unsanitary conditions." Because of Dr. Herman's fluency in Spanish, El Nido attracted a large number of Mex-ican expectant female patients and instructed them on their domestic roles as mothers.[6]

Creating Sacred Spaces

Religious expression formed an integral part of Mexican life in Corona. The Catholic Church provided a safe haven for Mexican immigrants who faced a hostile and alienating environment in the workplace and the community. Scholars have suggested that Mexican Catholics have used the church as a way to maintain their religious faith and transform their identities in the U.S. context. Consistent with this, Corona's Mexican Catholics, especially women, transformed St. Edward's Catholic Church into a center of social activity and cultural expression. Not all of Corona's Mexicans were Catholics, however; the Mexican Baptist Church established a small but active congregation that challenged the Catholic Church's dominance in the Mexican community.[7]

The earliest Catholic Church, St. John the Baptist Mission, was located in the town of Rincon, near Corona. In 1909 Father John McCarthy secured funds to build a small wooden church in the city, between Sixth and Merrill streets. Ten years later, the church congregation grew dramatically with large-scale immigration from Mexico. Father Clarence Kimmons faced a dilemma: many of the Mexican faithful earned meager agricultural wages and could not keep the church financially stable. The new pastor sought external support for the construction of a new building with the help of the Mexican congregation who were willing to donate their skills and physical labor.[8]

After the church received a substantial donation from the widow of Edward Alf, a longtime member of the Catholic Church Extension Society of Chicago, Father Kimmons secured the skills of a Mexican construction crew to begin building a "Mexican stone church." Mexican congregation members banded together and took over the construction of the church by gathering cobblestones from the Temescal creek beds and hauling them by horse and buggy to the building site. Mike Villa remembered watching his father apply his stone masonry skills, which he learned from his grandfather in Mexico, and work for more than three years on the church. In June 1919, Bishop John Cantwell of Los Angeles dedicated the new stone church, which was called St. Edward's. In his dedication, he stressed the need to provide charitable relief and to educate the new immigrants in American-style Catholic doctrine.[9]

Once the new church opened for regular mass services, though, Mexican attendance dwindled because of segregated seating practices. Mike Villa remembered that after his father helped build the church, the priest began segregating church members according to race. "As a

kid I used to go to church often until they started to separate us with a
rope. The usher would say if you were a Mexican you go over there, and
if you were Italian on that side, and if you're white on that side. . . . I did
not like the idea of being separated so I quit going to church for years."
Apart from racial discrimination, language served as an obstacle to
church attendance, as the Catholic Church's English-speaking priest-
hood alienated Mexican immigrants as well as the small Italian congregation.[10] Not until Father Miguel Santacana arrived in 1927 did church
attendance increase. In 1923 the church held two masses, one at 7:00
a.m. and other at 8:00 a.m., for its 400 members. By 1936 the parish congregation grew to 1,500, of whom 1,200 were Mexican, 225 were Anglo,
and 122 were Italian. Originally from Madrid, Spain, Father Santacana
conducted masses in Spanish and encouraged the practice of Mexican
customs and traditions.[11]

Although men built the stone church, Mexican women were central to the daily parish operations. Mexican women were considered the
"pillars of the church" for their volunteer work, which included preparing food for parish fund-raising events. The church depended on women
such as Frances Martínez, who used her musical talents for church services and other religious celebrations. Frances organized the church choir
and played the organ for funerals, baptisms, weddings, and other special
occasions, but without official status in the church she was not paid
wages and had to find work elsewhere. To earn extra money, she performed musical scores for silent movies at the local Mexican theater.
She was also the only female pianist in a jazz band that performed at
community benefit dances. Frances and other Mexican women carried
out important cultural work in the public sphere, which provided a
monetary escape from household labor and wage work, cemented new
friendships, and built community institutions.[12]

Mexican women built self-confidence and honed their leadership
skills during the planning of jamaicas (charity bazaars) to raise funds for
the Catholic Church. These charity events featured food booths, children's games, and music for dancing. Female volunteers donated their
time and energy in preparing the food and making homemade items to
sell, with the proceeds going to church coffers. Frances Martínez was
instrumental in organizing the first charity bazaars at St. Edward's.
"When I came to Corona in 1928 there was nothing going on. So I asked
the Spanish priest [Father Santacana] why not have jamaicas." This was
only the beginning of Frances's activist leadership in the community.[13]

Apart from fund-raising, women used these parish-sponsored
events to create social spaces for young people to congregate and forge

long-lasting friendships. As one organizer put it, "The *jamaicas* gave young girls a chance to meet and talk to boys in front of their parents." However, women still performed traditional roles as food producers and sellers in these settings. The *jamaica* event that allowed women to symbolically break gender norms was the mock jail in which women performed as police officers to arrest rowdy boys for misbehaving. One of the organizers of the mock jails, Margaret Muñoz, admitted, "That is how I met my husband." Gender norms were relaxed during these mock arrests. One researcher observed that "the boys delight in being arrested by a pair of attractive young girls, who at other times would appear shy, modest, and would be afraid to be seen by their parents."[14]

Despite the U.S. Catholic Church's efforts to Americanize Mexican immigrants, the Mexican Catholic faithful continued to celebrate long-standing public rituals and customs that reflected their Mexican Catholic identity. St. Edward's Church celebrated the Feast of Our Lady of Guadalupe, Los Pastores, and Las Posadas during the Christmas season, events that served as important cultural spaces to build a sense of community, ethno-religious identity, and the feeling of belonging. In the early morning of December 12, 1926, Mexican parishioners gathered to commemorate the appearance of La Virgen de Guadalupe. A solemn procession began through the barrio streets, with parishioners carrying candles and a large picture of La Virgen, and before they entered the church for mass a serenade with music took place outside. Mexican parishioners marched through the streets breaking into song and worship of their patroness, proclaiming their ethno-religious identity and, whether consciously or not, challenging the racism and nativism hovering ominously like a dark cloud on the Mexican community.[15]

Catholic priests often took advantage of women's cultural work in the parish and imposed "traditional" roles and values for Mexican women. One La Habra priest complained about the "improper" dress of young single girls and ordered them to dress in long skirts, long sleeves, collars that covered their necks, and veils. One young woman disagreed with the priest about the importance of chaste clothing. "We are not used to wearing these here. . . . I do not see what is the matter with him [the priest] that he makes us wear them." But an elderly lady reinforced the priest's views on feminine propriety. "I love to see the girls dress with modesty, like they have to dress in Mexico when they go to church." Mothers and fathers reinforced these strict gender norms for their daughters, and this often led to conflict. Daughters often defied parental authority and the Catholic Church when it came to courtship and marriage. One Mexican father, for example, appealed for help from the Catholic priest and the police when his fifteen-year-old daughter ran away with a twenty-six-year-old man. Father-daughter conflicts over sexual autonomy often led to elopement and marriages outside the Catholic Church.[16]

The Catholic Church attempted to keep its hold over its Mexican congregation despite Protestant evangelical efforts to woo them away. Protestant denominations, represented by Presbyterians, Methodists, Pentecostals, and Baptists, had been active in Mexico since the nineteenth century, and after the Mexican Revolution they continued their proselytizing efforts on both sides of the border. The influx of immigrants into southern California drew the attention of Protestant missionaries, who took up the task of evangelizing in Mexican barrios and *colonias*. Protestant missionaries made inroads in the Mexican community by combining religious instruction with social service and enlisting the help of settlement houses, girls' and boys' clubs, schools, community centers, and employers. One 1921 figure estimated twelve thousand Mexican Protestant members and three hundred Mexican churches throughout the United States.[17]

The American Baptist Church was one of the most active congregations in the Mexican community. Early Baptist work began in 1915 with the appointment of Mr. and Mrs. L. E. Troyer to the First Mexican Church in Los Angeles. Having previously worked in Puerto Rico and Mexico, the Troyers used their familiarity with Mexican culture and the Spanish language for evangelization among the Mexican populations. With support from the Southern California Baptist Convention, the Troyers established churches and missions in San Pedro, Wilmington, Bakersfield, Oxnard, Santa Barbara, and Corona.[18]

Mrs. Troyer described in her memoirs the early years of Baptist missionary work in Corona's Mexican community. Because "the Mexicans in the [Corona] district were not receiving the Gospel," the First Baptist Church decided to reach out to its Mexican neighbors. Troyer disclosed how Corona's leading citrus family and founders of the First Baptist Church, the two Jameson families, became interested in missionary work and helped build a church for Mexican Baptists. In 1919, Jameson donated a plot of land on North Main Street and paid more than twelve thousand dollars for construction of the church. Designed in Spanish mission style, the new church accommodated a medium-size congregation. The Mexican Baptist Church began with forty-five original members in 1920. A decade later it had grown to more than one hundred members, and by 1936 it claimed more than two hundred members. As one of the largest employers of local Mexican labor, the Jamesons wanted to keep close reins on the Mexican congregation. Troyer wrote: "The American [First Baptist] Church in Corona has carefully guarded all the interests of the Mexican Church and a beautiful new church now houses our Mexican people." Anglo Baptists practiced a kind of "pious paternalism" toward the Mexican congregation, believing that Mexicans were incapable of self-government.[19]

Reflecting the influence of the First Baptist Church, Mexican Baptists were encouraged to learn how to read English and embrace aspects of American middle-class culture. During church dedication ceremonies, Joy Jameson welcomed the attendees and offered a prayer "upon the new church and among the foreigners of our city." Riverside's Baptist minister predicted that "the church will do much toward helping the Mexican to become a better American." Invited guest Mrs. Troyer directed her comments to the possibility of Americanization through evangelization. "The Mexican should show much love and appreciation to the people of Corona for what they had done for them. . . . If every American church in Southern California would do what Corona has done, the Mexican problem would be solved." Protestant missionaries throughout the Southwest placed strong emphasis on the Americanization of immigrant populations, and special homemaking and child-rearing classes were designed to teach women their proper domestic roles.[20]

At the opening ceremonies, Rev. P. H. Pierson was chosen to become pastor of the Mexican Baptist Church because of his past missionary work in Mexico. Pierson led a group of guests into the Spanish-style building, showing them the main floor where church services and Bible study classes were held; the basement floor consisting of a spacious living room, kitchen, dining area, and living quarters; and the outside playground for children. Pierson spoke about his success with the night school that produced new pastoral leaders such as Manuel Enríquez. Teresa Enríquez recalled how her father became one of the leading Baptist pastors in southern California. "My dad got involved in the [Baptist] mission as [a] young man after he married my mom at 18 years old and settled down in Corona. Then he began working with the youth and leading Bible study."[21]

Baptist Mexican women, like women in the Catholic Church, volunteered their physical and emotional labor in the programming and daily operations of the church. Every few years, when a new pastor was assigned to the Mexican Baptist Church, "It was my father [Manuel Enríquez] in charge of welcoming him on behalf of the congregation and the women made the food for everyone," explained Teresa Enríquez. Apart from food preparation, women conducted Sunday school, ran the child care center, and taught songs and recitations to the children. Well known for her sewing skills, Teresa also was called upon to sew the capes of the male clergy. "Even the Catholic priest wanted me to make him a cape," she recalled. "So of course I made one for him."[22]

Being the daughter of a Baptist minister was not easy for Teresa Enríquez, especially after her parents divorced. She then lived with her strict grandmother while her father traveled from town to town spreading the gospel and opening new Mexican Baptist missions. Teresa understood at a young age the significance of the family's standing in the community, so when she fell in love she faced a difficult dilemma. Over the objections of her family, Teresa eloped and married a devoted Catholic. "My family was fine with it," Teresa said, "but his parents did not want me because I was not a good Catholic girl" even though her husband played in a jazz band and frequented the pool halls. The only way her mother-in-law would accept her was if she attended catechism classes and got married in the Catholic Church. So every Sunday morning for five years, she accompanied her husband to St. Edward's Church and studied catechism with Father Matthew Thompson. Finally her husband stood up against his mother and told her "he was not marrying the Catholic Church but marrying a good Christian and good woman." As Teresa proudly remembered, "We had a little ceremony at the home and later my husband became a Baptist. He stopped drinking [alcohol] and began to study the Bible." Teresa's negotiation of her religion with her husband and his family revealed how religious differences were as much an obstacle to intermarriage as were racial, ethnic, and class differences.[23]

Migrating to the Movies

During the 1920s young Mexican women, like many other immigrant women, flocked to dance halls, nickelodeons, movie houses, amusement parks, and other places of commercial entertainment looking for a "good time" and to escape the traditional controls of church and family. As Mexican women occupied more packinghouse jobs (47 by 1930 and 150 by 1940), they used their earnings to lessen their dependency on fathers and husbands and gain greater freedom in commercialized leisure spaces. One of the most popular leisure activities for American-born daughters of immigrant parents was going to the movies. Reformers, along with parents, regarded these heterosocial environments as potentially dangerous for unchaperoned women, who could engage in sexual promiscuity in the dark. As a result, some Mexican women were deterred; others defied the coercive powers of reformers and gained limited access to this new form of commercialized leisure.[24]

Compared to Los Angeles with its established theater districts, Corona had only two silent movie houses during the 1920s. The city's first movie theater, California Theater, opened in 1901 and catered primarily to Anglo audiences, with a racially segregated seating system. The public humiliation of discrimination still loomed large years later for those who experienced it. Alice Rodríguez recalled attending the Anglo-owned theater only once. "My mother would not let anybody push her around, so when she found out that we had to sit in the balcony of the theater she got mad and we never went back again." Juanita Ramírez's father responded differently when he was asked to move toward the unattractive part of the theater. She recalled, "He [usher] asked my father to move himself and us to the seats on the left side. My father then asked him, 'What, my money is no good? My money is not good like yours?' At that age, I felt so embarrassed that I wanted to crawl under my seat, but my father refused to be intimidated and stayed put." Feelings of pride mixed with acts of resistance represented early challenges to the city's unequal moviegoing system. As chapter 7 shows, this segregated system finally ended in the post–World War II years.[25]

The fear of declining revenues forced theater owners to admit Mexican patrons, as long they accepted racially segregated seating and the disparaging cinematic images of Mexicans. Some of the early Hollywood films screened in Corona's theaters depicted Mexicans as villains, cowards, and bandits. Among the films screened at the California Theater were *Bronco Billy and the Greaser, The Greaser's Revenge, Pedro's Treachery,* and *Bad Man.* These so-called greaser films reinforced many of the negative stereotypes held by politicians, newspapers, police, and those moviegoers who had very little contact with the Mexican culture. For the *Bad Man* premiere, the *Corona Independent* described the sombrero-wearing Pancho Lopez as a "poor peon" who terrorizes an Arizona cattle rancher. However, the newspaper reassured readers that "the Bad Man will only be on the screen. Needn't worry folks, he's in the film only and can't get loose." The anti-Mexican discourse in these films combined with segregated seating practices set the groundwork for Mexican businessmen to build their own movie theater.[26]

Instead of countering adverse anti-Mexican images, Progressive-era reformers concentrated on the corrupting effects of sexually lurid movies on young girls and children. The self-appointed guardians of motion picture morality were mainly Anglo middle-class women, affiliated with temperance unions, settlement houses, and civic clubs, who sought to censor "objectionable" movies with sexual promiscuity, drinking, and juvenile delinquency. In Los Angeles, where everyone including immigrant children and youths went to the movies, ethnically diverse movie crowds offended middle-class sensibilities. One Los Angeles critic attacked the candor and crudeness of the movies that attracted Mexican audiences. "In many cases the films shown in the theatres of the Mexican district, especially along North Main Street[,] are melodramatic and exciting in the extreme and not infrequently suggestive and more or less immoral." One researcher studying the movie habits in the All Nations Boys Club attributed movie attendance to enjoyment, killing time, and relaxation as well as "to neck" and "have fun with girls."[27]

In Corona, WIC led a campaign to impose restrictive measures on local movie theaters. WIC members adopted a "mothering" approach toward movie censorship and regulation that viewed female moviegoers as lacking in self-control and eminently corruptible. In 1910 the women's club lobbied the city council to pass an ordinance prohibiting "prize fight" pictures because they supposedly incited violence and promoted gambling. Six years later the city council debated an ordinance to close down movie theaters and placed it on the ballot. Despite opposition by the chamber of commerce and business owners, the Sunday-closing ordinance passed by a small margin. Movie theater owners joined by small business owners reopened the debate the following year by forcing another citywide vote.[28] Despite the defeat of the Sunday-closing ordinance at the ballot box WIC continued to work with state censor boards that led to the 1930 Hays Code. In a 1921 speech to WIC members, the president of WIC complained, "About 80 percent of the films produced here have such a thin veneer, covering the lust, crime, and vice portrayed, that they are unfit for children to see." WIC formed a committee to advocate for "better films" in Corona's theaters and toward this end sought support for a petition to be delivered to all the theater owners in town. WIC's efforts to reform the movie habits of Corona youths largely failed. Instead of heeding the reformers' wishes, theater owners paid more attention to patrons' changing movie tastes.[29]

Partly in response to segregated seating practices, anti-Mexican "greaser" films, and reformers' patronizing messages, Julio Cruz and his sons, who already owned a grocery store, built a theater named after the famous Chapultepec castle in Mexico City. Tony Cruz recalled why his father and his uncle built a theater. "I remember when my father went to the [California] Theater and was forced to sit in the balcony. This did not sit well with him, so he started thinking about building a theater. This theater gave the Mexican people a place to go and gather around on weekends. Everyone gathered to talk even after the show was over." El Teatro Chapultepec became an important social and recreational space for the entire Mexican community.[30]

In July 1926 El Teatro Chapultepec opened for business at the center of the barrio, between Fourth and Fifth streets on the east side of North Main Street. The Cruz brothers mortgaged their store and bakery to receive a sizeable bank loan to build the theater. The theater building cost at least twelve thousand dollars and measured 120 by 25 feet with 370 seats, a movie screen, and a stage for vaudeville acts, musical performances, comedy acts, and variety shows. One of the drop curtains depicted the Chapultepec castle with surrounding park scenery. Equipped with a modern projector supplied by the California Motion Pictures Equipment Company. El Teatro Chapultepec screened the latest silent motion pictures booked through the Film Booking Offices in Los Angeles. The opening ceremonies were attended by Mexican dignitaries from the Los Angeles consular office including the vice-consul, who addressed the attendees and formally dedicated the venue as a "Mexican theater." Although the theater catered primarily to Mexican audiences, the owner declared that the house would "welcome patrons of either American or Mexican extraction as the films will be carefully chosen to assure entertainment for both." Although management selected films for mass appeal to make the theater financially stable, Manuel Cruz acknowledged that films with derogatory images and negative stereotypes of Mexicans and Mexico were rejected.[31]

Patronizing El Teatro Chapultepec was one means by which Mexican moviegoers reclaimed their nationalist identity. The theater's name referred to the historic castle, Chapultepec, that became an important symbol of Mexican nationalism when "los niños héroes" plunged to their deaths in defense of Mexico against U.S. invaders. In addition, El Teatro Chapultepec hosted Mexican theatrical production companies that staged musical comedies (*zarzuelas*), dramas (*teatro de revista*), and variety acts (*variedades*). Traveling mariachi groups performed concerts to a predominantly older audience. The younger audiences were treated to first-run Hollywood films such as D. W. Griffith's *The Sorrows of Satan*, Cecil DeMille's *The Volga Boatman*, and Raoul Walsh's *What Price Glory?* featuring Mexican actress Dolores del Rio. Mexican spectators made their preferences known as they cheered, jeered, hissed, and taunted the characters on the screen. Teresa Enríquez recalled how motion pictures were rarely silent. "It was always so loud at the motion pictures. There was always somebody who would yell out at the picture or tell others to sit down." El Teatro Chapultepec invited Mexican audiences to form a reciprocal relationship with theater owners and shape cultural productions while at the same time allowing immigrants to perform a Mexicanist identity in the comfort of friends and family members and exposing younger audiences to aspects of American popular culture.[32]

Despite family and societal restrictions, Mexican women migrated to the movies, learning about the latest fashionable clothes, hair styles, and musical trends and becoming "star struck" over their favorite actresses. Whether meeting their boyfriends in dimly lit portions of movie houses or resisting chaperonage, Mexican women defined their own moviegoing experiences, which differed from ideal notions of femininity as defined either by Anglo middle-class reformers or by working-class parents. Most of the Mexican girls interviewed in the All Nations Girls Club revealed moviegoing as their favorite amusements and said that they were usually accompanied by siblings or friends. The researcher, however, showed concern with several informants who revealed their favorite movies (*Devil Dancer* and *Red Hot Dancer*) as having "sex appeal" and said that they enjoyed going to the movies alone or with boys.[33] Juanita Ramírez fondly recalled her first moviegoing experience. "My oldest brother took me to my first movie. I can remember a cowboy group of horses riding in the film toward me. I got so scared thinking they were coming right out of the film that I scooted under the seat and started crying." As a teenage girl, Ramírez developed a crush on actor Rudolph Valentino, who starred in the 1922 film *The Sheik*, but she could not attend Valentino movies without her older brother as chaperone.[34]

In some cases women defied their parents and attended movies without chaperones. Mexican parents were also suspicious of movie houses as potential spaces for courtship and promiscuous sexual mingling. For this reason, women were chaperoned by family members. Viola Rodríguez could attend Saturday matinees only if she brought along her younger siblings. "We would sell our souls to go to the movies. . . . [W]e would sell bottles to get enough money and we would have to take a sister or cousin."[35] Mexican fathers in particular insisted that their daughters conform to an ideal femininity that placed family obligations above personal wants and ambitions. "My father would chaperone me everywhere I went," explained Margaret Rosales. "He did not even let us wear nail polish." Parents instructed girls not to walk alone downtown, explained Margaret Santos, because "Corona from Fifth Street on down was a happening town, full of cantinas, pool halls, and movies and lots of music." Both Rosales and Santos, however, resisted chaperonage by leaving home with female friends and later abandoning them to meet their boyfriends at the movies. One Mexican boy admitted to an interviewer, "I go to the movies with my [male] friends and girlfriend. She sneaks out and says she is going to the show with a girl and comes with me. I meet her someplace."[36]

Apart from the allure of movies, women attended El Teatro Chapultepec to take part in the musical and dramatic performances produced by local community groups. Frances Martínez put it rather bluntly. "We depended on each other for entertainment." She added, "We used [Chapultepec] to put on programs, dances, fiestas and singing for entertainment." In 1928 the Cruz brothers hired Frances to play the piano for silent films. "I didn't have any [sheet] music so I decided what to play as I went along. . . . When the train was coming I would pound away, and when there was a love scene the keys would tinkle." When theater management began to rent theater space for functions, meetings, and events, Frances traded her piano playing for a meeting space for community groups such as the Club Mexicano de Señoritas. Scant sources revealed that this all-Mexican female group was founded in 1929 and modeled after a women's social club in nearby Ontario, California. The club held its meetings at El Teatro Chapultepec and then dissolved for unknown reasons.[37]

Frances lost her job in 1929 when the theater closed due to the stock crash and worsening national economy that forced owners into bankruptcy and the loss of their businesses. The closing of this community institution was a major blow to the local Mexican community, already beaten down by the nativist impulse and fearing the ensuing economic depression. To make things worse, the city's new movie palace, the Corona Theater, instituted segregated seating for Mexicans only. Ironically, the structure was built in the Spanish colonial revival style with balconies and towers. During the theater's grand opening festivities the owner, Glenn Harper, welcomed D. W. Griffith, Clara Bow, Al Jolson, Dolores del Rio, Laurel and Hardy, and many other Hollywood celebrities. Although the theater's gala opening received heavy publicity in local and regional newspapers, there was no mention of its racially segregated seating. In 1936 a new Mexican business owner took over the Cruz building and opened Teatro Circle that featured both Hollywood movies and Mexico-produced films. A year later Mildred Aranda inherited the theater business after her husband died, and she renovated it with new carpet, lighting, and air-conditioning in order to host more community events, including Cinco de Mayo festivities.[38]

Cinco de Mayo Fiestas

Cinco de Mayo became a major holiday on both sides of the U.S.-Mexico border following the victory of the poorly equipped Mexican troops led by General Ignacio Zaragoza over the better-armed French invaders in the famous Battle of Puebla on May 5, 1862. News of the impending victory spread throughout Mexican communities in the U.S. Southwest, prompting supporters to send money and supplies to aid the Mexican army. Mexican women in particular lent their moral support by publishing patriotic poems in San Francisco's Spanish-language newspaper *El Nuevo Mundo*. After Mexico reestablished its independence in 1867, Cinco de Mayo became a significant event for Mexican communities in the late-nineteenth-century Southwest. On May 5, Mexican residents reclaimed the streets to watch parade floats adorned with Mexican banners, and in their favorite festival attire they strolled the grounds in search of familiar faces, delicious food, lively entertainment, and patriotic speeches. The combination of print and public performance during these festivities encouraged expatriates to express their patriotic loyalty to the country they had left behind and create an "imagined community."[39]

In the early decades of the twentieth century, Cinco de Mayo provided an important cultural space for Corona's Mexican immigrants who faced an alienating environment with restricted job opportunities and racial segregation. Cinco de Mayo surpassed the Mexican Independence Day celebration of September 16 in popularity and festivity. El Club Zaragoza led the organizing efforts behind the city's 1917 Cinco de Mayo festivities. One of the club's original founders, Mrs. Delfina Canchola, allowed members to hold monthly meetings in her dry goods store. The *Corona Independent* said that the club, "whose executive board is composed of some of the brightest young Mexicans of this community, conceived of the idea of the local 'fiesta' for the purposes of uniting Mexicans for their general uplift and betterment." El Club Zaragoza later joined forces with other mutual aid organizations to form El Comité Patriótica, which in 1924 held the first festival queen contest. Every year on May 5, regardless of the day of the week, committee officials organized a daylong civic program complete with the coronation of the festival queen by the Mexican consul. A morning parade would be followed by patriotic speeches, cultural performances of traditional songs, and folkloric dances, concluding with an all-night street dance.[40]

By the mid-1920s the Mexican consular office in San Bernardino began to work more closely with event organizers as part of the Mexican government's ambitious efforts to promote Mexicanization through Spanish language schools, libraries, print media, and cultural events. Beginning in 1921, President Obregón instructed Mexican consular offices in the United States to organize Comisiónes Honoríficas Mexicanas (Mexican Honorary Commissions) within their designated districts. According to *La Opinión,* the political purpose of these organizations was to "maintain alive and constant the memory and love of Mexico . . . [and to] remind Mexicans of their duty to the Fatherland [and] serve as a connector between Mexicans in each of the small localities and the consulate." While in some cases Mexican consuls offered protection to the expatriate community, they also pursued their own geopolitical agendas that conflicted with the interests of the expatriate community, especially against radical labor organizers.[41]

In 1926 the consul-sponsored Comisión Honorífica Mexicana replaced El Comité Patriótica as the principal organizer of Corona's Cinco de Mayo festivities. The commission's first president, local businessman Julio Cruz, worked closely with Mexican officials from the San Bernardino consulate to organize the Cinco de Mayo festivities. Before a packed audience, Los Angeles consul F. Alfonso Pesqueira delivered a rousing speech on the stubborn rebels who had ousted French invaders from Mexican soil. As reported in the *Corona Independent,* the consul was abruptly interrupted by an audience member who complained about the nativist attacks and racial segregation in public schools and about "For the White Race Only" signs at the municipal swimming pool. Consul Pesqueira responded by offering "consular protection" and reminded the audience "to observe the local and community laws, being careful to keep themselves at all times above suspicion while living in an American community." Pesqueira emphasized "good citizenship during [Cinco de Mayo] as particularly necessary among the laboring classes because when not in their own country all infractions of the law will bring increased harm on the mother country." While downplaying the city's racial tensions, the consul's message emphasized individual responsibility, festival discipline, and, most of all, the need to convey a positive image of the Mexican community and the Mexican nation to the local Anglo population. The responsibility of presenting a positive community image to the larger American society fell upon immigrant leaders and an emerging second generation.[42]

94 CREATING LEISURE SPACES

Apart from crossing Sixth Street to work in the orchards, Mexicans would enter the Anglo side of town during the Cinco de Mayo parade. The local Spanish-language newspaper, *La Revista de Corona*, praised the organizers of the 1929 parade: "The Mexican Band of Corona led by Luis Miranda marched on Main Street stopping in front of city hall as bystanders watched with great admiration and then continued to Belle Street where dancers awaited them." The *Corona Independent* also reported on the success of the parade, saying, "Various Mexican societies with their colorful flags and banners, with floats gaily decorated in patriotic colors, pretty señoritas gowned in white, children marching and followed by scores of decorated cars, formed the parade attracting the attention of all city residents. The parade was [the] longest and the most colorful affair ever attempted by the Mexican societies of the city."[43]

On October 15, 1929, the stock market crash propelled southern California and other parts of the world into economic turmoil. Instead of blaming erratic fluctuations of the global economy, politicians, reformers, and Anglo citizens pointed fingers at the "Mexican problem," blaming Mexicans for the scarcity of jobs and overburdened relief rolls. In Corona, Anglo residents presented a petition to the chamber of commerce and the city council demanding job preferences for Anglo citizens. The petition stated: "Owing to the conditions in which many of the citizens of the white race of Corona are in, many being in need of assistance. We, the undersigned, ask that laborers of the white race be given the preference in order that they may live and also stimulate the business of the community." In this racially charged climate, combined with deportation and repatriation campaigns during the early years of the Great Depression, festival organizers canceled Cinco de Mayo celebrations.[44]

To cultivate contented and loyal employees, citrus officials argued, growers needed to promote their employees' Mexican customs and national holidays. One citrus ranch manager wrote in the *California Citrograph*, "There is such a thing as laying too much stress upon the Americanization of these Mexican laborers. We think that it is much better to develop their own native and individual manners." Rather than imposing American cultural standards upon them, the grower suggested "that our Mexican people give free expression to their own thoughts and ideals. The fifth of May is a great holiday for them and we encourage its observance." To promote this cultural celebration, the company built an open-air pavilion to stage musical performances, patriotic speeches, and dancing. "The program for the entire day is carried out with dignity and patriotism," commented one citrus grower. "Many of our native born

Americans could receive an inspiration and example from the [Cinco de Mayo] exercises given by these people and the decorum of the entire events." Another way growers promoted Cinco de Mayo was to allow workers to leave work early and pay them in advance. Corona Chamber of Commerce officials lauded "the cooperation received from all citrus houses whose paydays regularly fall on May 5 to advance paydays to May 3 as a goodwill gesture to employees."[45]

Part of the reason that Cinco de Mayo was more popular in Corona than Mexican Independence Day was the timing of the citrus harvest. Although lemons were harvested year-round, the height of the season, which generated more spending money for pickers and packers alike, was from March to July. After those months some families, especially those from Corona's barrio, migrated to Coachella Valley to pick peaches and other seasonal crops. According to former picker and city councilperson Onias Acevedo, "The people were all here because it was still harvest time. By May it was full harvest season and most families were in town to make the festival happen. In September, one-quarter of the people were picking crops in other places. Plus, [the festival] was in the spring, when it wasn't too cold and it wasn't too hot." As Reynaldo Aparicio explained, "May is the best month for some kind of traditional fiesta. It's springtime and many are celebrating getting out of wintertime."[46]

Men dominated the programming, financing, and public speaking events, while women predominated in food preparation, event decorations, the queen contest, and the dance contest. Indeed, all aspects of the day's festivities were highly dependent on women's cultural work, from the decoration of parade floats to working the food booths to organizing dance contests. Alice Rodríguez complained that "it used to be more women who helped to decorate floats than men. All my [female] friends and neighbors would come over the night before the parade. We'd spend almost all night working on the float." Eva Ortiz, owner of the Chapala Café, sponsored a float designed entirely by women. The float was a replica of a boat used in Mexico's largest lake, Chapala Lake. "We had a big parade with real floats like the [Pasadena] Rose Parade," explained Rodríguez. "Not just car [floats] with a little ribbon here and a little ribbon there. There were all real floats. Not with fresh flowers, but with paper flowers. Most of the women made the floats."[47]

At Foothill Ranch's Cinco de Mayo celebration, Mexican women were in charge of food preparation and serving dinner plates with different Mexican entrées. This annual celebration was part of the city's larger Cinco de Mayo programming that included the participation of company owners, managers, and their families. Former Foothill resident Manuel

Cruz remembered helping his dad and other adults set up the tables and benches. Cruz explained how the residents used the fiesta to forge cooperative relations with company management. "The [Foothill] women used to get together on the fifth of May and make a Mexican dinner with tamales, enchiladas, and *chiles rellenos* and invite all the bosses and their wives. They used to have a Mexican dinner fiesta, as a way to show their gratitude to the bosses." Once the band was set up, the women began cooking behind the booths, and couples gradually moved toward the dance floor. After the women organized the first Mexican fiesta at Foothill in the early 1930s, it became an annual tradition, with the company buying all the food and supplies and building the booths. In the short time that she lived at Foothill Ranch, Frances Martínez was impressed with the women and the generosity of the company president's wife, Mrs. Hampton. "There were some ladies that were really close to the owners and managers but they took the lead in organizing the fiesta dinners." Martínez described how Mrs. Hampton would meet with the Mexican women before the event to plan the meals, calculate the costs, and delegate to male supervisors the building of booths and the large wooden platform for the dances. Foothill women negotiated their loyalty to Mrs. Hampton and to Foothill's paternalistic ranch system but in return held the company accountable for their families' economic survival, especially during the Great Depression.[48]

The one public domain in which Mexican women, especially those who earned packinghouse wages, exerted some degree of control and attained social status within the community was the Cinco de Mayo queen contest. Becoming a fiesta queen was a complex process in which participants faced strict gender ideologies carefully weighted against economic realities and parental authority. Corona's 1923 Cinco de Mayo queen, Teresa Lemus, remembered how young Mexican women, ranging in age from sixteen to twenty years old, were expected to sell tickets around the community; the one who sold the most tickets earned the coveted queen title. Lemus was at first reluctant to enter the queen contest because of the amount of work involved—her new packinghouse job took up much of her time—but her mother encouraged her to enter. Selling tickets at ten cents each and convincing large working families to purchase a ticket was not easy. Lemus recalled during a newspaper interview that "collecting funds to hold a fiesta-dance was difficult because most people were poor [but] believe it or not we raised 100 [dollars]." After she was selected as the winner, the Mexican consul crowned Lemus during a widely publicized coronation ceremony. In the parade the next morning she wore a white georgette gown with a train of red velvet trimmed with white fur and rode on the queen's float, decorated with classic white pillars topped by the Mexican eagle and decorated in the Mexican national colors of red, white, and green.[49]

Within the patriarchal household young girls who aspired to become queen exerted some degree of control by lobbying older female members of their families. The case of Emily Delgadillo illustrates this point. Delgadillo was initially denied entry into the queen contest by her father, who refused to permit her to walk the streets selling tickets. Frustrated, she recruited her grandmother to convince her father to change his mind. Finally, he relented and decided to allow her to enter the queen contest on the condition that her sisters, mother, and grandmother chaperone her everywhere, especially when walking the streets. Mexican American queen contestants were carefully chaperoned by their parents, but that did not stop them from resisting parental authority by reclaiming public spaces for meeting friends and potential suitors. Because many of the female organizers and participants earned packinghouse wages, their limited economic autonomy allowed them to exert themselves and gain self-confidence to take on new challenges.[50]

Whereas Mexican men congregated in saloons, pool halls, and gambling joints, Mexican women came together in church-related events, movie theaters, dance halls, and religious and patriotic festivals. Unlike the male-dominated spaces discussed in chapter 3, women had fewer opportunities to create autonomous women-dominated spaces because of the strictures imposed on female power by family, churches, settlement houses, movie reformers, and employers. "Those were the days when young women were not allowed to go out without a chaperone," explained Frances Martínez. "During the daytime, we were permitted to go out with girlfriends. On Sundays after church we went to the park, theater, or dances by the river."[51]

Excessive protectiveness of daughters was tied to family honor and policing female sexuality, or what Vicki Ruiz termed "familial oligarchy." Parents had a strong ally in the Catholic and Baptist hierarchies that regarded the ideal woman as being sexually pure and upon marriage fulfilling her domestic responsibilities as wife and mother. Citrus employers and middle-class Anglo women, affiliated with WIC and the Corona Settlement House among others, played an important role in the implementation of the ideology of domesticity.[52]

While some females subscribed to these gender conventions, others clashed with women reformers and their own parents, and men in general, over traditional gender norms of domesticity and femininity within the limits imposed by the patriarchal system and the economy of a single-industry town. Voluntary service to Catholic and Baptist parishes provided women a social space away from home and opportunities to sharpen their fund-raising abilities. According to one feminist theologian, church activities provided Latinas "with the only arena in which they could legitimately, if indirectly, engage in developing themselves." At a time when movie theaters ushered Mexican patrons to designated seating sections, Mexican women began to rebel against movie censors and parents who sought to control their whereabouts. Apart from becoming movie spectators, they became active participants in transforming El Teatro Chapultepec into a cultural resource center and gathering place for women and families. At Cinco de Mayo fiestas, women took the lead in food preparation, parade float decoration, and most of all organizing the queen contest, which despite objectifying female bodies allowed women to assert themselves in the public sphere.[53]

Women demonstrated that they did not agree with narrowly defined gender norms that constrained their freedom and liberties, and as the story of Frances Martínez illustrates, women usually found a way to exercise their independence. Although Mexican women adopted many American fashion trends and behaviors, they understood that they would not be fully accepted as "American"; nor did they necessarily want to give up their Mexican heritage. Like their male counterparts, they still faced racial discrimination and class constraints at work and during their leisure time. Nevertheless, Corona women created their own spaces in churches, movie theaters, and festivals, where they could find a comfortable medium between so-called traditional and modern forms of femininity.

5   *Baseball and Sports Clubs*

"We were the best team around. We played all over Southern California and everyone wanted to beat us. Other teams would recruit the best players around so they could come to our town [Corona] and try to beat us," explained Natividad "Tito" Cortez as he proudly pointed to a large framed picture of the Corona Athletics baseball team on his living room wall. "Everyone used to come out on Sundays after church to watch the Athletics games and when someone hit a home run they would honk the car horns." Cortez remembered the all–Mexican American Corona Athletics as one of the most fiercely competitive semiprofessional baseball teams in southern California. First organized in 1933, this independent baseball club boasted a lineup of all-star players, claimed several tournament championships, and earned a reputation among baseball scouts for producing players with major league potential.[1]

Before 1947, American baseball's deeply entrenched color line kept African Americans, black Latinos, and dark-skinned Mexican Americans such as Cortez from playing in the major leagues. Despite racial segregation in baseball, Mexican American *peloteros* (ballplayers) took to the diamond fields every weekend afternoon to play independent sandlot and semiprofessional baseball. Community-based baseball clubs sprang up during the interwar years in southern California's barrios and *colonias*, introducing immigrant children to America's "national pastime" at a time when Mexican sports heroes were few and far between. In the context of economic exploitation, racial discrimination, and resurgent nativist attacks aimed at the Mexican population, second-generation Mexican Americans used baseball to proclaim their equality

99

through athletic competition without fear of reprisal and to publicly demonstrate community solidarity and strength.⌐

Baseball clubs had multiple meanings and uses among Mexican Americans in Corona during the 1930s. Employers and play reformers sought to use baseball clubs to Americanize and socially control the Mexican immigrant population. But Mexican American ballplayers in community-based semipro baseball brought their own attitudes and motivations to the game. In the face of racial discrimination and limited economic opportunities for Mexicans in Corona, baseball took on a symbolic and real social significance. In line with C. L. R. James's ideas about the political significance of cricket, Mexican Americans viewed baseball matches as mirroring larger racial, gender, and class struggles that transcended the playing field. Mexican Americans used baseball clubs to promote ethnic consciousness, build community solidarity, and sharpen their organizing and leadership skills. Baseball also taught men how to develop a masculine identity through competitiveness, fighting, emotional detachment, and domination over women. In doing so, they transformed the ball clubs into a political forum from which to launch wider forms of collective action.[2]

In arguing for baseball clubs as sites of resistance, however, one must consider how sporting venues reinforced gender hierarchies in the community. As chapter 6 will show, baseball collectivities contributed to the formation of unions. But baseball players who became union organizers or rank-and-file union members re-created a rough masculine culture that extended into the labor movement, thus reproducing unequal gender relations and helping to define the limitations of political opposition.

Play Reformers and the "Baseball Solution"

Baseball arrived in Latin America during the mid-nineteenth century, when American sailors and returning Cuban émigrés first introduced the sport in Cuba. From there the game spread throughout the Caribbean region. In Mexico, Cuban workers introduced the game to the remote southeastern Yucatan peninsula in the 1860s, but it was not until the Porfirian era (1876–1910) that baseball's popularity reached the northern parts of Mexico. With the influx of American capital into remote areas of central and western Mexico, railroad and mining company personnel treated workers to their first baseball games. American investors and Porfirian liberals recognized the game's potential of introducing modern industrial values such as teamwork and self-discipline to the

Mexican lower classes. Wallace Thompson, editor of a mining journal and author of five books on Mexico, observed the growing popularity of baseball with paternalistic approval. "A magnificent beginning has been made in the training of Mexican boys both in teamwork and in athletic development. . . . It seems that these features arc being developed by baseball, which there, as elsewhere, has stimulated the sense of play and is certainly as near a 'national sport' as Mexico has so far attained."[3]

U.S. companies subsidized baseball teams on both sides of the Rio Grande to increase worker productivity and foster company loyalty. As militant labor unions made inroads among immigrant workers during World War I, industrial and agricultural companies stepped up efforts to counter labor unions by offering recreation programs. One of the leading producers of agricultural fruit in the country, the California Fruit Growers Exchange (also known by its trademark, Sunkist), organized a sophisticated corporate welfare system that included Americanization classes, a housing program, recreational facilities, and sports clubs. Sunkist officials encouraged growers to organize baseball clubs to improve workers' physical fitness and mental preparedness for arduous, backbreaking field work. The director of Sunkist's Industrial Relations Department, G. B. Hodgkin, advised growers how to best "handle" Mexicans. "In order to produce the desired [Mexican] workers, they have to become a member of a local society or baseball team . . . to increase their physical and mental capacity for doing more work."[4]

Sunkist's baseball proposal persuaded citrus growers to form baseball clubs and build ballparks on ranch property. For example, Keith Spalding, son of sporting giant A. G. Spalding and author of *America's National Game*, owned and operated Rancho Sespe, a four-thousand-acre citrus ranch near Fillmore in eastern Ventura County. Spalding transformed this old Californio rancho into a "model scientific farm" complete with modern packinghouses, office buildings, "model" housing for workers, recreation facilities, a musical group, and a baseball diamond. In northern Orange County, the La Habra Citrus Association sponsored Los Juveniles, consisting of Mexican citrus workers. The association formed this baseball club to replace the popular sport of cockfighting conducted clandestinely inside citrus orchards. "The entire [Mexican] colony has become baseball conscious in a short time," observed a university researcher, "and the interest exhibited in this great American sport has seemingly supplanted the former Sunday diversion of cock-fighting, which is common to many Mexican colonies in Southern California." To become "baseball conscious," according to the association, required compliance with manly codes of conduct. The team's "good sportsman" rules consisted of being "dependable, truthful, trustworthy, and never late for baseball practice"; the sportsman "is never heard to use bad language at work or at play [and] never displays his temper." La Habra's baseball program linked baseball with modernity, manliness, and progress, defined in opposition to the uncivilized, culturally backward, and unmanly character of cockfighting.[5]

Popular among Mexican communities throughout the southern California citrus belt, cockfighting was typically conducted away from the public eye, inside citrus orchards and in remote locations. Despite being declared an "illegal sport" under county ordinances, cockfighting would sometimes draw up to two hundred people at a time. The Limoneira Ranch supervisor wrote to his boss, Charles C. Teague, owner of the Limoneira Company, about the "game cock fight" broken up by local police officers. In response, Teague complained that "the raiding by the Sheriff's office of this affair gives a lot of very undesirable publicity to our company and I think that we should take every possible step to prevent a recurrence of anything of this sort." He then recommended "making a rule that no game cocks will be permitted on the ranch." Another reason for the political elite's strong opposition to this largely ethnic, working-class, and highly masculine sport was the possibility that this leisure space could be transformed into a politicized space of opposition. The editor of the *Corona Independent* revealed this understanding of the subversive potential of this gambling sport when he wrote, "A Corona Mexican and others were taken into custody after a cock fight raid and one of the persons was found carrying communist literature." Workers used cockfighting as an important social space to (re)assert their cultural identity and to resist company officials and law enforcement agents who aimed to control, oversee, and regulate their everyday behavior.[6]

While employers sought to mold a workforce, play reformers sought to redirect immigrants from their own "unwholesome" amusements into "Americanized" forms of recreation and sports. As shown in chapter 3, the associated male leisure activities of public drinking and gambling in saloons and pool halls along North Main Street threatened the moral and social order of the community. Play reformers targeted immigrant children in schools, playgrounds, churches, and settlement houses to mold them into a submissive working class with middle-class Anglo Protestant values. Cary Goodman has shown how the reform movement transformed autonomous street play into more controlled and organized play to counteract the perceived moral decay of cities and street life that reformers thought caused juvenile delinquency. The head of the Los Angeles Department of Playgrounds and Recreation encouraged mass participation in sports that would "instill ideals of good sportsmanship, fair play, team work, clean living, and plant loyalty . . . bringing about a happy spirit of cooperation between employer and employee." Dr. Emory Bogardus and his sociology students at the University of Southern California produced research studies on the significance of sports and recreational activities in Los Angeles Mexican communities. "Wholesome recreation for Mexican immigrants is largely missing. The main amusements are talking and siestas, cheap motion pictures, playing pool, dancing, boxing matches, gambling and cock-fighting." What was missing, according to Bogardus, was baseball, a pastime well suited to counter these "unwholesome" amusements. Years later Bogardus observed that "the Mexican 'takes' well to the national pastime of the United States, namely, baseball. More significant, through games such as baseball, he acquires a new meaning for teamwork."[7]

Segregated "Mexican schools" also organized sports teams for young men and women. School principal Katherine Murray offered detailed steps to promote the assimilation of young Mexican immigrants, described as the "lowliest type"––"primitive people close to nature and elemental in customs and home life." Because of the supposed racial inferiority of Mexican immigrants, Murray suggested, schools should help form community groups such as mothers' clubs, men's welfare committees, young men's groups, and young women's groups. "The next step is a young men's club organized through a night school, an orchestra or perhaps a baseball team. These young fellows need wholesome activity and are really hungry, with the same hunger of their elders, for the better things in life."[8]

These efforts to reform workers' cultural lives were not limited to young men. Women were also introduced to recreation programs and sports teams in schools, churches, the YWCA, playgrounds, and settlement houses. For example, during the early 1930s the San Diego Neighborhood House built a baseball diamond to "give girls an opportunity for recreation away from their numerous home responsibilities [and to] instill cooperation among the girls." The Neighborhood House helped form a Mexican American women's baseball team that routinely played against men's teams. Mexican American women also took up softball, organizing and participating in softball league tournaments throughout southern California with help from company sponsors, schools, and settlement houses. All-female softball teams were often ridiculed or cheered for their team names and colorful uniforms. Some examples of team names included Los Tomboys (Orange), Las Debs (Corona), La Jolla Kats (Placentia), and Mexico Libre and Four Star Eagles (Los Angeles). Despite the sport's popularity, women's softball was considered a novelty attraction for male spectators and was usually scheduled as exhibition games before men's baseball. Softball had a different meaning for women, however, than for male spectators and team promoters, allowing them to form female friendships and gain public visibility outside the home and workplace.[9]

Baseball was also viewed as promoting racial harmony in the workplace. Around the same time, Hawaiian sugar planters were introducing baseball clubs to their ethnically diverse workforce. One researcher observed, "Foremost among the sports in promoting racial harmony and understanding is baseball, both amateur and professional. Baseball as a form of play or recreation has been for many years in Hawaii a valuable social medium through which many races have been drawn together in friendly common projects." Similarly, the citrus industry used baseball to bridge cultural differences between Anglo supervisors and Mexican workers.[10]

As noted above, many American companies sponsored some sort of recreational program and provided facilities for organized sports such as football, basketball, softball, and baseball. One that did so was the Corona Foothill Lemon Company, the largest employer in Corona. In 1928 the Foothill Lemon Company cleared several rows of fruit orchards on its nine-hundred-acre ranch property to build a diamond for its newly formed softball team, the Foothill Lemoneers. Foothill management supplied team uniforms emblazoned with the company's name and logo and sponsored tournaments against other company teams. The company viewed the team "as a means of expressing appreciation to the [Mexican] men for their cooperative service in the ranch work throughout the year."[11]

The Lemoneers consisted of five Anglo ranch supervisors and four Mexican workers. Ranch supervisor Carl Herklerath served as team captain for several years, in charge of scheduling games, providing equipment, and recruiting players. Former player Santos Garcia recalled that when he served as the team's batboy, "I had to pick up all the equipment at the ranch store and carry it to the baseball diamond where everyone would get together and play ball all day on Sundays." Because the Mexican ballplayers worked eight- to ten-hour days, six days a week, picking fruit, they could practice only occasionally in the evenings and played only on Sunday afternoons. Despite the sport's popularity among community residents, the company team was limited to older adults and played only softball. Teenagers and young adults were relegated to being spectators, batboys, and substitute players. When Tito Cortez was asked how he learned to play baseball as a teenager at the Foothill Ranch, he responded, "The younger kids around my age used to play pickup games in the ranch, with rocks and sticks . . . [and] some of us also learned from watching the older players like Blas Garcia, Salvador Rios, and Manuel Muñoz who played for the ranch team." Cortez and his peers continued to play ball despite being sidelined to spectator status, even if doing so interfered with their job responsibilities. Cortez remarked that he and his friends "used to get together and sometimes we played all night" and that "lots of folks used to sleep in and were late for work, but the foremen did not really say anything."[12]

Several years later, a group of second-generation Mexican American youths demanded that the company provide equipment and uniforms for their newly formed baseball team, the Foothill Aces. The company responded by providing bats, balls, uniforms, and access to the Foothill diamond. But for some players, limited company support was not good enough, so after only two seasons the Foothill Aces disbanded. Also, work schedules limited playing time, and the company diamond's remoteness from town reduced spectator numbers. Former ballplayer Zeke Mejia explained, "Teams popped up at the local citrus picking ranches where many Hispanics lived but they did not last long. . . . [T]he games did not attract much attention because they were too far away from the town." The ability to attract a larger audience limited Mexican American ballplayers' hopes of acquiring social status and public visibility for major league scouts who appeared unannounced among the spectators. Cortez explained how, after two seasons, the company failed to deliver on its promise to keep up maintenance on the diamond. "The team ended around 1933 because they [the Aces players] were too tired of the baseball field. . . . [I]t was not as good as the one in town where the Athletics played. You see many of these players picked fruit and did other kinds of ranch work so they could not find the time to keep it up."[13] While the company hoped this sporting activity would encourage Mexican males to identify more closely with management, the failure to deliver a more comprehensive sports program served instead to widen the gap between company management and second-generation workers. The Great Depression forced some companies to reduce their welfare offerings, but with the large labor strikes that rocked the California countryside, citrus companies continued their recreation programs through the 1930s. Unlike the Lemoneers, the Aces made repeated demands on the company to fulfill its promises to maintain a manicured diamond field and supply the team with equipment and transportation. When the company failed to meet these demands and scaled down its welfare offers, workers decided to look elsewhere for sporting opportunities. With the demise of the Foothill Aces, several ballplayers (Tito Cortez, Silvestre "Silve" Balderas, Alfredo Uribe, Sammy Lopez, and Ray Zaragosa) opted to play for the independent all–Mexican American Corona Athletics Baseball Club.[14]

Community Baseball and Sports Clubs

The appeal of baseball was not limited to Mexican immigrants, of course; the sport attracted all segments of the American working classes. Early commentators hailed baseball as the nation's "melting pot" sport with the greatest potential of Americanizing foreign-born youngsters and children of immigrants, but the game's strict racial and gender system shattered this myth. While sports journalists celebrated the substantial influx of players of eastern and southern European descent who entered the major leagues during the mid-1930s, they overlooked the more than fifty Latin American and U.S. Latino players who joined the major leagues before 1947, the year Jackie Robinson broke the color line. Players originating from Mexico included Melo Almada, José Luis (Chile) Gómez, and Jesse Flores. With its East Coast bias, major league focus, and white-black binary framework, baseball history has virtually ignored the sporting experiences of Mexican Americans, Asian Pacific Americans, and Native Americans in amateur and semi-professional baseball leagues throughout the American West.[15]

While other racial minority groups also adopted baseball as their favorite sport, Mexican American baseball was unique, in large part because of the close proximity of the U.S.-Mexico border and interior Mexico. From its inception Mexican baseball was a transnational phenomenon, straddling both sides of the border to entertain crowds who filled the stands to cheer for their favorite teams. Baseball teams from Mexico routinely crossed the border to participate in southwestern tournaments. For example, Mexico's championship team, San Luis "Mexico," was invited to participate in several Los Angeles–area tournaments during the 1930 season. Los Angeles–based teams were also invited to tournaments in Hermosillo, Sonora, and Mexico City. During these international games the Mexican consul was occasionally invited to throw the first pitch.[16]

Mexican baseball teams often sprang up from within the community as part of sports clubs, mutual aid organizations, churches, and small businesses. A chief promoter of sports was the Asociación Deportiva Hispano Americana, organized in 1927 by the city's leading Spanish-language newspaper, *La Opinión*, and a board of directors made up of Mexican consular officials, middle-class professionals, and small business owners. Another big promoter was the Asociación Atlética Mexicana del Sur de California, formed on the eve of the 1932 Los Angeles Olympics with the assistance of the city's recreation department. Persuaded by baseball's rising popularity among second-generation Mexican American youths, La Asociación helped form a separate baseball league, Asociación Mexicana de Baseball del Sur de California (Southern California Mexican Baseball Association), which fielded more than fifteen amateur and semiprofessional teams. Some of the 1933 teams included the El Paso Shoe Store Zapateros, the Oxnard Aces, the La Habra Juveniles, the San Fernando Missions, the Hermosa Mexican Club Pescadores, the Santa Paula Limoneros, the Placentia Merchants, and the Corona Athletics.[17]

The original Corona Athletics Baseball Club was organized in 1931 by Mexican American youths who worked in Corona's citrus industry. Many of the original members were introduced to baseball through a network of company-sponsored teams including the Corona Foothill Lemon Company Lemoneers, the Exchange Lemon Products Company team, and the American Fruit Growers Blue Goose team. However, when companies failed to meet player demands for equipment and a playing field, the youths decided to form their own team. Although freed from company control, the Athletics were still dependent on Corona's Mexican community for financial backing and moral support. The idea of forming a community baseball team was also supported by members of the Club Deportivo Mexicano de Corona. Founded in 1928, the Club Deportivo Mexicano organized amateur boxing matches, featuring local Mexican prizefighters, for Corona's Mexican community. Besides sponsoring boxing matches, Club Deportivo encouraged its members to organize baseball tournaments. In 1929 the club announced plans to help organize a community baseball team. "The Club Deportivo Mexicano is thinking of organizing a Mexican baseball club to compete against the clubs from San Bernardino, Riverside and other Mexican colonias who have the fortune of having their own clubs." For unknown reasons this proposed team was never formed. It took a few more years of planning to inaugurate the first community baseball club.[18]

Boxing was also a popular sport in southern California's Mexican communities. Labor and civil rights leader Bert Corona commented on the popularity of boxing. "There was a lot of interest in boxing and other sports among Mexicanos in the thirties. Two or three world champions from California, such as Bert Colima, often fought at the Olympic Auditorium or at Gilmore Stadium in Hollywood, where as many as twenty-five thousand would attend these fights." In Corona, amateur boxing matches were held at the Main Street Athletic Club or a new fighting arena built on the site of the old ballpark on West Sixth Street. In 1928, play reformers pushed for a city ordinance to restrict boxing matches to spectators over eighteen years of age and require the presence of a deputy sheriff to enforce the age limit and the dry law. Corona's favorite prizefighters were Anglo American Jimmy Ragsdale; Italian American Joe Marabella, and Mexican Americans Kid Flores, Pete Casas, and Jimmie Barba. Many of these matches were advertised in the *Corona Independent* and the *Revista de Corona.* One ad announced the impeding arrival of Bert Colima, known as the "Idol of Whittier," a popular prizefighter throughout southern California: "El Club Deportivo Mexicano de Corona wishes that the entire city will get to know the champion of the Pacific Coast, Bert Colima." The chief purpose of this bout was not mere entertainment but to raise money for a destitute family. *La Opinión* reported on the amount raised: "The Club Deportivo organized a fundraiser for a family who lost their home in a fire. They earned 28 dollars that was given to the Felix family."[19]

Most of the fifteen Mexican American ballplayers who made up the Corona Athletics Baseball Club resided in Corona's barrio, while several lived in outlying citrus ranch communities. Within the circular city, Sixth Street was considered the racial borderline that divided Mexican on the north side from Anglos on the south side of town. Among the few reasons that Anglo residents would venture across Sixth Street into the Mexican barrio was to catch a glimpse of the Corona Athletics. The players all attended Washington Elementary School, designated as a "Mexican school." Very few continued on to high school because they needed to contribute to the family income, so they followed in their parents' footsteps—picking and packing citrus fruit.

Facing a bleak future in agricultural work, Mexican American boys readily embraced baseball. Zeke Mejia decided early on to dedicate himself to school and sports. "I did not want to pick lemons like my father and needed an incentive to stay in school so I started playing sports, especially baseball. It taught me something about myself. I hated to lose then and still hate to lose now." Those who could not escape agricultural work, though, found that the backbreaking field work could be useful conditioning for playing sports. As former Athletics ballplayer Tito Cortez explained, "Working inside the [citrus] groves, carrying a heavy sack, climbing up and down the ladder, using a quick eye to pick lemons helped with my pitching and [baseball] training." Cortez insisted that working six days a week, ten hours a day, did not interfere with his baseball performance. "Everyone used to comment how we would work like a dog all week picking lemons, then played baseball all day on Sundays. But you see, that was the only thing to do since there was no television." While their work experiences may have helped the ballplayers hone their game, historian Steven Gelber contends that baseball culture in turn reinforced workplace values such as appreciation of rationality, personal accountability, teamwork, and competitiveness between groups.[20]

Although relegated to the lowest rungs of the agricultural industry, Mexicans potentially could move up as coaches and managers of a baseball team and thus gain valuable leadership and organizational skills. This was the case with Marcelino Barba, Gilbert Enriquez, and Marcos Uribe, three Mexican American community leaders who began their careers through participation in baseball teams and sports clubs. Barba worked in the packinghouses as a fruit crate assembler and machine operator while at the same time managing the Athletics Baseball Club from 1931 to 1939. As manager, Barba spent many hours scheduling ball games, soliciting sponsors, and organizing tournaments. Gilbert Enriquez worked in a shoe store while he coached the Athletics team and Washington Elementary students after school. He later became involved in city politics, becoming the first Mexican American on the city's recreation commission and the founding editor of the Spanish-language newspaper *El Imparcial*. Marcos Uribe worked as a citrus picker until he lost his right arm in a work-related accident, becoming known as "El Mocho." Despite his handicap he replaced Barba as the Athletics manager (1940–48) and later managed an ice cream truck. Because of his leadership experience and winning record, he eventually became an effective labor organizer.[21]

Apart from honing leadership skills, baseball allowed players to travel and make new friends outside their immediate surroundings. During the summer months, when the lemon harvest ebbed, the Athletics team traveled north to Santa Barbara, to Coachella Valley in the eastern desert, and south to the border towns of Mexicali and Tijuana.

To offset transportation expenses the manager sometimes borrowed a hauling truck from local packinghouses. Former Corona baseball player Zeke Mejia fondly remembered his traveling experiences. "I liked to travel to new places because I liked meeting new friends. I remember traveling to Lake Elsinore, which was a long way in those days. But the only ride we could get was from a friend who hauled fertilizer in his truck. So all the guys crawled inside the truck and tried not to breathe during the ride. By the time we arrived to play we all smelled like fertilized fields. We did it because we loved the game." These sporting networks established during away games and tournament matches became important for community organizing and labor struggles.[22]

While baseball tours helped weld informal social networks and alliances, they also provided masculinized forms of sociability. In keeping with the game's competitive machismo ethic, postgame drinking parties became a popular pastime among ballplayers. Following each team victory the manager would purchase food and beer for the team. Former Athletics pitcher Tito Cortez remembered, "After the game the managers would buy us *cerveza* [beer] and tacos. Sometimes we had a barbeque out there [with] roasted goat." These postgame celebrations, however, were contingent on how much money they collected during the game. When they were short of funds they visited their main sponsor, Jalisco Bar, where they received free drinks. This popular male drinking establishment was jokingly referred to as "El Resbalador" (the slippery place) because of the high number of inebriated ballplayers who accidentally slid into imaginary bases.[23]

Baseball's masculine culture on the playing field excluded women from participating in the game. But many Mexican women attended Corona baseball matches nonetheless and helped fund-raising efforts by selling Mexican food at the games. Emily Delgadillo claimed to have made more than one thousand burritos at Corona City Park to raise funds for her husband's softball team. Some Mexican American women also played on all-women softball teams that became popular during World War II. Following his tenure as the Athletics manager, Marcos Uribe helped organize an all–Mexican American women's softball team in 1949 called the Corona Debs, or Las Debs de Corona. Sponsored by the American Dry Cleaners and coached by Uribe along with two Anglo Americans, Dee Anderson and Don Ragsdale, the team consisted of fifteen girls dressed in blue and gold uniforms with the sponsor's name emblazoned on the back of their shirts. To join the team each player had to meet three requirements: understand the rules of the game, attend regular practices, and show excellent performance on the field. The team held its practices and matches on the Athletics field.[24]

Despite their willingness to play ball, women still encountered gender barriers at home. Some young women played until they got married, at which point domestic responsibilities left little time for practice or weekend tournaments. Possibly the husbands may also have objected to their wives' involvement in sports. Other women negotiated their domestic role and athletic interests. As one former Debs ballplayer remembered, "We used to love playing softball. Even though some of us were already married, we still never missed practice." Despite the male coaching staff, the women forged a uniquely female sports culture. Annie Bravo remembered the sense of community within the team. "I used to play for the American Cleaners team. I played second base. We used to help each other to get better, and after the game all the girls got together at someone's house." Softball offered women public visibility and self-confidence outside the home and opportunities to form a female support network.[25]

As mentioned in chapter 2, racial segregation in city parks and recreation facilities before World War II forced Mexicans to look elsewhere for recreational resources. Like other southwestern cities, Corona maintained a segregationist policy that barred Mexicans from using the city park's baseball diamond and swimming pool. Mexican ballplayers thus gravitated toward empty lots or agricultural fields that became makeshift baseball diamonds. The Athletics team transformed an empty railroad yard, located in the Mexican barrio, into a ballpark with bleachers and a concession stand. Because the managers of the Santa Fe Railroad were baseball fans, they allowed the Athletics to lease the land for a dollar per month. Another reason the Athletics preferred the railroad yard was to avoid city restrictions on alcohol consumption and food sales.

For Corona's Mexican working-class community, the Athletics' baseball field represented an important cultural space. The ballpark's free admission policy appealed to families, children, youths, and elderly people with limited discretionary incomes. While watching their favorite teams, fans could reunite with extended family members and friends. This Sunday afternoon ritual fostered cultural pride among Mexican residents that cut across class, gender, generational, and citizenship divides. Following the baseball games, Mexicanist-oriented organizations, aimed at preserving a Mexican national identity, occasionally staged patriotic celebrations complete with mariachi music, food, and speeches. Baseball historian Samuel Regalado has suggested that "baseball in the barrios did more than help to preserve a strong sense of Mexican heritage within these communities"; it also promoted "a sense of unity amongst the people—especially for those who had been in the United States only a few years."[26]

Children of Mexican immigrants, either born or raised in the United States, also gravitated toward America's national sport. During the 1930s, second-generation Mexican American youths filled the stands of ballparks every Sunday afternoon, hoping to realize their own "field of dreams." One recreation director surveyed Mexican American youths in Los Angeles and Phoenix about their favorite American sports. Respondents preferred baseball, followed by softball, boxing, basketball, and football. Another researcher observed, "The young [Mexican] men like baseball. It seems to be the only sport that appeals to them."[27]

The Corona Athletics game was one of the main attractions at the city's fiftieth anniversary and Cinco de Mayo fiesta in 1936. Although excluded from the main theatrical performance, *The Golden Circle* (see chapter 1), Mexican Americans participated in the five-day jubilee celebration by organizing events for the last day, which fell on May 5. This widely publicized event attracted people from all over Southern California, including a *Los Angeles Times* reporter who observed that "many prominent figures in Mexican circles of Southern California spoke on the [Cinco de Mayo] program which was replete with readings, music, marching bodies, and a hundred decorated automobiles in the parade." That same afternoon more than five thousand spectators packed the city park to watch the Mexican American baseball team, the Corona Athletics, square off against the Anaheim Merchants. Along with traditional Mexican dances such as Jarabe Tapatio (Mexican Hat Dance) and Chiapanecas (group folk dance from Chiapas, Mexico), festival organizers added the Jitterbug Dance Contest to the lineup, with jazz and swing music performed by a local Mexican American band, The Highlights. The band and dance contest attracted a large young crowd "who were all on their best behavior." One Mexican American committee member expressed his gratitude to the city mayor and Anglo civic groups for their participation. "Without their assistance we could not have presented such a contribution to our city's anniversary celebrations. . . . We trust that our [Mexican] people's efforts have left a memory of a splendid conclusion to the city's jubilee." Festival organizers and ballplayers attempted to convey a positive image of the Mexican community with the hope of improving race relations in Corona.[28]

For Mexican American ballplayers such as the Athletics, there was no contradiction in emphasizing both their Mexican heritage and their American citizenship. Rather, defining an ethnic and cultural identity, as historian George Sánchez has suggested, involved a complex and ambiguous process contingent on historical circumstances The ballplayers' bilingual and bicultural skills were necessary to solicit sponsors, negotiate contracts, and gain supporters in city government.[29]

To cover team expenses, Athletics managers passed a baseball hat around the bleachers for those who could contribute. They also sought financial support from local Mexican and Anglo businesses. Former Athletics coach Jess Uribe explained the fund-raising process: "From all the people that came to watch us we would pass around a basket to collect money to support the team but it was never enough. Only coins you would see because people were so poor. But still many people helped us cover the costs. For 15 expensive uniforms we had to find support from the local businesses." He added, "We used to get sponsors from the Mexican businesses, especially bars. Each business would buy a baseball uniform and placed their name on the back." The Athletics club also held fund-raising dances at the American Legion Hall to help offset transportation costs. These dances, announced in *El Imparcial* and on the local Spanish-language radio station, featured traditional Mexican ballads by Al Lopez's band and swing music performed by the Mexican American band The Highlights. "Many people both local and from out-of-town have enjoyed this wholesome addition to the town's recreational activities," read one newspaper advertisement. "The purpose of the dance is to raise money to cover necessary expenses since passing the hat at each game is not enough." Apart from these fund-raising efforts, baseball managers also enlisted the support of Anglo business establishments such as Corona Hardware, American Dry Cleaners, and Western Auto Supply.[30]

While some parents encouraged their children to play baseball, others were suspicious of the national pastime because it competed with family obligations. Former Detroit Tigers pitcher Hank Aguirre, a six-foot San Gabriel native nicknamed the "Tall Mexican," told his biographer of his father's disapproval. Because the Aguirres owned and operated a family grocery store, his father had little patience with his son's budding baseball career. However, when Aguirre received his first bonus for signing with the Detroit Tigers in 1951, his father "put behind forever his lack of interest in baseball and his scathing views of the game as a waste of time." Major league pitcher Jesse Flores also encountered family resistance. Born in Guadalajara, Mexico, Flores migrated to

La Habra with his family and later dropped out of school to work in the citrus orchards with his father. When Flores joined the Chicago Cubs in 1942, his mother was not very pleased. "She didn't really like the idea. She used to go to church and pray for me when I was pitching. She thought I was going to get hit in the head with the ball." Unlike his mother, Flores's father and brothers attended all his games and supported his career choice. When he pitched a two-hitter against the Red Sox he was "reminded of all the times I had picked lemons and oranges." Flores played for seven seasons on three different teams until he ended his career in 1950; years later he became a successful scout for the Minnesota Twins. Reflecting on his seven-year pitching career, Flores concluded that "I think without baseball I would have been just another worker."[31]

Despite family obligations, Mexican American ballplayers still took a chance at making it big in the major leagues. The Corona Athletics played in semiprofessional leagues not associated with the professional leagues and its minor league appendages. The local sports columnist reminded readers that "the record of the Corona Athletics is well known. Their string of victories is a very long one with few losses interrupting the usual outcome of games." After achieving a winning average of .700 during the 1936 season, they were invited to participate in the California state championship tournament at Wrigley Field, Los Angeles. Although they lost the tournament, the Athletics demonstrated that they had the potential to play in the major leagues. Not until Jackie Robinson broke the color line in 1947, however, did scouts begin to pay attention to the Athletics. Between 1947 and 1949, major league teams recruited three Athletics players—Tito Cortez, Ray Delgadillo, and Remi Chagnon—to play for their farm teams. Bobby Perez and Louis Uribe also signed contracts with the Brooklyn Dodgers in the 1950s but continued playing minor league ball. Although no Athletics player achieved major league star status, simply belonging to one of the most fiercely competitive baseball teams in the region was enough for some. Some ballplayers showed off their athletic prowess in photographs taken by a local photo studio. These photos were occasionally distributed like baseball cards at tournament games.[32]

Before 1947, major league scouts recruited two semipro players of Mexican descent from southern California. In 1933, Baldomero "Melo" Almada became the first Mexican American to play in the major leagues; he played for seven seasons, first for the Boston Red Sox, then for the Washington Senators, and finally for the 1939 Brooklyn Dodgers. Born in Huatabampo, Sonora, Mexico, to a wealthy land-owning family,

Almada moved to Los Angeles and played sports in the city's public school system during the 1920s. As the star pitcher for the Los Angeles High School and El Paso Shoe Store teams, Almada became an instant celebrity in the English- and Spanish-language print media. The English media constructed an image of Almada as an assimilated "American" athlete referred to as "Mel" and occasionally mistaken for an Italian American. One sports journalist wrote, "Although proud of his Mexican lineage and completely loyal to it, he doesn't even look like a Mexican, being taller, broader and considerably fairer than most of the citizens of our sister republic." In contrast, *La Opinión* and the Mexico City newspaper *El Excelsior* proclaimed Almada as a "Mexican national hero." On July 23, 1933, the Mexican Consul helped organize Melo Almada Day at Wrigley Field, featuring Hollywood film star Rosita Moreno and Mexican prizefighters Kid Azteca and Baby Face Casanova. Although lighter-skinned Latin American and Latino major league players, including Almada, benefited from "whiteness," they still faced ethnic stereotypes and subtle forms of discrimination.[33]

Mexican American semipro players became optimistic about their major league prospects when Jackie Robinson broke the color line. As a rising sports star at the University of California, Los Angeles, Robinson appealed to many young aspiring athletes from the surrounding area. Tito Cortez was one of these players with major league dreams. Between 1937 and 1947 Cortez pitched five no-hitters for the Athletics. In 1947 the Cleveland Indians recruited Cortez to play for their farm team in Tucson, Arizona. As a starting pitcher for the Tucson Cowboys, he helped the team reach the minor league playoffs. Cortez described his Tucson experience: "I received $125 a month plus $20 a month for rent. I stayed in a dormitory. When they signed me up I began as a relief pitcher, then a starter pitcher. I was the only Mexican American in the team." Cortez's promising career, however, was cut short when he was hit on the left eye by a ball that left him partially blind. Cortez remembered breaking the news to the Arizona Cowboys. "When I told them I had an accident, they did not believe me. They sent me a contract and then another one. Finally I just tore it up." After ignoring their letters he discovered later that he was blacklisted from playing on the major league farm teams. The Cowboys suspected that Cortez was one of a dozen American ballplayers recruited by the Mexican League, which offered higher salaries and bonuses. In response, baseball commissioner A. B. Chandler blacklisted for five years all players who joined the Mexican League. Although Cortez and other Mexican American ballplayers did not achieve major league status, they demonstrated a capacity for athletic ability, leadership, and organization capabilities that could extend far beyond the realm of sports.[34]

Masculinity On and Off the Playing Field

In the racially charged climate of the Depression years, characterized by segregation, discrimination, and nativism, baseball took on wider social significance within Mexican communities. A University of Chicago sociologist long ago observed, "The whole [Mexican] colony is always keenly interested in the baseball games especially when they play against outsiders. It is as though the honor and status of the colony were at stake." This observation underscores how Mexican Americans' struggles to gain acceptance on the playing field involved symbolic and real racial contestation. Victories by the Corona Athletics over all-Anglo baseball teams challenged notions of white superiority and stereotypical notions of Mexicans as docile, culturally inferior peons. Semipro player Frank Ruiz explained the wider racial significance of Mexican-Anglo matches: "They all wanted to beat us. If they couldn't beat us with the runs, they would try to beat us with the umpire, because we were a little better than they were. I guess they didn't want the Mexican kids to beat them, you know, the Anglos over there. We had a little rough time sometimes, but then we'd score more runs. There's no way they could say they won without enough runs." Mexican American ballplayers such as Frank Ruiz also demanded respect and equal opportunity beyond the playing field. Ruiz's bitter memories of "No Mexicans Allowed" signs posted at the local swimming pool and the city park made him question whether "true" equality existed in America's national pastime. "Being a [poor] Mexican, well, you might say you had two strikes against you," Ruiz said. "And we had good players. They could have made the big leagues."[35]

Racial differences were quite visible on the baseball diamond, especially when the all–Mexican American Corona Athletics played their main rival, the Corona Cardinals, an all-Anglo team. A local sports columnist described the rivalry as a "baseball civil war" to be hard-fought at the city park diamond.[36]

For male players, baseball's highly charged hit-and-run plays, aggressive batting, and game brawls became part of its appeal and served to publicly demonstrate players' virility. The competitions between Mexican and Anglo men represented a struggle over racial, class, and masculine pride. As Michael Messner has suggested, "Subordinated groups of men often used sport to resist racist, colonial, and class domination, and their resistance most often took the form of a claim to 'manhood.'" In the highly masculinized arena of baseball, Mexican American men attempted to reassert their racial and masculine identity. In this sense, players became heavily invested in winning because it was one of the ways they could challenge racism while maintaining their masculine pride, honor, and respectability.[37]

In some cases verbal and physical threats to ballplayers' masculinity and racial pride led to fights on and off the playing field. Tito Cortez remembered one incident during a game between the Athletics and a team called the Colored Giants: "One time the Athletics was playing a black team from Los Angeles and one of the guys playing shortstop was batting and made a 'sissy' remark to the pitcher. Something about pitching like a girl, but the catcher heard what he said. He got up and took off his mask, chest protector and ran after him. You could only see his spikes kicking dirt behind." The "sissy" remark provoked the pitcher to respond aggressively so as not to appear weak, powerless, and most of all outwardly effeminate in front of teammates. The fear of feminization and emasculating discourses on the playing field drove male athletes to perform hegemonic forms of "heterosexual masculinity" while suppressing "homosexual masculinities."[38] Additionally, altercations between black players and Mexican American players sometimes bristled with racial tension, but at other times the groups developed friendly relations. Former semipro player Jess Guerrero played for the Los Angeles Colored Giants and fondly remembered playing alongside the famous Negro League pitcher. "I couldn't play with no white team but I played with the colored teams. I played with Satchel Paige." In the culturally diverse region of southern California, the Corona Athletics played against other ethnic teams such as the Los Angeles Nippons (Japanese American), the Sherman Institute Baseball Team (Native American), and the Los Angeles Colored Eagles (African American). Guerrero attempted to play major league baseball, but he faced racial barriers. He bitterly complained, "I have been playing baseball since I was 13 years old. I've been playing all sports. The only problem that kept me from making the majors was my color."[39]

The Athletics club served as a gendered space from which Mexican American ballplayers reproduced a collective masculine culture and identity. Displays of masculine behavior were built around excessive drinking, gambling away hard-earned money, abusive language, competitive behavior, and physical prowess. In some cases this aggressive behavior led to domestic violence. Irene Contreras, the former sister-in-law of one Athletics ballplayer, complained about the player's excessive drinking that interfered with family obligations and domestic relations. Pool halls were another favorite stomping ground for postgame celebrations. The disruptive, exuberant, and wildly aggressive working-class masculine behavior of Athletics players overlapped with a more middle-class masculine behavior that stressed self-discipline, obedience, and acceptance of hierarchy. Athletic players displayed both versions on and off the playing field. On the one hand, an aggressive and combative masculine behavior celebrated on the diamond contributed to winning a game, but on the other hand, this disruptive behavior could threaten efforts to build a disciplined team. These competing forms of masculine behavior, however, maintained a rigid gender hierarchy.[40]

Baseball helped establish strong bonds of male solidarity and companionship that provided the basis for teamwork on and off the field, but the ballplayers' rebellious behavior also led to divisions within the team. For example, when one Athletics player missed several practices and displayed "aggressively rowdy" behavior during a match, the team manager benched him for several games. After his father protested to the manager, a verbal fight ensued. After several attempts at reconciliation, the disgruntled player left the team altogether and convinced several other players to join him in forming a rival baseball club, the Corona Cubs. Organized in 1946, the Cubs played at the city park diamond wearing uniforms donated by Pancho's Garage. A bitter rivalry ensued between the teams during the late 1940s, with both claiming to be the best "Mexican" team in the city.[41]

Despite the increased popularity of baseball among second-generation Mexican Americans, employers and play reformers were only partially successful in their Americanization efforts. From their perspective, baseball offered an alternative to the perilous thrills of cheap amusements such as gambling, drinking, cockfighting, and other perceived antisocial behavior. In their view, immigrant workers could potentially become "baseball conscious" and adopt American middle-class values of sobriety, thrift, and discipline, both on and off the playing field. While some players did adopt some aspects of Americanism, bicultural Mexican Americans imposed multiple meanings on this national pastime and transformed baseball clubs into masculine cultural and political spaces. In his pathbreaking essay on baseball's role in nineteenth-century Cuban nationalism, Louis Perez notes that Cuban baseball players became "conscious of new meanings and mindful of new possibilities" of baseball and began "to reinvent themselves self-consciously as agents of change." So too with Mexican American *peloteros*. By negotiating their commitment and loyalty to the national sport, Mexican

Americans created a social space to assert their own cultural values and masculine pride and, when circumstances warranted, used baseball clubs to forge a politics of opposition.[42]

While baseball brought the Mexican community together on Sunday afternoons, it did so at a time when companies and play reformers sought to organize and control the community's sporting life. In the early decades of the twentieth century, American companies organized baseball clubs to increase the discipline, obedience, and productivity of their immigrant workforce. Play reformers also believed that baseball would ensure the eventual assimilation and Americanization of immigration populations. Baseball mitigated class conflict since everybody, from business owners to company management to the working classes, played the game. Indeed, some ballplayers accommodated baseball's promotion of capitalist values and Anglo middle-class notions of masculinity—stressing discipline, aggressive independence, and acceptance of hierarchy—but others resisted and imposed their own meanings on these games.

For Mexican American *peloteros*, baseball matches represented more than mere athletic competitions. Within the context of unequal Mexican-Anglo relations, they provided a venue for symbolic and real confrontations between the races. Moreover, Mexican Americans politicized baseball clubs into social spaces that became the basis for wider forms of collective action. As the case of the Corona Athletics Baseball Club demonstrates, members learned valuable leadership, networking, and organizational skills that spilled over from the playing field into the political and labor arenas. As chapter 6 shows, Corona Athletics members who became labor organizers activated their sporting networks and honed their organizing and leadership skills in an attempt to challenge the power of agricultural companies.

While the ballplayers' competitive masculine behavior and leadership capabilities as displayed on the playing fields and picket lines helped mount a militant challenge, they also reproduced male domination by excluding women from leadership positions. This contributed to the ultimate failure to achieve class solidarity. The baseball club's combative masculine identity and the exclusion of women from participation—and to a lesser extent from spectatorship—revealed the limitations of working-class resistance when the gender hierarchy is extended from the workplace to the playing field.

PART THREE

From Leisure to Political Activism

6 Labor Unionism and the 1941 Strike

"The strike saved my life," recalled Fred Martínez. "Because I was arrested, spent two months in jail, and was charged with inciting a riot, unlawful assembly, and disturbing the peace, the military didn't take me to war." Martínez was referring to the 1941 labor action that brought industry in Corona to a standstill and ended in a violent riot in front of the Jameson Company packinghouse. "Some of the [police] officers were hit with rocks. One of them was hit with a branch and they thought it was me." A year later, Martínez received a 4F exemption from the draft board because of his arrest record, causing his friends to nickname him "4F." Today, Martínez's nickname serves as a reminder of the failed two-month strike for better wages and working conditions that created divisions among company management, employees, and sectors of the Mexican community.[1]

Unionization efforts of Mexican citrus workers in this citrus-dominated open shop town were extensive during the late 1930s and early 1940s. Assisted by the progressive union, United Cannery, Agricultural, Packing, and Allied Workers of America (UCAPAWA), activists demanded an increase in pay from four and a half cents a box to six cents plus overtime pay; free equipment and transportation; six holidays including Christmas, New Year, and Cinco de Mayo; and union recognition. UCAPAWA was affiliated with the left-wing Congress of Industrial Organizations (CIO) and became one of the leading Popular Front organizations that supported New Deal programs, civil rights, democracy, and antifascism at home and abroad. Several CIO union leaders were former baseball players associated with the Corona Athletics who honed their leadership skills and organizational abilities on the playing field and transferred them to the picket lines. Mexican women were denied leadership positions within the union structure but, nevertheless, participated in the picket lines and lined up strike support from surrounding areas. Unlike Corona's barrio residents who rallied behind the strikers, the employee-residents who lived and worked on surrounding ranches faced special economic constraints that prevented them from joining the strike. While some supported unionization efforts, others opted to support the status quo, demonstrating that conservative community norms often clashed with labor militancy. After the arrests of forty-nine strikers following the riot, police deputies patrolled the area, intimidating workers and threatening further arrests. Finally, growers imported Anglo strikebreakers, forcing the union to give up the struggle.

Labor Unionism in the Citrus Industry

Despite the failure of spontaneous labor actions and union organizing attempts during the First World War, Mexican citrus workers once again turned to labor unionism during the 1930s in an effort to improve their economic conditions. During the summer of 1936, Orange County pickers launched one of the largest strikes in the state, forcing growers to resort to brute force and violence. One of the leaders of the antiunion Associated Farmers called the strike "a little Mexican revolution." But not all sectors of the Mexican community formed a united front, as Gilbert González has shown. Mexican consular representatives expelled suspected radicals from union ranks and negotiated an agreement with growers. In the strike's aftermath, Mexican workers abandoned their independent union to join the CIO and the American Federation of Labor (AFL).[2] After facing a conservative Mexican consulate and the staunchly antiunion Associated Farmers, Mexican citrus workers turned to more progressive national labor unions for assistance.

After splintering off from the conservative AFL in 1935, the more progressive CIO became a staunch defender of the Mexican working class throughout the United States, not only in regard to wages and working conditions but in matters of racial discrimination, housing, education, and civil rights.[3] Encouraged by the New Deal legislation, although it excluded farm labor from its provisions, the CIO enlisted the help of Democratic Party liberals and Communist Party members to forge a Popular Front to elect social democratic politicians into office, carry on campaigns against fascism, fight racial discrimination at home, support civil liberties, and come to the defense of black and Mexican American youths. Mexicans joined and led Popular Front organizations such as the Congress of Spanish-Speaking Peoples and Asociación Nacional México-Americana. By participating in CIO-led unions and Popular Front struggles, a new generation of Mexican men and women began to merge labor and civil rights and redefine what it meant to be an American.[4]

The entry of the CIO into the citrus industry began with the passage of the 1935 National Labor Relations Act (also known as the Wagner Act) that allowed industrial employees to hold elections and required employers to negotiate with elected representatives of a majority of the workers. Established under the Wagner Act to settle worker-employer disputes, the National Labor Relations Board (NLRB) helped organized labor by reclassifying packinghouse employees from "agricultural workers" to "industrial workers." Organized labor and the citrus industry had battled over interpretation of the Wagner Act's agricultural exemption clause until a 1937 court case that ruled against the North Whittier Heights Citrus Association. Citrus industry attorney Ivan McDaniel argued that the same agricultural laborers who picked also packed the fruit in orchard fields. The NLRB rejected this argument, since picking and packing were simultaneous tasks performed in separate workplaces and by different employees. Despite several appeals, the California Ninth District Court finally upheld the NRLB decision in 1940.[5]

Concerned about the NLRB decision and with the militant struggles of the orange pickers in 1936 still fresh in their minds, the California Fruit Growers Exchange, the American Fruit Growers, and the Mutual Orange Distributors formed the Agricultural Producers Labor Committee (APLC). To ensure that packinghouse workers remained outside federal protection, the APLC worked closely with the Associated Farmers to form company unions and to "break farm-labor unionism and suppress strikes by means of more or less direct action." W. E. Spencer, chairman of the APLC, asserted that employers must hold their ground against unionization. Apart from lobbying members of Congress, the APLC posted bulletins in every packinghouse in southern California, warning employees that the industry group would fight to maintain "open shop" conditions.[6]

Packinghouses faced another challenge that same year when the CIO chartered UCAPAWA to organize agricultural, cannery, and food-processing workers. This left-leaning union, with some members belonging to the Communist Party, established a diverse following among black sharecroppers in Alabama, black and Anglo workers in Memphis, and Filipino workers in Seattle and Alaska.[7] Between 1937 and 1940, the union made great inroads among California's field and food-processing workers, establishing thirty-five locals and securing wage increases and improvements of working and living conditions. After a series of defeated strikes in the San Joaquin Valley, UCAPAWA faced financial woes and hostility from the Associated Farmers. As a result, UCAPAWA organizers decided to abandon the fields and refocus their energies on food-processing sites where workers lived in the towns year-round.[8]

In southern California, UCAPAWA organized strong worker-controlled cannery and packinghouse locals under the effective leadership of Luisa Moreno and Dorothy Ray Healey. According to Vicki Ruiz, the union benefited from the active participation of rank-and-file Mexican women, some of whom became staunch leaders of their locals. Encouraged by the favorable NLRB ruling, UCAPAWA proceeded to organize the entire citrus industry in the summer of 1937, beginning with packers. One of the first CIO citrus unions emerged in the Riverside–San Bernardino district.[9]

After a series of successful organizing drives in the greater Los Angeles area and the establishment of a Spanish-language supplement in the union newspaper, UCAPAWA stepped up efforts in summer 1940 to organize citrus packinghouses in inland southern California. Corona's citrus packinghouses became a key testing ground for the UCAPAWA campaign. Lead organizer Emil Geist reported on the progress of Corona's Citrus Workers Organizing Committee: "Corona is so much in need of unionization that representatives of all kinds of workers have asked UCAPAWA to take them in, indicating [the] possibility for building a strong CIO base in the heart of this ASSOCIATED FARMER stronghold." Geist added that packinghouse workers were "disgusted with their 'phony' [company] union" and wanted the "CIO to take them over." He predicted that out of the seven major packinghouses, "UCAPAWA will very likely win the elections petitioned with NLRB."[10]

UCAPAWA organizers turned to baseball clubs for assistance in their organizing efforts. The Athletics Baseball Club offered its playing field as a union meeting site. "The CIO came into Corona to organize the workers, and of course the ranchers did not want us to organize," explained Rudy Ramos. "We used to meet on Sheridan and Grand Boulevard. There used to be a baseball field . . . where the famous Athletics played. . . . [T]his ballpark is where we used to meet because it was hidden from view and away from the police." Workers pointed out that Sundays were reserved for church services, moviegoing, baseball games, and other leisure activities. During meetings, workers formulated union demands and discussed the importance of days off and overtime pay for Sundays. Battle for control over leisure time and space became part of the broad efforts to win collective bargaining and union recognition.[11]

Within a few months, UCAPAWA organized a majority of employees at the Jameson Company and the Corona Citrus Association, and the NRLB ordered an election at both packinghouses. In response, the local chapter of the Associated Farmers resorted to intimidation. According to one organizer, "Each Associated Farmer undertook to visit three workers and try to influence them against voting for the CIO. . . . Thinly veiled threats were made as to what would happen to the workers and the industry if the CIO won." In addition, the local newspaper printed a front-page editorial titled "The Stakes Are High" that accused UCAPAWA of trying to impose a closed-shop contract system to benefit "imported, high-priced, radically-inclined labor leaders." Another editorial accused UCAPAWA of "boring from within—that is the object of Communist International as it spreads its talon-like network over the nation in [an] attempt to paralyze our political and industrial life." These red-baiting articles portrayed local workers as being "duped" by CIO organizers and instructed them "to do a little clear thinking of their own . . . before they cast their ballot in an election of vital importance to the future welfare of Corona's main industry."[12]

Acting on their own initiative, workers went to the polls on July 22, 1940, and voted 54–14 in favor of the union. "The significance of the election cannot be overlooked," declared one UCAPAWA official. "It is the opening wedge in the organization of the huge citrus industry in Southern California which employs over 20,000 workers in the sheds and fields. This plant was organized despite tremendous opposition of the Associated Farmers." After the successful election, the Los Angeles Industrial Union Council sent a Spanish-speaking organizer, Alfonso Ortiz, to expand the organizing to other packinghouses. During a victory celebration, Ortiz distributed flyers printed in English and Spanish that announced the next union meeting, where he gave a rousing speech: "Every packinghouse worker in the entire citrus industry knows what the complaints are. . . . It's long hours, short pay all over California; it's lack of job security, lack of seniority rights, abuse of the stand-by, petty tyranny from petty bosses that is forcing the worker to look for protection in the CIO. The only way we can change our working conditions, and raise our wages and protect our jobs is by organization. The packinghouse workers in Corona have found the answer and want to say that CIO IS HERE TO STAY!" Following the four-to-one vote, the company refused to meet and negotiate a contract with the newly formed UCAPAWA union, the Agricultural Citrus Workers Union Local 342, so members resorted to more direct action.[13]

Concerned about the possibility of a strike, the city council introduced a new antipicketing ordinance. It expanded the definition of "picketing" to include the following: (a) threat of bodily injury, (b) threat of bodily injury to a family member, and (c) threat of damage to property owned by the individual. The council introduced the antipicketing ordinance at the urging of Corona growers. The minutes of the Queen Colony Fruit Exchange revealed the growers' intentions: "The matter of a 'picketing ordinance' for the city of Corona was discussed. It was thought advisable that we contact the city council regarding such an ordinance." Similar antipicketing ordinances were adopted in thirty-four counties across the state, granting police more power to keep labor unions at bay.[14]

Bitter Lemons

After six months of stalling tactics from employers, union organizers decided to strike in the early morning of February 27, 1941. More than eight hundred people gathered at the ballpark to coordinate picket line duty and plan their next moves. Once round-the-clock picketing began, the newly formed Corona Citrus Growers Association (CCGA) called upon law enforcement officials to patrol the packinghouses, groves, and ballpark. According to the *Riverside Daily Press*, "The meeting began at the ballpark [and] then the crowd adjourned and gathered at another open field due to interference by police and stool pigeons." Immediately afterward, the Corona City Council passed a resolution to designate the baseball field's surrounding areas "no parking zones." In response, union supporter and Athletics manager Marcos Uribe led a group of workers to city hall to protest the "no parking" resolution. Uribe spoke to the city council: "We petition the council to reconsider their undemocratic action. . . . We ask this in order to allow the citizens of Corona the opportunity and the unabridged right of liberty." The city council rejected their complaints, and the union moved their meetings to the outskirts of town.[15]

Concerns about potential strikebreakers from the surrounding citrus belt districts prompted union members and supporters to publicize their struggle. Strike committee leader Heliodoro Medina, for example, visited *La Opinión* headquarters and urged the newspaper to tell its readers to spread the word and discourage people from strikebreaking.

Medina explained the strike demands and highlighted the exploitative nature of the company store. "We want the end to the company store that exploits workers and keeps us indebted to the company." The company store at the Foothill Ranch forced workers into a web of chronic indebtedness with little opportunity to save money and improve their economic condition.[16]

Seasoned baseball players who became labor organizers activated their sporting networks for strike support. Medina recruited several baseball players to contact Casa Blanca's barrio and meet with baseball managers to warn their players not to intervene in the labor conflict. Athletics ballplayers Tony Balderas and Charles Uribe visited ballparks in Placentia, Ontario, Santa Ana, Oxnard, and San Fernando to solicit support from baseball teams. Baseball tournaments in nearby towns also helped to spread the word about the Corona strike.[17]

A key supporter of the Corona labor struggle was the UCAPAWA baseball team from Orange, California. In 1937, UCAPAWA Local 120 organized a CIO baseball team that toured southern California, winning semipro baseball tournaments and discussing with opponents the values of unionization. Under the coaching skills of Ray Zuñiga, the CIO team won numerous matches, some of these against baseball teams in Tijuana, Mexico. According to the *UCAPAWA News*, "This local has distinguished itself in continuous struggle, without fear of any sort, raising high its banner against the winds." Although the CIO team and sporting networks that extended throughout the region helped cultivate support for the Corona strike, they did not prevent growers from resorting to repressive measures.[18]

After two weeks, the strike reached a stalemate. Corona mayor Dan Huckins stepped into the fray by reminding both sides that "Corona is essentially a citrus town, dependent on the citrus industry, so let's get busy and settle our problem." The mayor's advice was ignored, however, as the picket lines expanded to seven ranch properties. Soon thereafter, the strike spread to nearby Casa Blanca, prompting the chief of police to request more police and additional guns and ammunition. Increased police presence raised tensions. Edward Willits, president of the Corona Foothill Lemon Company, admitted that the growers "had control of the sheriff." So when picket lines began forming, the packinghouses responded by paying workers in two-dollar bills. This way, according to Willits, "The town was thick in two-dollar bills, to make the people in town realize how much their business relied on" the citrus industry. These coercive maneuvers highlighted the political and economic muscle of Corona growers. One of the most powerful growers,

Joy Jameson, earned a reputation for his autocratic style. As one Italian packinghouse manager put it, "What Jameson said was the word in those days, and it carried a long way."[19]

Tensions between Italians and Mexicans emerged during the strike. When the CIO union placed picket lines in front of the Jameson Company packinghouse, Italian employees had to decide whether to walk out in support of the union and be reprimanded by Italian managers or continue working and possibly face harassment from picketers. John Guirbino wrote about crossing the picket line. "The pickets were out all night grouped around bonfires. It was our primary job to see that they did not burn the wooden plant down. I knew most of them on the picket line. Periodically throughout the night they would yell and call me a 'scab.'" Guirbino's story revealed how relations between both groups had deteriorated, a breakdown that continued well into the striker court trials.[20]

Italian managers were preferred for their ability to speak Spanish and keep close surveillance on the Mexican female workforce. According to Angelo, his father, Mike Lunetta, learned to speak three languages. "My dad got the job in running the Foothill packinghouse because he spoke good Spanish. He was very fair to the Mexican people. It was not like having an American boss who could not speak their language."[21] His relationship with Mexican employees soured, however, when a majority opted to join the CIO union, despite his efforts to convince them otherwise. "Since my dad was part of management he had to break the picket line," explained Angelo, so "he wore a sheriff's badge to show some authority." When asked why the unions could establish a stronghold in the citrus industry, Lunetta responded, "Well, most of these [Mexicans] were not the type to get mixed [up] in unions; they were contented [and] did not object one way or another." This explanation resembled Corona growers' paternalistic language of race that attributed labor militancy not to workers themselves but to outside agitators. Mexican workers were supposedly incapable of self-organization and lacked the ability to fight on their own, but they proved the growers wrong.[22]

Claiming it was losing 25–33 percent of its fruit, the CCGA appealed to the local community for support and vowed to "never permit outside organizers to gain control of the jobs of *our* agricultural workers and control of farming operations here." Joy Jameson was reported as saying that his employees were "very happy" and earning "never less than $5 a day" and that "pickers' wages [were] running as high as $9." In the growers' view, the real labor problem was not with their "loyal employees" but with "outside agitators." By using the rhetoric of "localism," growers attempted to de-legitimize the CIO organizers who resided elsewhere and supposedly placed their own interests above local workers. However, Corona's Mexican community understood the importance of seeking outside help from organized labor. As Frances Martínez explained, "We had outsiders coming in to help us, and we needed the help, but they really stuck it to them [and] the strike got too hot."[23]

To counter growers' legitimacy about representing the best interests of the "local" community, the union called for a citywide election. CIO organizer Theodore Rasmussen asked the grower-controlled city council to hold a special election by secret ballot. All field and packing-house workers on current payrolls would be eligible to vote on the question "Do you want to be represented by the CIO for the purpose of collective bargaining?" CIO representatives promised that if they lost the election they would never interfere with the local citrus industry again, but if they won they should be eligible to conduct industry-wide negotiations over wages, hours, and working conditions for both citrus packinghouse and field workers. Corona growers considered the CIO proposal "impossible and ridiculous" since pickers were excluded from federal protection. Barnes accused Rasmussen of "trying to make it an industry-wide election whereas the strike is against the individual growers and associations." In spite of growers' and the city's reluctance, the CIO conducted the election on the steps of city hall. Out of 572 who voted, 568 voted in favor of the CIO. By voting for the union, workers became more conscious of their civil rights and provided moral justification for their struggle. Following the election, Rasmussen declared that "we now ask the growers and helpers to recognize this local expression favoring the CIO as a bargaining unit, and sit down around a table to discuss wages, hours and working conditions."[24]

After the election victory, organizers visited the outlying citrus plantations in an attempt to organize pickers who worked and lived on company property. After several visits, Heliodoro Medina reported that "although they were afraid to sign a pledge card because of company intimidation, they feel the necessity of a union, and will vote for the CIO."[25] However, unionists faced daunting challenges in organizing citrus ranch pickers. First, unlike packinghouse workers, citrus pickers were classified as agricultural workers and thus were exempted from federal protection. Because the ranches resembled an autocratic plantation system, worker-residents experienced a higher degree of company control than city residents. For ranch residents, joining a union meant reprisals from company management and the risk of losing not only their jobs but also their homes. Moreover, because they lived and worked on company property, ranch workers were not easily accessible to organizers. When picket lines formed around the citrus ranches, growers posted armed guards in the groves and instructed pickers to pick only in the inner groves to "protect" them from union organizers.

As discussed in chapter 1, owners of the Foothill Ranch used a series of paternalistic measures—job benefits, company homes, company store credit, a community center, and recreational facilities—to cultivate loyalty and allegiance among its employee-residents. Although the union included the elimination of the company store as part of its overall demands, many families relied on company store credit for day-to-day needs and for emergencies. According to one Foothill Ranch supervisor, "As far as our employees were concerned, there was not a whole lot more they could obtain from the union. They already had free housing. . . . So that is one reason they did not join. The company as a whole had pretty good relations with the workers."[26]

Given these constraints, some residents went along with the company's wishes, while others used the paternalistic system to win concessions from their employer and waged subtle acts of resistance that often went unrecognized beyond the ranch boundaries. Take, for example, Luis Cruz, who worked for Foothill for more than twenty years, and one day decided to leave when his demand for a wage increase was ignored. "They treated me pretty nice and everything. But the only thing is [they] didn't pay enough." Luis left Foothill for a construction job in Orange County that paid twice as much. When Cruz returned to pick up his last paycheck, the company owner asked why he had left. Luis responded rather angrily, "Why? I live in a free country where we can go any place we want. . . . There is no sense for me to tell you that I was moving because I know that you will not let me go."[27]

When the labor conflict erupted in town, the decision to support or not support the union was first of all an economic one. Ranch residents were well aware of the power the company wielded over their lives and understood that joining the strike or the union would mean the loss of their job, home, family stability, and friendships. The issue was an intensely personal and familial one as well. When asked why he did not join the strike, Manuel Cruz said he felt that he did not have a choice since all his older brothers were good friends with ranch supervisors.[28] Although most ranch workers did not join picket lines or the union, they did engage in slowdowns, workplace sabotage, walkouts, fruit theft, feigning sickness, and talking back. In effect, ranch employees were neither deeply co-opted nor fully oppositional in a collective sense. Rather, they determined their best options based on years of self-assertion and resistance and within the limits set by the company. While working inside the groves, Reynaldo Aparicio heard that a strike had begun in the packinghouse and was spreading to the groves. In response, picking foremen pushed workers to pick faster before the picketers arrived. Aparicio showed his solidarity with the union by telling the foreman that the "union was not asking for too much." The foreman immediately fired him. "That was the biggest break I got," Aparicio said. "I did not want to pick fruit all my life."[29]

To keep ranch residents from going into town for shopping and entertainment purposes, the company provided incentives to stay put. "Since the advent of the union here," Alfonso Ortiz told the newspaper editor, "the growers increased bonus payments, [improved] working conditions in groves and lower[ed] prices in company stores." Manuel Cruz recalled that "the company did not want us to come downtown because they were afraid that [the strikers] might gang up on us, so they bought us some ping-pong tables, checkers, cards, and entertainment, because we could not go to the [movie theater] show." When residents did go to town they risked verbal harassment and reprimand from union supporters. "Once you revealed that you lived in Foothill, you were immediately branded a scab," lamented Cruz. "They held it against you because you worked at the ranch. Some friends would not even talk to me."[30] Onias Acevedo, who grew up on the Call Estate Ranch and later became Corona's first city councilman of Mexican descent, defended his decision to stay put. "We were afraid of being kicked out and left with nothing. We were like damn goats tied up with a rope. There was only so far we could go."[31]

Physical confrontations also broke out between strikers and non-striking workers. When ranch residents refused to walk out of the groves, fights broke out. For example, ranch resident Heracio Magaña, who refused to walk out on strike and voiced opposition to the union, was allegedly attacked by a picketer. Magaña escaped injury, while the attacker was arrested and sentenced to six months in the county jail for assault and battery. The combativeness that arose from the masculinized picking culture became a source for worker militancy against company authority but also worked against bridging class and gender divisions in the community.[32]

During the strike, Mexican women participated in the picket lines, cooked food for strikers, raised money for the strike fund, and solicited support from local businesses. According to the *Corona Independent*,

"Three women representing the C.I.O. were circulating at city business establishments to learn whether or not they were employing union labor. A beauty parlor even was asked whether or not it was giving services to 'scabs.'" But while they occupied the majority of packinghouse positions (as graders, packers, and sorters), Mexican women did not occupy leadership positions within the union structure, and their specific grievances (such as sexual harassment from male foremen) were not part of the overall union demands. In addition, boyfriends, fathers, and husbands discouraged women from joining the picket lines. According to Alice Rodríguez, "My husband did not want me to join the [picket] line, so I stayed home. When the Italian foreman came to the house to convince me to go back to work, I told him that I did not want to go against my friends." Despite her husband's reluctance, Rodríguez supported the strikers by printing flyers at home, babysitting, and providing moral support to the strikers. By simply staying home, withholding their labor power and refusing to cross the picket lines, women such as Rodríguez engaged in a form of resistance.[33]

Although women benefited from wage increases and union recognition, most of the demands concerned the jobs of male pickers hired by packinghouse associations, including free transportation to the groves, a fifty-cent per hour minimum pay during wet waiting periods, seniority rights for pickers, an eight-hour workday with overtime pay, and a six-day working week with double pay for holidays. Although pregnant with her second child, Frances Martínez attended one of the union meetings. She remembers that "there was a [union organizer] talking in the baseball field; he was talking like a preacher, and they were saying that he was a communist. . . . [W]hen I heard him talk he was telling the people to demand their rights." The majority of attendees were male pickers who were voicing their grievances. According to Martínez, "As I understand it the [men] were complaining about the 'wet' system. Even for the women it was really hard, because the [men] were not working and would come home saying, 'No te levantes, honey' [Don't get up, honey]." This statement meant that the wife did not have to get up early to pack a lunch for her unemployed husband. In other words, male pickers faced job insecurity that threatened their masculine breadwinner role within the family. For this reason, according to Martínez, "The pickers went on strike, and [packing]house workers joined them in sympathy. But afterwards they put the men in jail."[34]

Those Mexican women who walked out in support of their brothers, husbands, and boyfriends proved themselves to be fierce fighters on the picket lines. Several fights broke out between Mexican women and

Anglo women recruited from Orange County packinghouses to replace striking packers. For example, during the strike Mrs. Blackman, wife of the Jameson packinghouse foreman, charged directly through the picket line, but before she reached the front door, striking Mexican women stopped her and engaged in a "verbal outburst." The striker was arrested for disturbing the peace and later released. To prevent further confrontations between strikers and employees who refused to walk out, fifteen to twenty deputies from the Riverside Sheriff's Office were stationed in front of the packinghouse entrances.[35]

After twenty-four days with no sign of resolving the labor conflict, Corona growers resorted to more repressive tactics. On the afternoon of March 21, 1937, a barrage of rocks was thrown at passing police cars from the picket lines. The assailants broke a car window and hit a police officer on the head. Police responded by throwing fifteen or twenty tear gas canisters into the picket line, which had about 150 to 200 strikers. Rudy Ramos recalled the chaotic scene. "The police threw tear gas at us, but we'd picked it up and threw it back." Then, he said, "the people spread out and three girls took me away from the field." The police escorted 49 male strikers to jail and booked them on charges of disturbing the peace, inciting a riot, unlawful assembly, and aggravated assault with a deadly weapon. Some of the leading union organizers arrested included Heliodoro Medina, Marcos Uribe, Tony Balderas, and Angel Altamarino. Medina was accused of being one of the "instigators of the present labor difficulty" and urging picketers to attack the police.[36]

The day after the incident, police arrested two more union organizers, George Becerra and Gilson Gray. Gray, an employee of the CCGA, was congregating with the remaining picketers when he suddenly was whisked away by police officers and "thrown into jail and held incommunicado." Gray was released after posting fourteen thousand dollars in property bonds; he was the only defendant to make bail. None of the remaining defendants could post bail, which was set at one thousand dollars per person. Harry Kaplan, lawyer for the Los Angeles CIO, attempted to secure their release from jail through habeas corpus proceedings, charging "illegal restraint and detention without filing charges within the statutory time." A Riverside Superior Court judge denied the petition, claiming that the defendants were "under lawful processes." After three were released to juvenile court, one pleaded guilty and received probation and the remaining forty-five defendants were scheduled for separate trials.[37]

The press reported on the community-wide interest in the court trials, which were held in Riverside. "Despite rainy weather the steps of the city hall were crowded with spectators and families of the defendants who were unable to get into the courtroom." In front of an all-Anglo jury, prosecuting attorneys blamed CIO organizer Theodore Rasmussen's speech during a union meeting held before the "riot," in which he was quoted as saying that "we want action on the strike." These words, according to prosecutors, "were interpreted to mean violence of some sort." Kaplan cited the inability of the police to differentiate among a crowd of two hundred to three hundred individuals; he thus argued that the case rested on mistaken identity. During closing arguments, Kaplan claimed that police officers had attempted to create a "disturbance" by first dispersing all women and children from the scene and then launching tear gas canisters at the picket lines. The trial ended in a partial victory when the jury found all defendants not guilty of "rioting" except four persons who were found guilty of "unlawful assembly."[38]

The last defendant, Manuel Martínez, went on trial a week later, charged with "intent to commit great bodily harm" against two deputy sheriffs. Described as a short, heavyset twenty-seven-year-old citrus worker who hauled fertilizer and picked fruit, Martínez pleaded not guilty and maintained his innocence. Court transcripts of witness testimonies revealed the possibility of mistaken identity. Deputy Reginald Meier testified that when he arrived on the scene, he observed a "loud, noisy demonstration." He saw another police officer, Fred Householder, attempting to arrest an unidentified man who allegedly had been throwing rocks at passing police cars. As Deputy Householder approached the picket lines to arrest the suspect, "he was beset upon on all sides by [Mexican] people who were surrounding him." As Householder tried to free himself, he was struck with a club. But when asked whether the club was in the hands of Manuel Martínez, Meier was not sure, admitting that he "didn't see the blow descending" and saying that "from the short glance I got of him, he appeared to be a Mexican, I would say between 20 to 30 years old, young, of medium height and build." And when asked again if the defendant hit Deputy Householder, Meier said, "I believe he did." Later he admitted that twenty to thirty officers approached the picketers with tear gas in hand to scare them away, but strikers stood firm. Another deputy sheriff called to testify for the prosecution could not definitively identify Martínez as the assailant. Nonetheless, an all-Anglo jury found Manuel Martínez guilty on two felony assault charges. The judge rejected the defendant's pleas for probation and sentenced Martínez to San Quentin State Prison to serve two concurrent five-year sentences.[39]

During the court trials, Anglo and Italian employees of the Jameson packinghouse testified against the Mexican defendants. According to a newspaper account, "Mimi Corselli, Nick Corselli, Mimi De George, Charles Muratore and Ralph Pallireto . . . testified they left the plant about 6 p.m., the same night of the alleged riot. They identified some of the defendants as being in the crowd." At the end of the strike, both Mexicans and Italians returned to work with cold stares, bitter feelings, and deeper awareness of how much they had grown apart. The strike and court trials further widened the rift between both groups. Frances Martínez put it rather bluntly. "They did pretty well. The Italians packed their way out of the barrio." Motivated by the promises and privileges of whiteness, Italians climbed up the socioeconomic scale within the citrus industry and moved into the outlying suburbs of Southside Corona.[40]

The litigation lasted five weeks and drained the union coffers. Alfonso Ortiz reported to the Los Angeles Industrial Union Council on the cost of the trials, complaining that "the court fights have cost $600 [and] UCAPAWA is very broke. We are asking for contributions." He asked if the council would be "having an organizational drive going in L.A." to support the Corona defendants. The lack of CIO financial support left fund-raising efforts in the hands of family members and friends, making some question the commitment of labor organizers who lived outside of Corona. Onias Acevedo did not support the strike and explained his reasons. "There were three guys who used to come from L.A. and would be rebel rousing and raising hell with us for two or three days and then take off and go home. But we were still here."[41] Some *huelguistas* (strikers) began to question why "the [CIO] guys were being paid by the union" while they were left to raise strike funds. When the rioting took place in the front of the packinghouse one picketer complained, "Where the hell are they [CIO] when we need them?"[42]

Additionally, during the court trials, the Corona Foothill Lemon Company established a tent city for two hundred Anglo migrant workers and their families whom they imported "to defy the union men who had walked off the jobs." Although the tents were on Foothill property, the workers were assigned to the citrus orchards affected by the strike and received extra protection from private security guards. Originally from Oklahoma, Arkansas, and Texas, these Anglo migrants initially lived in trailers and tent housing, then later moved to the nearby Home Gardens neighborhood. The local newspaper described this "new community as rapidly assuming the appearance of a typical California labor camp." The combination of these strikebreaking tactics and mass arrests forced the union to redirect its efforts toward defending the strikers. Harry Kaplan admitted that "the mass arrests have weakened the strike morale to some extent." This ultimately crippled the strike and ended the fledgling CIO union movement in Corona.[43]

Strike Aftermath

Despite some success in organizing union locals and rousing the state's agribusiness establishment, UCAPAWA had run out of funds and could no longer afford to organize packinghouse and field workers. The majority of UCAPAWA's total income was supplied by only twenty-three non-farmworker locals located in bigger cities. UCAPAWA organizer Dorothy Healey admitted that "we could sign up a lot of people and we began winning strikes, but we never developed a stable member or system of regular dues collection." In terms of membership, at the end of 1937 about three thousand farmworkers belonged to UCAPAWA, but two years later the numbers decreased to twenty-five hundred . Moreover, the California CIO, like its AFL counterpart, failed to make agricultural workers an organizing priority and instead left the responsibility to the federal government and the "public conscience."[44]

Mexican women have long participated and often led major labor actions throughout the United States.[45] During the Corona strike, however, Mexican American women were excluded from union leadership positions despite occupying more than two hundred packinghouse positions in 1940. Another contributing factor was the uneven gender ratios in the industry. Out of fifteen hundred persons in the citrus labor force, there were approximately nine hundred male pickers compared to six hundred women packinghouse workers. Unlike female packinghouse workers, the agricultural exemption in the Wagner Act deprived male pickers of collective bargaining rights. The "agriculture-industrial" differentiation led to feelings of resentment among the men who could not fulfill their breadwinner role.[46]

Although intense police suppression and worker divisions orchestrated by the citrus companies played an important role in undermining the union effort, it is also true that union organizers failed to incorporate women as integral leaders of the union and seemed rather insensitive to women's issues. In effect, the union's marginalization of women reproduced the male domination in the community and contributed to the labor movement's defeat. Baseball players who became union organizers extended their physical prowess and "rough" masculine behavior from the playing field into the labor struggle. In addition, the industry's gender division of labor, which separated men into field-related jobs and women into packinghouse-related jobs, contributed to the divisions in the community. Despite the strike's defeat, women organizers and participants mounted a strong challenge to company officials and continued to resist in other ways such as work stoppages, petition drives, and individual confrontations.[47]

These gender divisions and interethnic conflicts combined with paternalistic and repressive tactics orchestrated by Corona growers, with the help of the Associated Farmers and APLC, were too much for the fledgling UCAPAWA. The union's funds were depleted after mass arrests and court trials. Although Corona did not provide "the opening wedge" to bring the unions into the citrus industry, this setback did not stop UCAPAWA from trying again two years later. In 1943 UCAPAWA organizer and civil rights leader Luisa Moreno formed the Citrus Workers Organizing Committee (CWOC) to launch an organizing drive in the Riverside-San Bernardino area. Unlike the UCAPAWA male leadership in Corona, Luisa Moreno made sure that female workers occupied leadership positions in the new locals. Two years later, CWOC (now affiliated with the Food, Tobacco, Agricultural, and Allied Workers) declared thirteen victories and sixteen defeats in packinghouse elections. These new unions were short-lived, however, and the Corona citrus district was excluded altogether. The *Corona Independent* reported, "So far as is known there are no CIO or other union labor organizations in Corona and no organization work nor elections for this vicinity have been under consideration in the citrus industry." Reflecting on the difficulties in organizing citrus workers, Luisa Moreno wrote that "the complete history of organization in citrus will be written some day. It will include many bitter struggles—ending again and again in defeat or ineffectiveness for both AFL and CIO."[48]

Corona was not the only citrus town that experienced a bitter labor defeat. The lemon industry towns of Ventura County experienced a six-month-long strike led by Mexican citrus workers affiliated with the AFL union, Agricultural and Citrus Workers Union (ACWU), Local 22342. In a rare show of solidarity between the CIO and the AFL, the defeated Corona workers supported AFL efforts to extend their "secondary boycott" to the Exchange Lemon Products Company plant. On May 2, 1941, twenty strikers placed a picket line on the local plant to prevent the owners from processing "hot cargo" lemons from Ventura County. Corona by-products workers refused to cross the picket line and assisted with picketing duties. Upon advice from Charles C. Teague, by-products plant president, Joy Jameson refused to shut down the plant and instead dumped sixty carloads of Ventura County lemons near the railroad tracks. Former plant manager George Stanley recalled the lemon-dumping scene. "Farmers came with their shovels and were unloading lemons into a big hole in the ground [when] strikers ganged up to drive the farmers out of the boxcars. That was the basis for the claim of violence and we got a court injunction against the union." Ultimately, AFL union efforts were defeated by the court injunction and the mass eviction of five thousand Mexican families from the company homes of Ventura County's citrus plantations, including Limoneira Ranch.[49]

In the aftermath of the Corona and Ventura County citrus strikes, Carey McWilliams, director of the California Commission of Immigration and Housing, sent a sharply worded letter to Nelson Rockefeller, head of the Office of the Coordination of Inter-American Affairs (OCIAA). McWilliams protested the mass eviction of Mexican families in Ventura County as "further evidence of Yankee intolerance," thus undermining the ideals of the Good Neighbor Policy toward Latin America. McWilliams pointed out that "this incident was widely reported in the Spanish language press in California and had the most unfortunate repercussions in Mexico." The rest of the letter outlined a strategic plan to improve Latin American relations that included (1) a study of the discrimination affecting resident nationals of Latin American countries; (2) a program to encourage long-resident Mexicans to become American citizens; (3) increased recreational, housing, public health, and educational opportunities for Mexican communities; and (4) sponsorship of lectures, art exhibits, and cultural events to give citizens a better understanding and appreciation of Mexican history and culture. McWilliams added that "if we really want to demonstrate goodwill towards the Latin American nations, then no more obvious tests of the sincerity of our policy could be suggested than our attitude toward resident nationals of these countries." He concluded by stating that "because of local indifference, prejudice and misunderstanding, it is the federal government which should assume leadership . . . [and then] states and communities would fall into line and do their part." In response, the OCIAA established a Spanish-Speaking People's Division to coordinate programs and study the social conditions in the southwest.[50]

The Corona strike represented a significant challenge to the great power that the citrus growers wielded over the lives of working men and women. At the same time, the strike also demonstrated problems in achieving working-class unity across gender, racial, ethnic, and class divides. First, it illuminated the ways in which the citrus ranches and company paternalism had polarized the Mexican community, and the question of whether to support the labor action forced people to weigh competing loyalties to their families, the union, the company, and the larger community. Verbal and physical altercations between those who opposed the union and those who showed sympathy erupted during the strike. These divisions revealed that not all members of the Mexican community went along with the union but showed ambivalence and conservative norms that supported the status quo. Second, although Mexican and Italian immigrants shared cultural and linguistic similarities that fostered a unique interethnic community, by the 1930s these relations had begun to erode. By 1941 Italians had moved into top-level managerial positions and moved out of the segregated barrio neighborhoods and elementary school, so when the strike broke out there were few opportunities for the two groups to unite. This rift also revealed how Italians used their "white" color privilege to achieve a higher economic and residential mobility. Last, despite the participation of Mexican women in the labor movement, women were excluded from union leadership positions. In effect, the union's marginalization of women effectively reproduced male domination that contributed to the labor movement's defeat.

Although the efforts to unionize citrus workers in Corona were ultimately unsuccessful, the CIO-led labor movement in Corona laid the political foundation for the Mexican American civil rights movement that emerged in subsequent decades. Labor union activists and returning veterans founded civil rights organizations to fight for the desegregation of public schools, local theaters, and recreational facilities and help bring about the election of Corona's first city councilperson of Mexican descent. In doing so, Mexican American activists translated the official Good Neighbor Policy to gain community resources and attain social justice at the grassroots.

7 *The Struggle for Civil Rights*

"If it hadn't been for the war, I'd still be planting, fumigating, and picking," remarked Onias Acevedo. "[World War II] opened your eyes while you were in other parts of the world, so you could see beyond your own little domain. . . . So you change your way of thinking." Nick-named "Ace" by his friends, Acevedo was one of 90 Mexican American soldiers who left Corona to fight overseas in the Second World War. In 1928, when he was six years old, Acevedo had arrived with his parents and siblings at the Call Estate Ranch and immediately started picking citrus fruit with his father. After his father died in 1939, Acevedo dropped out of school and returned to the groves full-time to support his family. After serving in the U.S. Army for three years, he returned to Corona in 1946 with the intent of getting an education under the GI Bill, opening his own barbershop, and organizing the Mexican community to achieve greater political power. As Acevedo bluntly stated, "Many of the boys that went to war got their claws out when they came back home."[1]

Civil rights battles for more educational, recreational, and political opportunities for Corona's Mexican population took shape in the wake of World War II. On the heels of the Congress of Industrial Organizations (CIO) labor union defeat, Mexicans regrouped under grassroots community groups that used Popular Front and Good Neighbor Policy rhetoric to support their local struggles. Two key groups, the Los Amigos (Friends) Club and the Joe Dominguez American Legion Post, mobilized support for the desegregation of schools, movie theaters, and swimming pools; they also contested negative images in the print media and registered voters to increase political representation. Cinco de Mayo festivals became important leisure spaces for mobilizing support to build a youth recreational center. Led by Frances Martínez, Mexican American women occupied key leadership roles during these civil rights campaigns, thus challenging patriarchal authority within organizations and the larger community. Ultimately, the Mexican community gained limited political power with the election of the first Mexican American city councilperson and the building of a recreational center. Still, with the exception of some war veterans who benefited from the GI Bill, the majority failed to gain upward mobility in the postwar years.

"Good Neighbor" City

Mexican Americans participated in local efforts to promote inter-American unity, a phrase used by advocates of the Good Neighbor Policy to promote goodwill relations with Latin America. The election of Franklin Roosevelt in 1933 marked a shift in U.S. foreign policy toward Latin America; the Good Neighbor Policy sought to move away from an aggressive interventionist past, improve trade relations, and promote cultural exchange. Headed by Nelson Rockefeller, the Office of the Coordination of Inter-American Affairs (OCIAA) promoted the "policy of good neighbor" through press, radio, motion pictures, and cultural activities. Much in the same way that the New Deal sought to help workers gain a greater share of the country's wealth, the Good Neighbor Policy presumably entailed giving Latin American workers a "new deal" and "a fair share" of their country's resources. In México, the election of President Lázaro Cárdenas in 1934, the founding of the Confederación de Trabajadores Mexicanos (CTM) labor union in 1936, and the nationalization of the foreign oil companies gave workers renewed hope that the promises of the Mexican Revolution would finally be fulfilled. The true intention behind this new U.S. foreign policy, however, was the containment of economic and political nationalism in Latin America.[2]

Although the Good Neighbor Policy initially left out domestic issues, U.S. labor and civil rights activists reminded Nelson Rockefeller that promoting democracy abroad without practicing it at home smacked of hypocrisy. After strong lobbying efforts by Mexican American educators and politicians, including the proposal sent by Carey McWilliams in fall 1941, the OCIAA began to pay more attention to the "Latin American problem" in the Southwest. In 1942 the Southern California Council of Inter-American Affairs (SCCIAA) was formed in Los Angeles to "acquaint the people of Southern California with the culture, language and literature and problems of our neighbors south of the Rio Grande . . . and it endeavors to eliminate any discriminatory practices in Southern California." Within a year the Local Mexican Affairs Coordinating Committee was formed to advise the SCCIAA on eliminating racial discrimination in the workplace and community, coordinating visits of Mexican government officials, and providing more recreation outlets for youth.[3]

Concerns about "delinquent" youths loomed large in the aftermath of the 1942 Sleepy Lagoon court case, in which twenty-four Mexican youths were rounded up and beaten and faced murder charges for the killing of José Díaz near a swimming hole.[4] The anti-Mexican bias in the courtroom and the press brought together organizers from the CIO, Congress of Spanish-Speaking Peoples, the Communist Party, and other Popular Front groups to fight for the release of the convicted men. In a letter addressed to the SCCIAA, Manuel Ruiz, a lawyer and advisory member of the Local Mexican Affairs Committee, wrote, "From the evidence read, the fundamental rights of the defendants were impinged upon and were deprived of a fair trial."[5] After the defendants languished in jail for two years, the Sleepy Lagoon Defense Committee won their release on appeal. Charges of pervasive racism toward Mexican youths were confirmed in June 1943 when military servicemen attacked Mexican youths wearing zoot suits. These week-long disturbances received press attention throughout Latin America, generating accusations of Yankee racism and possibly endangering the Good Neighbor Policy and the wartime alliance against the Axis powers.[6]

The entry of the United States into World War II in December 1941 forever changed those Mexican Americans who enlisted for military service and Mexican American men and women who took advantage of civilian jobs that opened up on the home front. Out of 950 Corona men and women who were drafted or voluntarily enlisted in the armed forces, there were 190 of Mexican descent. Like other Americans, Mexican Americans rallied behind the war effort by organizing war bond drives; rationing tires, gasoline, clothing, and other scarce commodities; joining the local draft board; reporting suspicious aircraft; and parading the streets with raised American flags. Upon return from military duty, Mexican American veterans found their old citrus jobs replaced by Mexican contract workers under a wartime emergency agreement between the U.S. and Mexican governments. They opted instead to take advantage of the GI Bill to get a college education or learn a trade. Some of these veterans opened small businesses (barbershops, photography studios, jeweler shops, television and appliance shops) catering to all

Corona consumers. However, many still encountered discriminatory hiring practices. Dr. Carlos Castañeda's 1944 field investigations for the Fair Employment Practice Committee (FEPC) found widespread discrimination toward Mexican Americans in war-related industries. John Perez, a Corona veteran who enrolled in a technical college in San Bernardino, spoke of his difficulty in finding a defense job. "Nobody would take me because I was Mexican." Despite modest gains by a small middle-class veterans group, the Corona barrio still faced substandard housing conditions, racially segregated schools, lack of recreation outlets, and lack of representation in city government.[7]

In this wartime climate, Mexican Americans in Corona appropriated the liberal pluralist discourse of the Good Neighbor Policy to make demands upon government officials to improve barrio conditions. During a meeting of the grassroots community group Los Amigos members discussed an article that appeared in the Mexico City magazine *El Tiempo* addressing Corona's "racial problems" in the schools and the "pachuco problem" in the streets. The article focused on a racist editorial from a Home Gardens Anglo resident and the response from an Anglo resident of Casa Blanca who considered Mexican residents "good neighbors" and argued that they had demonstrated their patriotism by buying war bonds and filling defense jobs and justly deserved praise, not antipathy.[8] A few months later, Amigos members attended a meeting of the Local Mexican Affairs Coordination Committee in Los Angeles. The committee's president, Reynaldo Carreon, spoke of how some "Americans are doing their best to make the [Good Neighbor Policy] work" and warned that "if any racial or religious discrimination exists within this country, the old world will accuse the Americans of not practicing what they preach." They also attended the Cinco de Mayo festivities in front of city hall, where they listened to a speech from the Mexican secretary of foreign affairs, Ezequiel Padilla. Energized by the speech and motivated by the democratic ideals of the Good Neighbor Policy, Los Amigos members committed themselves to making Corona a "Good Neighbor" city.[9]

Mobilizing the Home Front

While soldiers were facing life-and-death situations on the front lines, Mexican American men and women organized themselves to wage another battle on the home front. In an attempt to remedy these conditions, a grassroots community organization, Los Amigos Club, took up the challenge of "arous[ing] interest and educat[ing] the citizens of

Mexican descent as to their rights, privileges and duties as American citizens." The *Corona Independent* described the club's beginnings in 1943 and its fearless leader. "One could not speak of Los Amigos Club without mentioning Mrs. Frances Martínez, respected young matron of Corona, whose earnestness, hard work, friendliness, and excellent sense of humor had a large part in the formation of the club and their interesting and worthwhile activities." During one of the club's meetings at the St. Edward's hall, Jesus Moreno, vice president, gave a pep talk about unity. He told a story about a ranch worker whose tractor turned over and fell into a ditch and how it required the strength of forty people to pull him out and save his life. "In unity there is strength," Moreno concluded, urging "all veterans and citizens of Mexican descent to take part in [the] running of the country." Los Amigos waged campaigns against segregated schools, raised funds for student scholarships, lobbied the city for more youth recreation, and advocated social change through the ballot box.[10]

The idea for the club's founding began with Frances Martínez after witnessing a police brutality incident. In September 1943 Frances brought her two young children to a Catholic church–sponsored *jamaica,* and the event was interrupted by police sirens. "There was a drunk, and a cop cuffed his hands behind his back. The cop dragged him along the ground on top of his bound hands. It was hurting him." Then, Frances's friend Frank Ortiz approached the police officer and asked him "not to drag" the man. The officer responded angrily, told Ortiz to back away, and pulled his gun. Then a large crowd gathered to watch the police arrest Ortiz. The next day Martínez took the day off work to attend Ortiz's hearing but could not find him. "So I asked the lawyer to explain to me what happened to Frank Ortiz. He told me they gave him a fifty-dollar fine and thirty days in jail. All this because he was trying to help. . . . I was infuriated."[11]

Outraged by the police brutality episode, Frances felt that there needed to be some kind of collective response from the community and sought advice from sympathetic Coronans. She enlisted the support of Father Matthew Thompson at St. Edward's Catholic Church. Father Thompson was a cigar-smoking Irish American priest who had arrived in May 1943 from the Catholic Church in Calexico, California. Having worked with Mexican congregations in Imperial Valley and San Diego, Father Thompson attributed many of the problems facing the Mexican community to "political apathy." Frances recounts her meeting with the priest: "I went to see Father Thompson at the church and told him about [the incident]. He told us it was kind of our fault because we did not vote." Father Thompson offered the St. Edward's church as a meeting place to begin a voter registration campaign.[12]

After graduating from Corona High School in 1932, Frances, one of only four Mexicans in her graduating class, eloped with George Martínez and moved to Guadalupe, New Mexico, for several years.[13] She witnessed her mother-in-law stand up against a theater manager. "She refused to sit in the Mexican section of the local theater and challenged the ushers to remove her from her seat." Frances was also influenced by Hispanas' participation in local and state electoral politics.[14] When Frances moved back to Corona in the late 1930s, she found a "sleepy town" with nothing happening politically. Immediately, she got involved in organizing party fund-raisers to raise money for student scholarships and youth recreation. These included amateur talent shows, *tardeadas* (afternoon dances), *jamaicas,* and community dances featuring local musical groups and sometimes Hollywood celebrities. "One time I got Danny Thomas to come out for our function. I went to his house in Hollywood. Since he was a Catholic, I told him that it is a benefit to build a new church." Her leadership ability in mobilizing resources and recruiting celebrities for these fund-raising events earned Martínez the nickname of "Sacafiestas" (party organizer). Frances preferred to work behind the scenes and so never ran for the city council or the school board. When she became president of the Washington Elementary School PTA in 1939, she decided to "stir things up" and led a group of parents to school board meetings to protest the separation of schoolchildren on the basis of race and nationality. Facing strong resistance from school board members and Anglo parents, Frances pressed the American-born generation to use its political power at the ballot box.[15]

Low naturalization rates among U.S.-born children of Mexican parents combined with low high school graduation rates had long been major obstacles to political empowerment. Despite the upsurge in naturalization rates due to the Nationality Act of 1940 and the pressures of wartime patriotism, Mexican Americans were still not registered to vote. As more men went off to war, the task of voter registration fell upon women such as Frances Martínez. After Frances received a registrar license, she set out by foot with her youngest child in a baby carriage and went house to house in the Corona barrio. "I registered about three hundred people, and shortly after that our votes were effective in the school board campaign." Another way to register voters and raise funds, according to Frances Martínez, was to organize dances. Los Amigos Club held outdoor *tardeadas* with a voter registration table stationed nearby and conducted Americanization classes to encourage adults to become U.S. citizens.[16]

Drawing on the antifascist and prodemocracy discourse of the CIO movement and the Pan-American unity themes of the Good Neighbor Policy, Los Amigos sought a more progressive, multiethnic, and internationalist version of the term "Americanization," one that resembled Gary Gerstle's notion of working-class Americanism and the international dimensions of the Popular Front.[17] Unlike the 1920s Americanization programs that sought to assimilate immigrants into American middle-class life, Los Amigos Americanization programs included courses in English and Spanish, naturalization, and civic duties in regard to electoral politics. One Los Amigos member outlined the program's main objectives, which were to (1) improve the conditions among the Mexican Americans and Mexicans living in Corona, (2) promote mutual understanding and better cooperation between the Mexican Americans and Americans, and (3) use education to overcome problems of prejudice, segregation, discrimination, social inequality and inferiority complex.[18]

Not all members of the Mexican community, however, supported Los Amigos's voting registration campaign and Americanization program. The most vocal critics were members of the Comisiónes Honoríficas Mexicanas, first organized by Mexican consular offices in the 1920s, that played an early role in organizing Cinco de Mayo festivities. "The Comisiónes got mad at [us] because [we were] registering Mexicans during the fiesta," declared Frances Martínez, who challenged the immigrant generation. "They said we [were] trying to make *Americanos* out of *Mexicanos.*" Although fund-raising, canvassing, and other promotional events had gone on during the festivities, some Comisiónes Honoríficas Mexicanas leaders believed it was inappropriate to convince participants to renounce their Mexican citizenship while celebrating Mexican history and culture. "You see, the older Mexican people still had dreams of one day returning to Mexico," explained another Los Amigos member, Reynaldo Aparicio, "so they held on tight to these [Mexican] traditions." Intraethnic conflicts were commonplace during this period.[19]

Because the Comisiónes Honoríficas Mexicanas functioned under the supervision and control of the local consular offices, Los Amigos members turned to the Mexican consul in San Bernardino in an attempt to resolve the dispute. As the representative of Los Amigos, Frances Martínez argued that the Comisiónes Honoríficas Mexicanas was hindering the political development of the city's Mexican American community and undermining efforts to make Corona a Good Neighbor city. Serving as an intermediary for the quarreling groups, the consul organized a community meeting. In the end, the Mexican consul sided with Los Amigos. As Martínez explained, "The consul told them [Comisiónes Honoríficas Mexicanas] that they were guests here and if they wanted to separate themselves, they should go back to Mexico, where they need active people. But for those [Mexican Americans] who are citizens, they have a duty to exercise their rights." While recognizing the important role of the Comisiónes Honoríficas Mexicanas in the fiesta, the consul praised the bicultural skills of the Mexican Americans and suggested that they had the most potential for harmonizing race relations in town and improving conditions for all Mexicans.[20]

Mexican consulates played a major role in shaping community organizing and patriotic events along conservative and nationalistic lines in the 1920s and early 1930s. However, when President Lázaro Cárdenas took office, he began to implement long-awaited social and political reforms and appointed more consulates sympathetic to progressive causes. In addition, Cárdenas embraced some Popular Front strategies, and when the United States declared war on the Axis powers in 1942, Mexico became an important U.S. ally. On the Los Angeles home front, Mexican consular officials showed some support to the Sleep Lagoon Defense Committee and assisted Mexican American veterans in organizing their own American Legion post after they were rejected from an Anglo-only veterans group. In other parts of the Southwest, Mexican American activists turned to the Mexican consuls for assistance and seized the Good Neighbor Policy discourse to gain more resources and political power for the Mexican community.[21]

Although some immigrant elders criticized the registration campaign, Los Amigos received support from returning veterans. Because they had risked their lives fighting abroad, Mexican American veterans reasoned that they deserved equal treatment and citizenship rights such as their Anglo counterparts had.[22] Yet upon their return, Corona's *soldaderos* (soldiers) were treated like "outsiders" and denied admission into the all-Anglo W. H. Jameson American Legion Post 216. Jameson Post members suggested that the Mexican American veterans "would be better off if they formed their own post." The Mexican American vets walked off in disgust. Referring to Anglo and Mexican American soldiers serving in the armed forces, Onias Acevedo put it rather bluntly: "We slept together, we ate together, we fought together, so the heck with them." At the next Los Amigos meeting, members discussed the discriminatory incident and heeded Frances Martínez's suggestion that they hold a general meeting with all Mexican American veterans about forming their own American Legion post. As Frances put it, "Look, I told them, you can go to Washington [D.C.], and represent yourself. You don't have to stand behind the tail of any one of them [Jameson Post members]."[23]

Frances Martínez organized the first meeting by mailing letters to all veterans of Mexican descent, paying for postage, and securing the St. Edward's church hall for the meeting. On July 19, 1946, more than eighty male veterans attended the meeting and listened to speeches by other Mexican American veterans who had formed their own separate charters. The post's first commander, Reynaldo Aparicio, recalled the successful first meeting: "We decided to be on our own, because if they can do it we can do it too." A week later twenty-nine veterans applied for a separate charter, and on May 1, 1947, they received final approval. The post was named after Joe Dominguez, the first Mexican American soldier from Corona to die in action. Dominguez was unanimously elected because "he was a local boy of good character, a graduate of Corona High School, and all-around good athlete [and] was well known and liked by his comrades."[24]

During wartime, Mexican American women played an active role in the war effort, selling war bonds and war stamps; writing letters to their soldier husbands, brothers, or boyfriends; and helping returning veterans readjust to home life.[25] They bought and sold war bonds to aid the efforts of the Corona War Council, headed by Joy Jameson, a major packinghouse employer. Their involvement in community groups and in supporting the war effort coincided with their increasing entry into citrus packing-houses. Prior to the arrival of Mexican contract workers (*braceros*) Corona's orchard fields, many Mexican American women worked as cit-rus pickers. Esperanza Olvera remembered the cuts and bruises she acquired picking lemons. "I got cut really bad because of the big thorns on the tree branches, and my feet would hurt after five or six trees." Women's entry into the orchards challenged traditional notions of femi-ninity, prompting one male picker to comment, "I don't know how they take it [picking fruit]. I guess they're tougher than they look."[26]

As Mexican American women began earning their own wages, they began to make informed choices about how and where to spend their time and money and when to marry. Los Amigos member Guadalupe Ramírez Delgadillo worked at the Orange Heights packinghouse, earning enough to buy her own car and delaying marriage plans until her late twenties. "I learned how to drive right away and had lots of friends to go shopping in Orange County."[27] Her parents ultimately conceded to her wishes but prohibited her from dating braceros.[28] In 1944, Corona Growers, Inc., contracted more than three hundred braceros and housed them in Camp Temescal, a labor camp located on the outskirts of Corona. Longtime Foothill Ranch employee Manuel Muñoz was charged with transporting braceros to work and supervising their leisure time. He recalled several altercations in the pool halls, cantinas, and cafes between braceros and Mexican American men. "The Good Neighbors from the south" were becoming a problem, according to the local newspaper, so citrus growers built a recreation center at the camp and supplied "a quantity of baseballs and bats for the men and Spanish reading material for the benefit of the workers."[29]

As baseball players went off to war, Athletics games were discontinued during the World War II period. Los Amigos member Ray Delgadillo received a 3A exemption from the military and soon thereafter got a contract to play baseball in Mexico. His playing career ended when he returned to Corona "because I was 3A and still went to Mexico. They [the military] found out I went to Mexico so they punished me by drafting me." As discussed in chapter 5, Mexican American women played in softball teams such as the Corona Debs, thus building up self-confidence in the public sphere and opening more spaces for women to play sports.[30]

Another public domain in which Mexican American women attained limited control and social status within the community was the Cinco de Mayo queen contest. But working on a seasonal basis and earning meager piece-rate wages limited their ability to subsidize their own candidacies, since they had to purchase their own dresses and meet other contest expenses. For this reason, each queen candidate needed to solicit a business sponsor. One of the main sponsors was Doña María Ortíz, owner of Chapala Café, a popular restaurant-bar frequented by Mexican braceros. Ortíz often acted as mediator in courtship disputes between Mexican American men and arriving braceros who sought female companionship in town. Doña Ortíz used her influence on male customers to determine the queen contest winner. At the 1945 contest, for example, contestant Gloria Granado visited Chapala Café to increase her chances of winning. After some awkward moments, she received the support of Doña Ortíz, in part because of her "light skin color." Doña Ortíz convinced Mexican nationals to purchase four hundred tickets from Granado during the last fifteen minutes of voting, bringing her total earnings to one thousand dollars and thus earning her the Cinco de Mayo crown.[31]

The politics of Cinco de Mayo queen contests revealed the larger racial and class divisions within the Mexican community. Queen contestants with European or Spanish-like features were typically preferred over dark-skinned Indian and mestiza candidates. Because of white privilege, Granado's long-standing friendship with a darker-skinned queen contestant became strained. After Granado won the crown, her friend became jealous and made for an uncomfortable drive to Los Angeles to buy dresses. Fiesta participants also expressed their racial and class preferences by buying ticket-votes. For example, the 1946 queen, Margaret Muñoz, proudly declared during an interview that she became the first queen from the Foothill Ranch. Her proud smile turned to scornful dismay, however, when she talked about disparaging comments from a female audience member. The audience member commented on her dark skin and her poor upbringing at the Foothill Ranch. When her mother heard the comment, she became angry and abruptly cut the woman off, telling her, "Hey, lady, what do you think the queen of Mexico is? A white girl? No way. She is also *morenita* like my daughter."[32]

Although women gained greater public visibility, they still faced gender divisions in community organizations such as the Joe Dominguez Post. The Dominguez Post women also cooked, cleaned, performed secretarial and office work, and accompanied their husbands to meetings. Women occupied these traditional gender roles within the Dominguez Post even though Los Amigos women were responsible for getting the post started in the first place. "The [veteran] men never mentioned how they got there," remarked Frances Martínez. She cleverly understood that some men had a problem with women taking charge and standing up for themselves. Donald McGaffin, a *Press-Enterprise* reporter who covered many of Frances's fund-raisers, explained that when "she took the City Council head on, she inevitably took a Mexican American male with her to the Council . . . [where] she fed answers to the male and he got his name in the paper. Frances operated sotto voce." Guadalupe Ramírez Delgadillo was more blunt about the Dominguez Post male veterans, whom she described as "just takers. They did nothing until they came back home from the service. We were doing it way before them. We were already fired up." Wives and daughters of male veterans extended their roles by forming the Ladies Auxiliary in 1948 with the chief aim of "raising funds for scholarships and actively supporting local child welfare programs."[33]

Lemon Fiestas

Los Amigos Club and the Joe Dominguez American Legion Post sought to use Cinco de Mayo festivals as forums to express their grievances, most notably about the lack of recreation for youths. Beyond such immediate concerns, they sought public recognition as a political force in city affairs and economic advancement for workers in the lemon industry. One way to ensure that their claims and demands were understood by the power elite was to invite city officials to the festivities. City officials, for their part, viewed the event as an opportunity to attract tourist dollars and show their support for the Good Neighbor Policy. One newspaper advertisement sought to entice southern Californians to Corona's Cinco de Mayo fiesta: "Corona will don festival attire in preparation for the coming fiesta when Corona's Mexican population lays down its citrus tools and dons fiesta regalia to celebrate Cinco de Mayo."[34]

Corona city officials viewed these festive occasions as an opportunity to improve intercultural relations, so they joined forces with the Mexican consular office, the Corona Recreation Commission, and the Corona Chamber of Commerce to form the Corona Coordinating Council (CCC) that sought to promote "city-wide cooperation and good-neighborly feeling." Invoking the spirit of the Good Neighbor Policy, CCC officials viewed Cinco de Mayo as a vehicle for pursuing the policy's liberal goals at home and abroad. Hector Jara, vice consul from the San Bernardino office, assured the Corona City Council that "no doubt the fiesta will tend to [foster] a better understanding and to strengthen the friendly relations between our two people, and I sincerely believe that the city's Mexican population will continue to receive your help and cooperation in various endeavors." Toward this end, CCC officials encouraged the Anglo community to participate in the fiesta by sponsoring booths or attending events. The mayor reminded Anglos that "the fact that the Mexican people make up a permanent part of Corona's population and are an integral part of the city's social and economic life is reason enough for cooperating with them." The mayor attempted to lead by example in the 1945 festival when he participated with the consul in crowning the Cinco de Mayo queen.[35]

Following their meeting with the Local Mexican Affairs Coordination Committee in Los Angeles, Corona leaders decided to incorporate Pan-American themes in the 1946 fiesta. The festival planning was led by Los Amigos Club, with help from the Joe Dominguez American

Legion Post. Los Amigos boldly outlined its main objective as follows: "The chief purpose is to improve conditions among the Mexican Americans and Mexicans living in Corona. Believing in our American institutions and in the democratic way of life, we believe that by raising the social level of Mexican American people and improving their living conditions we are helping to improve our community."[36] During the parade procession, the musical band stopped in front of city hall to perform the "Star-Spangled Banner" and then the Mexican national anthem. Another symbol of Pan-Americanism at the 1946 festival, according to Los Amigos member Alice Rodríguez, was the mestizo Uncle Sam that took part in the parade. "We had a dark mestizo person on the parade float, and we needed somebody to represent Uncle Sam standing in front of a big globe of the world. As the parade float went by, he was dressed in star and stripes, Uncle Sam in brown face, carrying the Mexican and American flags, and people were looking and laughing." Fiesta organizers and participants sought to gain public recognition of their working-class "American" ethnic identity by demonstrating their commitment to democracy and civil rights and emphasizing their indigenous ancestry and mestizo background.[37]

At the 1946 celebration, Los Amigos decided to raise funds for building a youth recreation center to be known as La Casita. This was prompted by police arrests of ten Mexican American youths with zoot suits at a dance party. During a meeting at Teatro Circle, the festival organizing committee expressed disdain for the local newspaper article that described Mexican American youths as "hoodlums" with "guns, steel chains, and pointed shoes that could be used as deadly weapons." Corona's police chief recommended to the city council that "in the interest of the public welfare . . . the Mexicans be granted no more dance permits," adding that "in normal times the Mexican dances might be properly conducted but with the advent of the 'zoot suit' era, trouble is almost certain to develop." The city council heeded the police chief's advice and denied dance permits to Mexican groups (except the Cinco de Mayo festival committee) and passed a night curfew ordinance. The entire Mexican community was targeted, according to Frances Martínez, who felt it was unjust to deny dance permits because of a few "bad actors." She recalled that "I went before the council and read the Constitution before them. I then asked the police to give me the names of the troublemakers" and advised the council to "give troubled Mexican youth proper recreation rather than [prison] correction." She met with the boys and their parents and warned them about the consequences of wearing a zoot suit amidst the anti–zoot suit wartime climate. Afterward there were fewer disturbances between youths and the police, but the lack of recreational outlets for youths went unresolved.[38]

Although the city recreation department was willing to donate land for a center, the community needed to raise approximately ten thousand dollars for construction. At the 1946 Cinco de Mayo festival, organizers raised more than two thousand dollars. While this was not close to the total amount needed, the Los Amigos Club president praised the community's efforts, saying, "Residents of Corona should be justly proud of living in a community where the Good Neighbor policy is not only a figure of speech but an actuality. . . . The Mexican people are deeply grateful to each and every one who had any participation in the Cinco de Mayo. . . . [W]ords fail us to properly thank all the Corona Good Neighbors. Let us cooperate with one another in a truly democratic city."[39]

Despite framing their discourse and actions within the Good Neighbor Policy, Mexican American organizers were still short of funds, so in 1947 they turned to the citrus companies for assistance. In a controversial move, Mexican American organizers associated with the Los Amigos Club proposed to citrus industry officials and the Corona Chamber of Commerce that the city move away from the "old Cinco de Mayo idea" toward a "Lemon Fiesta" theme "in recognition of the importance of the lemon industry in the development of prosperity for Corona." Apart from promoting the Good Neighbor Policy that supplied imported bracero help, Corona growers were also interested in promoting their new Sunkist Concentrate for Lemonade product, which had recently premiered in most local grocery stores. The proposed three-day weekend celebration, to be called "Spring Fiesta and Lemon Festival" or "Lemon Fiesta," was not well received by some members of the Mexican community. The most vocal critics were members of the Comisiónes Honoríficas Mexicanas, who accused festival organizers of "selling out" and "de-Mexicanizing" Cinco de Mayo by succumbing to the hegemonic control of the local citrus industry and corporate America in general. One critic sarcastically asked what lemon-related events such as a "lemon baking contest" and "lemon box derby race" had to do with the Battle of Puebla.[40]

Nonetheless, three Mexican American groups in Corona—the Los Amigos Club, the Joe Dominguez American Legion Post, and the newly organized La Casita Recreation Center Council—decided to participate in the Lemon Fiesta. A Joe Dominguez Post member, Reynaldo Aparicio, explained their reasons. As well as needing to raise an additional seventy-five hundred dollars to build the recreation center, the groups

wanted to "bring more resources to the community by improving relations with the city and getting better-paying jobs in the lemon industry." Frances Martínez defended her group's decision against the
criticism of the Comisiónes Honoríficas Mexicanas by citing the luke-
warm support from the Mexican consul, who made a public appearance
at the festival and crowned the queen but failed to provide real financial
help in organizing the event. She also blamed it on unemployment as
the nation shifted from wartime to a peacetime economy, "so we
needed to get help from the city, [company] sponsors, and Anglos."[41]

In the end, the Comisiónes Honoríficas Mexicanas decided to
organize a separate Cinco de Mayo celebration on May 5 that featured a
queen contest with different candidates, a marching band from Mexico,
and patriotic speeches extolling the virtues of the Mexican nation.
Lemon Fiesta organizers meanwhile maintained much of their bicultural programming and added new lemon-related events that symbolized the increasing commercialization of this ethnic festival. The first
day of the Lemon Fiesta was devoted to lemon-related events organized
by the Corona Chamber of Commerce, including lemon pie baking contests, a lemon box derby, free lemonade drinks, a giant lemon pie placed
in front of city hall, and tours of what was touted as "the world's only
lemon by-products plant." On the second day, Mexican American
groups led Mexican cultural activities, including many of the traditional events featured in previous celebrations: the morning parade, the
queen contest, a baseball tournament, and Mexican expressive forms
such as mariachis, *charros* (cowboys), and *ballet folklorico.* On the final
day both teams worked together to organize a big dance at the future
site of La Casita.[42]

In a bilingual pamphlet distributed to all attendees, organizers clearly
outlined the 1947 fiesta's mission. "The [Lemon Fiesta] will again make
La Casita Recreation Center the recipient of its efforts. This is done in
the hope that an appreciable advance may be made in the immediate
usability of this project. In future years it is anticipated that other interests of the community will receive the yearly Fiesta offering." At the
festival, the Mexican consul praised the work of Mexican American
organizers in promoting closer intercultural and inter-American relations: "The close and friendly relationships between Mexico and the
United States are reflected in the [La Casita] recreation project. Like
Corona, other cities will also be building recreational centers." Despite
the consul's praise, the La Casita Recreation Center Council received
little financial help.[43]

There were other important changes in the 1947 festival, including shifts in the roles and recognition of women. An addition to the program highlighted Mexican women's roles during the Battle of Puebla, including that of Doña Josefa Ortiz de Domínguez, who risked her life to warn the Mexican army that a trap was being set up by French troops, thus enabling them to prepare for the decisive battle. The queen contest also was increasing in prominence, having evolved from a marginal part of the program in the 1920s to one of the most popular events in the late 1930s and early 1940s. However, by the postwar years queen candidates found themselves seeking corporate sponsors to pay for their dresses, the crowning ceremony, and parade floats. One of the biggest employers of Mexican American women, the Harvill Company, sponsored only its own female employees who entered the contest. The 1947 queen contestant, a Harvill employee named Emily Delgadillo, posed for several photos inside her workplace. Several months before May 5, these photos were featured in the *Corona Independent* for publicity and advertising purposes. One of the photos was published with the following caption: "During and after the war many beautiful girls contributed greatly to the operation of [lemon] die-casting machines." The photo featured a Rosie the Riveter–like image that stressed loyalty and obedience to the company and the American nation and promoted the industriousness of Mexican American women.[44]

While such portrayals ignored women's low wages and their subordinated racial and gender position within and outside the workplace, the corporate sponsorship of queen candidates nonetheless threatened the masculine roles of some Mexican American men, who believed that queens should solicit votes solely from individuals, groups, and small businesses. One Comisiónes Honoríficas Mexicanas member complained that "the small [Mexican-owned] businesses were not being asked to be sponsors because the companies have gotten too involved with the queens." For Mexican American queen candidates, however, a corporate sponsor meant less time and energy spent selling ticket-votes door to door, and they could potentially use their public role to negotiate better working conditions and higher pay.[45]

Another significant change during the 1947 Lemon Fiesta was the introduction of a new parade route. The new route began in front of city hall (located in the Anglo south side of town) and moved northward, passing the main commercial streets and company packinghouses and finally arriving at the proposed site for the new recreation center, located in the center of the Mexican barrio. The main parade float featured the queen, her nephew and niece, and her court surrounded by tree branches with lemons. This public procession acted as a "political ritual," dramatizing the community solidarity behind this worthwhile cause, as well as took on symbolic importance as Mexican American participants passed by the centers of power—a reminder of whose labor power had been used to build the city. In assessing the success of the Lemon Fiesta, it is important to consider the ways in which cultural practices and symbols have the capacity of resisting and accommodating to politico-economic structures of power.[46]

Despite widespread support for the recreation center, the 1947 Lemon Fiesta raised only $1,953, and during the 1948 and 1949 Lemon Fiestas the amount totaled $3,500. The small amount revealed the limitations of the fiesta: although the event drew support from the Anglo community and the citrus industry, this kind of support did not always translate into significant economic gains for the Mexican community. By 1949 the La Casita Recreation Center Council still needed more than $7,000 for the center's completion. Another reason for the shortage of funds stemmed from the rapid unemployment that followed World War II.[47]

To raise the remaining amount, festival organizers reminded CCC members about their commitment to become "Good Neighbors" and put the city council on notice about their rising political power in future elections. In a newspaper editorial, Frances Martínez complained to city council members that "it will take twenty years of holding fiestas to get the money needed to finish the La Casita building. . . . They [Mexican youths] need a place where the children can meet and it should be a public enterprise." Martínez personally handed over to the city mayor a check of Lemon Fiesta funds raised with the expectation that the city council would subsidize the remaining costs. After intense political pressure from members of Los Amigos Club and the Joe Dominguez Post, the city council finally allocated $6,500 of city funds to complete the construction of La Casita in September 1950.[48]

The use of the festival to raise funds for the recreation center had a long-term impact beyond the immediate gain of acquiring recreational space for the community. It enabled Mexican Americans to sharpen their leadership and organizing skills and to establish networks of support that proved invaluable for future civil rights struggles. In nearby Los Angeles, progressive Mexican American activists also used cultural festivals to conduct a range of social, cultural, and political activities to mobilize an increasingly politicized Mexican American community.[49] During the opening ceremonies for La Casita, one city official praised "those [Mexican Americans] who not only made a fine new recreation center possible, but have cemented lasting friendships among two races who reside side by side within Corona." Using these new friendships and social networks to their advantage, Corona's Mexican Americans continued to press for social change and civil rights. Successes included the eventual desegregation of public schools, recreation facilities, and public spaces and election of the first Mexican Americans to the Corona school board and city council.[50]

Making Lemonade

The schools were one of the first arenas of struggle. Unlike Italian parents who successfully enrolled their children in Southside schools in 1934, Mexican parents met with strong resistance from the all-Anglo Corona School Board when they tried to have their children attend predominantly Anglo schools. Hilarion López, who attended Lincoln Elementary School in the early 1920s, wanted to enroll his son in the same school but was instructed by the superintendent to enroll him at Washington, the "Mexican school." He recalled that unlike the Lincoln and Jefferson schools, Washington Elementary School "did not even have air conditioning." López shared his story during one of the board meetings to discuss school zone boundaries. School board members defended their position by citing the Mexican children's supposed lack of English-language proficiency, cultural differences, and deficient personal hygiene. The school superintendent, F. E. Bishop, declared that children from the all-Anglo neighborhood of Home Gardens "were normal, cleaner and faster learning than many Mexicans and that being sent to school with large groups of Mexicans might affect them unfavorably." A Mexican parent responded angrily: "It is not a matter of health that was involved, but of rights."[51]

After studying the 1930 Lemon Grove and 1946 Westminster school desegregation suits, Mexican Americans felt they were on safe legal ground and began lobbying school board officials to allow Mexican children to attend the Lincoln and Jefferson elementary schools.[52] As Frances Martínez explained, "We tried talking to the school, but since the Mexicans who were American citizens never voted, they laughed in our faces." The newly formed Mexican Coordination Council, made up of Los Amigos members and Mexican parents, mounted a formidable challenge to the school board's discriminatory zoning policy. At a meeting on September 1944, more than 150 Mexican parents voiced their frustration with the board's inaction and threatened to withhold their children from school. Gilbert Enriquez, Corona Athletics manager, school coach, and member of the Mexican Baptist Mission, spoke on behalf of the Mexican Coordination Council, stating that "the [school] zoning plan is not democratic. . . . [T]hese Mexican young people, who some day will become citizens of the United States, should be permitted to attend the school nearest their residence." Enriquez reminded the board of the valiant efforts of Mexican American soldiers fighting abroad and defending the rights of all Americans. He accused the school board of betraying the ideals of the Good Neighbor Policy since the zoning plan had "never create[d] goodwill and proper cooperation."[53]

To pressure the school board, the Mexican Coordination Council enlisted the support of Anglo supporters and Mexican consul Edmundo González from the San Bernardino office. At the school board meeting González stated that "segregation of Mexican children is not justified and is opposed to the fundamental principles of education which are to prepare children for good citizenship." The consul threatened legal action if the Mexican children were not allowed to attend the school nearest their home. Not all Coronans supported the school board. One Anglo parent expressed the opinion "that Americans cannot draw a line as to color or race and that the Mexican children as citizens of this country are entitled to the same consideration as other pupils." The Mexican Coordination Council got support from some Anglo members of the Corona Coordination Council who helped organize the Lemon Fiesta. These included the city mayor, Charles Miller; Father Matthew Thompson; Donald McGaffin, reporter for the Corona Bureau of the *Riverside Enterprise*; and Jessimine Hampton, wife of the Foothill Company president and chairperson of the Corona Recreation Commission. While living at the Foothill Ranch, Frances Martínez cultivated a friendship with Mrs. Hampton that lasted into subsequent decades, and Mrs. Hampton became a key supporter of Mexican American civil rights.[54]

After continued pressure from Mexican parents and their supporters, the school board decided to redraw the school zone boundaries. The new zone for Washington Elementary School extended from north of Sixth Street in both easterly and westerly directions, thus allowing Mexican children from outlying ranches to attend Jefferson Elementary School, while Anglo children from Home Gardens and Mexican children from the north-side barrio would attend Washington Elementary School. As a result, 375 Mexicans and 225 Anglos (a majority from Home Gardens) enrolled at Washington Elementary School. Not all Mexican parents were pleased with the new school zones. Hilarion López did not agree with the plan because it maintained gerrymandered boundaries. He partially blamed Gilbert Enriquez, and his connections to Baptist church and city officials, for giving in to school board officials when they approached him to accept the plan.[55]

The new plan also fueled backlash among Anglo parents in the unincorporated neighborhood of Home Gardens, many of whom originated from Oklahoma and arrived as strikebreakers at the Foothill Ranch. Home Gardens parents began a petition calling for a separate school for their children. The petition stated: "This new zoning plan has been a blow to property values in our community and we are going to fight it bitterly. We are not satisfied to send our children to [a] Mexican town, with the busses hauling them farther than the building to which we prefer them to go. If the situation is not corrected we will declare an absolute boycott against Corona." Two months later Home Gardens parents succeeded in forcing the school board to set up five classrooms in a small building provided by the War Production Council that later became known as Home Gardens School.[56]

Despite the advocacy by Mexican parents, a large majority of Mexican children still attended Washington Elementary School until it was demolished in 1948 when the school board refused to improve the deteriorated buildings. Around this time, however, Mexican parents began sending their children to the newly built St. Edward's School, a private Catholic elementary school. While Mexican Americans were fighting for school desegregation, Mexican parishioners had been raising funds for a new Catholic school and rectory. Father Thompson supported the school desegregation efforts, encouraging Mexican American parishioners to "stick up for their rights." In a speech before the Corona Exchange Club, Father Thompson stated that "we often hear of the Mexican problem. . . . The Mexican is no problem. But he has problems. . . . There are signs of improvement in the Mexican problem in Corona [but] many still live in substandard houses with inadequate sanitation facilities. Migrant labor keeps many almost in servitude. The Mexicans are the same as the rest of us. They also are looking for their place in the sun." On September 7, 1947, Bishop Charles Buddy dedicated St. Edward's School, and over the next few years enrollment gradually increased to four hundred students.[57]

Mexican parents continued to advocate for school reforms and representation on the school board. The next step was to use their voting power as a swing vote to ultimately elect one of their own. The combined efforts of Los Amigos and the Mexican Coordination Council paid off when Cipriano Hernández was elected to the school board in 1948 and continued as a board member for sixteen years. Hernández recalled years later, "There was a whole bunch of us of Mexican descent. . . . We wanted to start someplace in being elected. Nobody else wanted to try it, so I said I'd give it a try."[58]

The successful election of Cipriano Hernández to the school board served as a stepping stone for future city elections. Ten years later, in 1958, Onias Acevedo was elected to the city council, winning the highest number of votes, 1,709, more than any candidate in any previous election; Charles Jameson, son of citrus tycoon Joy Jameson, garnered 1,080 votes. Acevedo's victory revealed the rising political power of Corona's Mexican American organizations. Upon returning from the war, Acevedo attended barber school in Los Angeles on the GI Bill and soon opened his own barbershop. Returning veterans attained relative economic independence from the citrus industry by opening their own businesses, which included photography studios, jewelry shops, and restaurants. The barbershop became a center of social activity among men, who would voice their grievances and discuss their problems. Because most of his customers were citrus workers who got their haircuts after work in the evenings, Acevedo used the daytime hours to attend college, and years later he opened a real estate and insurance business called Ace Insurance and Real Estate (after his nickname, "Ace"). Members of Los Amigos Club, the Joe Dominguez American Legion Post, and the new Corona chapter of the League of United Latin American Citizens (formed in 1957) urged Acevedo to run for office to represent the interests of the Mexican community. Having learned from their success in the school board race a decade earlier, "We did the same thing in the city council [race]," stated Frances Martínez. "We were there to back him up."[59]

Acevedo explained why he decided to run for office. "The city council and city hall didn't give a damn for the Mexican community. They were nothing but trouble, I heard one Anglo [city official] say; they are always getting in trouble, drunk, and incarcerated." The desire to counter this negative image prompted many to campaign and vote for Acevedo. Even the *Corona Independent*, which had often contributed to the racialization of Mexicans, praised Acevedo's victory. "Certainly the Americans of Mexican descent had an 'ace' in the hole when 'Ace' Acevedo was swept into office in the [council] race. . . . Certainly the Americans of Mexican descent deserve to have a representative as part of the city government, constituting a large percentage of the population."[60]

During his four-year term (1958–62), Acevedo pushed the city to hire more bilingual Mexican American employees for the police and fire departments and appointed Mexican Americans to the city's planning and recreation commissions. In addition, he helped start the effort to bring much-needed paved roads and streetlights to the Corona barrio. His main achievement, of which he was proudest, was the battle to move city hall to the old high school site instead of building a new one in downtown Corona. This move angered downtown business owners, who desired higher real estate values. Acevedo's approval of a new shopping center on Main and Ontario (south Corona) and new hospital further angered downtown business owners, who lobbied against his reelection, and Acevedo was voted out of office. Another factor in the election was the smaller turnout by Mexican American voters. "I was somewhat bitter and disappointed with my own community," lamented Acevedo, "because they did not back me up a second time." Reflecting on his short political career, Acevedo said that "in politics you can't go out there and just raise hell like a community activist; you also have to play ball. You have to measure your steps because there are five city councilmen and you are only one person."[61]

Aside from participation in electoral politics, Mexican Americans engaged in individual and collective forms of resistance against segregated public spaces such as swimming pools and movie theaters. As in other southern California communities, Corona's swimming pool restrictions publicly demonstrated the profoundly antidemocratic practice of de jure segregation afflicting Mexican Americans. They took their cues from the many local campaigns against segregated public facilities waged by ordinary African Americans in Mississippi and elsewhere.[62] Reynaldo Aparicio defied the plunge policy by showing the instructor his draft letter and asking for swimming lessons during the week, except on Mondays. According to Aparicio, the instructor "agreed to give me lessons the rest of the week, but I had to come after they closed the premises. I had the pool all to myself." Aparicio invoked the patriotic discourse of wartime to convince the instructor to give him swimming lessons beyond Mondays. Although he learned how to swim, the long-standing practice of discrimination remained intact until news of the first Mexican American casualty in World War II stirred the conscience of the plunge staff. On December 27, 1943, the manager of the city plunge, Nettie Whitcomb, heard the news that one of her former swimming students of Mexican descent had been killed, and she decided to remove the racial restrictions. Without approval from the city council, Whitcomb burned the sign saying "For the White Race Only" in the city park while some onlookers gawked in disbelief and others cheered. In the nearby city of San Bernardino, Ignacio López, editor of the Spanish-language newspaper *El Espectador* and founder of the Unity

Leagues, filed a class action lawsuit against the city of San Bernardino for being denied access to the swimming pool.[63]

While Mexican Americans eventually won the right to swim any day of the week, discriminatory practices persisted at the Corona Theater. Inspired by her mother-in-law's activism to desegregate movie theaters in New Mexico, Frances encouraged other members of Los Amigos to defy the orders of ushers, ticket-takers, and theater management. Gilbert Enríquez confronted the owner of the Corona Theater, Glenn Harper, after being denied entrance to the theater balcony. According to his niece, Teresa Enríquez, her uncle wanted to sit in the balcony but was abruptly instructed by the usher to sit on the Mexican side of the theater. He complained until the manager conceded. "So we sat next to white people who kept staring at us. He then told me next time you come to the show, 'Sit anywhere you want.'" Gilbert refused to return to the Corona Theater and later became the manager of the Circle Theater, the successor to El Teatro Chapultepec that featured first-run Hollywood and Mexican films and musical performances. Although they did not launch boycotts or legal challenges, Mexican American patrons in Corona used individual acts of resistance to challenge the city's unequal moviegoing system that finally ended in the post–World War II years.[64]

In demanding recognition as first-class citizens, Mexican Americans also had to battle the negative images and stereotypes in the print media and in American popular culture in general. Frances Martínez criticized the negative portrayal of Mexicans in the local newspaper, which prominently featured murders, arrests, fights, riots, and other such incidents involving Mexicans. In 1943 Frances marched into the office of the *Corona Independent* to question the editors over their policy of printing the racialized descriptor "Mexican" in connection with people, places, and incidents in the news, when other ethnicities were not named. Incidents involving Mexican youths, for example, were reported under such headlines as "Mexican Youth Stabbed by Sailor," "Cuttings Mark Mexican Dance," and "Mexican Youths Admit Robberies." Frances bluntly told the editor, "If you put one nationality, you have to put them all." After the editor promised to change the newspaper's coverage, he asked Martínez to become a contributing writer with a particular focus on the local Mexican community. Martínez's columns covered the religious, cultural, and political activities of local Mexican Americans. In 1949 the newspaper allocated space for a Spanish-language column, "La Sección Mexicana de Corona," written by members of Los Amigos and the Joe Dominguez Post.[65]

Mexican Americans put forth their own images and expressed their opinions through the Spanish-language print media and radio. In 1949 Gilbert Enríquez founded a Spanish-language weekly newspaper called *El Imparcial*, which featured local and regional news, sports, and entertainment along with announcements of weddings, funerals, and group activities. Enríquez operated the newspaper from his home on Ramona Street and, with the help of family members, sold it for a nominal fee of five cents per copy in Corona and in inland cities. Modeled after *El Espectador*, *El Imparcial* protested against discrimination and advocated civil rights for Mexican Americans. Enríquez wrote an editorial column titled "Carta Abierta" (Open Letter) that called for the unification of all Mexican-origin groups and encouraged "their participation in the economic, political, civic, and cultural affairs in the city in order to eliminate racial hatred and prejudices based on color, religion, and nationality."[66]

Corona Mexican Americans made "lemonade" out of the "lemons" handed them in life. In a citrus industry town that billed itself as the Lemon Capital of the World, wages were low, open-shop conditions prevailed, and jobs outside agriculture were scarce, so in effect Mexican immigrant families did what they could to survive. World War II opened new job opportunities for returning Mexican American male veterans who took advantage of the GI Bill and founded their own businesses or secured manufacturing jobs instead of returning to the groves.

Mexican American women organized community support for the home front defense of their civil rights. Once women could secure jobs in the packinghouses and to a lesser extent in the orchards, they used their earnings to supplement family incomes, satisfy individual desires for consumer goods, and take part in community fund-raisers. Their entry into the workforce coincided with their increased participation in community groups such as Los Amigos Club and the Joe Dominguez Post, even though many often worked behind the scenes with little recognition. World War II also made possible greater leadership roles for Mexican American women.

Corona's Mexican Americans translated the ideals and goals of the Good Neighbor Policy to promote their civil rights struggles. According to Carey McWilliams, the Good Neighbor drive provided an impetus to rising political activism among Mexican Americans. "As more and more Mexicans began to participate in Good Neighbor conferences and institutes, the discussion shifted from a probing of conditions long deplored to a consideration of ways and means by which the Mexican people themselves might be given a chance to improve these conditions."[67] Leisure activities, and specifically the Cinco de Mayo festival, played a key role in these developments. In the beginning, Corona's Mexican Americans used the festival to defend themselves from external racist and nativist attacks and to reaffirm a cultural bond to Mexico. Later, younger organizers, including some veterans, transformed the Cinco de Mayo celebration into a vehicle for gaining access to community resources and demanding full participation in American mainstream institutions. In the process, Cinco de Mayo evolved into a bicultural Mexican American event aimed at promoting good-neighbor relations between Mexicans and Anglos and between the United States and Mexico. In negotiating the cultural and political terrain of the fiesta, Mexican Americans showed neither complete endorsement of corporate values and dominant Anglo culture nor direct opposition to the political-economic order. Instead, they opted for an unstable middle-ground position from which they could appropriate the Good Neighbor Policy's ideology and commercial components of the fiesta to make demands upon city government officials and Mexican consular representatives. While these developing intercultural relations helped Mexican American civil rights efforts in Corona, economic mobility within the citrus industry remained elusive. Despite new job opportunities in defense-related industries for Mexican Americans, they still faced low wages and racial and gender barriers in the workplace in the postwar years.

Corona's Mexican American festival organizers eventually used Cinco de Mayo to fund and build La Casita, which served as a recreational center for youths and a venue for community groups. Throughout the 1950s, La Casita provided an important social space for the Mexican community—but, according to city officials, it was built on city property, and since they needed money for moving city hall, the city decided to sell La Casita to a group of Anglo businessmen, without the consent of the Mexican community. Los Amigos member and photographer Rudy Ramos reminded the city that "the fund which financed construction of the building was begun by Mexican Americans with proceeds from Cinco de Mayo celebrations. . . . It wasn't the city's money."[68] This move soured relations between the city and the Mexican community and highlighted the limitations of electoral politics and the Lemon Fiesta. In addition, in the politically charged climate of Operation Wetback, McCarthyism, and Cold War hysteria during the 1950s, many of the festival organizers redirected their energies toward raising families and making a living. The Cinco de Mayo festivals were discontinued until the early 1970s, when a new generation of community activists revived and redefined the festival as part of the emerging Chicano and Chicana movement.

Mexican Americans affiliated with Los Amigos Club and the Joe Dominguez American Legion Post advocated the desegregation of public schools and recreation facilities. They sought more community resources, contested negative images in the print media, and demanded inclusion in the American political system. The first Mexican American city councilman, Onias Acevedo, took office in 1958 largely as a result of the Mexican American vote, although his stances on controversial issues cost him his seat in the next election. At the 1964 election, former Foothill Ranch resident and carpenter Manuel Cruz's bid to "represent the average working man" was narrowly defeated by twenty-five votes. Not until 1978 was another Mexican American, David Felix, elected to the city council.[69]

Epilogue

"It was a cozy little town. I hated the quiet back then; now I wish we had it back," remarked Frances Martínez during an interview. The sleepy little rural town surrounded by lemon groves and a circular boulevard that she encountered when she arrived in the late 1920s underwent dramatic changes in the 1960s and 1970s, becoming yet another southern California suburb. The most significant economic change was the influx of new industry and the decline of the citrus industry. Then other changes followed: housing tract developments built on former orchard land, an urban renewal plan for downtown businesses that included a shopping mall, and the construction of Highway 91 through Corona's Mexican barrio. The city population barely reached 10,000 in 1950, but by 1970 it boomed to 27,519 and by 1996 had topped 100,000.[1]

Corona could no longer maintain its small town charm and stave off the rapid suburbanization that had already swallowed up most of southern California. The most notorious symbol of these new times was the Highway 91 Riverside Freeway. The 91 freeway was completed in 1962, stretching from Riverside to Orange County and cutting through the heart of the Mexican barrio on the north side of town. Now considered one of the most traffic-congested freeways in the state, Highway 91 transformed Corona into a bedroom community of Orange County. Soon thereafter urban redevelopment arrived with the hope that it would revitalize the downtown area with a new shopping mall and higher tax revenues for the city. Despite major opposition from different sectors of the community, including Mexican American groups, the urban renewal project was completed in 1975, leaving the city sharply divided and forcing small family-owned businesses to close or relocate elsewhere. Some residents expressed regrets about losing Corona's "old town" charm.[2] The last and most dramatic change was the rise of industrial parks and the decline of the citrus industry in the Corona area With the realization that the citrus industry's days were numbered, due to higher land prices and taxation, worsening air and water pollution, and increased population growth, growers either sold their land or switched into the land development business. In 1968 the Corona Foothill Lemon Company formed a land company to supplant rows of citrus fruit trees with housing tracts. With fewer lemons to process, the Exchange Lemon Products plant shut its doors in 1982.[3]

Amid the political and economic transformation of Corona in the 1960s and 1970s, Mexican Americans and a younger generation of Chicano and Chicana youths waged political battles for civil rights. After the completion of La Casita in 1949, Los Amigos Club dissolved and in 1964 former members founded a local chapter of the Mexican American Political Association (MAPA). Founded in 1960, MAPA grew out of the many Mexican American grassroots groups throughout California that tried to elect their own representatives to local and state government. MAPA opposed the urban renewal plan and vowed to run a candidate for the spring election. By 1969 Mexicans comprised one quarter of the city population, wielding enough political power to swing city council elections. That same year tensions between Corona police and the Mexican American community reached the highest point when police "pointed guns" at four Chicano youths hanging out in the street and almost created a "near riot." This incident set off a protest march led by MAPA and Chicano youths in front of police headquarters. MAPA called for a police review board to prevent Corona from becoming a "police state town." MAPA member Frances Martínez read the angry editorials accusing "Mexicans" of instigating a "race war" and penned a biting response: "These so-called 'Mexicans' are one hundred and one percent Americans—second and third generation Corona born Americans—many of whose ancestors were on the American continent before any Anglo had set foot on United States soil." She appealed to both Anglo and Mexican American groups to take a crash course on U.S. and Mexican history to better understand the problems facing Chicanos, because "these young people are strictly a United States product."[4]

Frances Martínez never lost her fierce determination and effective organizing skills to transform Mexican Americans into a powerful political force in Corona. Key to her organizing success was using her artistic talents, her dance and musical abilities, to organize fund-raisers for political empowerment of the Mexican community. In the 1970s Frances continued to be active in MAPA, at St. Edward's Catholic Church, and on the Human Relations Commission, the Corona Hospital District Board, and the Corona Public Library Board. She also became a key player in the Corona Democratic Club. Frances organized fund-raiser dinners for Senator Ted Kennedy and Congressman John Tunney during their campaign stops in Corona.[5]

In 1973, Corona's Cinco de Mayo festival was revived by a group of Chicano and Chicana activists associated with the Community Action Program (CAP), funded by President Lyndon Johnson's Great Society antipoverty initiative. "We decided to revive Cinco de Mayo," explained Albert Varela, one of the founding members, "because we wanted the youth to get a sense of who they are as a people. So we can help them understand their cultural roots and place within the community." As part of the Chicano movement, community and student activists redefined Cinco de Mayo as a reaffirmation of cultural nationalism and anti-imperialist struggle. Like the previous generation, festival organizers sought to use Cinco de Mayo for community-building projects and raising funds for a new youth recreation center. In the mid-1970s Chicana organizers, influenced by the feminist movement, transformed the queen contest from a beauty contest to a public-speaking and talent competition to build self-confidence and prevent rivalries among female contestants. "The secret to our success," explained Varela, "is that we now stay local and don't make an effort to bring famous movie stars or celebrities to serve as grand marshals, only local heroes and role models." The grand marshal at the 1986 Cinco de Mayo festival and Corona's centennial celebration, for example, was eighty-two-year-old Teresa Lemus, the city's 1923 Cinco de Mayo queen. During the 1990s, the festival became an official civic event organized by the city recreation department and attracted thousands of visitors from out of town. Every year the organizing committee raises money from local businesses for the student scholarships to local high school seniors. Like many other Cinco de Mayo celebrations across the state, the committee rejected alcohol industry sponsorship and the selling of alcoholic beverages because it threatened the family-oriented environment and would lead to alcohol-related incidents.[6]

Chicano organizers also used athletic sports for cultural expression and to build community solidarity. After the Corona Athletics Club disbanded in 1960, former players went on to become coaches of softball teams in later years. Jim "Chayo" Rodríguez, for example, became Corona's leading softball coach and was inducted into the Inland Empire's Hispanic Hall of Fame. At the height of the Chicano movement, Rodríguez formed a softball club, Los Chicanos, to steer youths away from gangs and prisons. The players selected the Mexican Revolutionary leader, Pancho Villa, as their team mascot. Los Chicanos players lived up to their team mascot's fighting ability, winning several championship titles in southern California softball tournaments. Every spring until the team disbanded in the early 1980s, Los Chicanos hosted the Chicano Fast Pitch Softball Tournament in Corona, attracting more than sixty teams from as far as Mexico competing for first prize and hundreds of fans cheering for their favorite team.[7]

Mexican Americans used Cinco de Mayo festivals and baseball games and to a lesser extent pool halls, movie theaters, and church-related events as vehicles for reaching a wider audience with their demands for full participation in the city's political, economic, and social affairs. The involvement of Mexican men and women in commercial leisure, cultural festivals, and sports clubs gave them the kind of self-confidence and organizational and leadership skills that could be translated into grassroots advocacy and political action. Although citrus workers did not gain significant upward economic mobility, especially after the failed unionization drive, they achieved more equal treatment in public recreation and civic life. Traditional labor actions, principally the strike, needed to be replaced with more strategic and effective uses of leisure to fit the unique political and economic power structure of an "open shop" town dominated by a group of citrus industry elite. In the end, Corona's Mexican Americans appropriated the democratic ideals of the Popular Front, the Good Neighbor Policy, and World War II to legitimize their demands and help shape U.S.-Mexico relations in general and the treatment of Mexican Americans in the United States in particular.

Throughout this process, leisure activities provided cultural spaces to build solidarity that would positively impact the lives of future generations. While certain male leisure forms proved instrumental for collective actions, they also reinforced gender inequality by intensifying male privilege over women in the home, community, and political arena. Not all forms of leisure were resistive or necessarily emancipatory; some gave pleasure to those who sought escape and fellowship and oftentimes reproduced conservative norms and antisocial behaviors that negatively impacted the community. Male pursuits for pleasure in saloons, pool halls, brothels, and gambling and bootlegging spaces often led to brawls, scuffles, excessive drinking, and sexual control of women. The rowdy behavior they displayed while asserting a masculine autonomy served to reinforce unequal gender relations, thus undermining family and community unity. Narrowed economic resources nurtured by capitalist exploitation and racial and gender hierarchies led to a mix of militancy, accommodation, and conservatism among Corona's Mexican population. Mexican Americans thus made "lemonade" out of the "lemons" handed them in life—low pay, limited economic and educational opportunities, residential segregation, and racial discrimination—by becoming a political force to be reckoned with.

NOTES

Introduction

1. Kevin Starr, *Inventing the Dream: California through the Progressive Era* (New York: Oxford University Press, 1985); Mike Davis, *City of Quartz: Excavating the Future in Los Angeles* (New York: Verso, 1990); Scott L. Bottles, *Los Angeles and the Automobile: The Making of the Modern City* (Berkeley: University of California Press, 1987); Steven Ross, *Working Class Hollywood: Silent Film and the Shaping of Class in America* (Princeton, N.J.: Princeton University Press, 1998); Becky Nicolaides, *My Blue Heaven: Life and Politics in the Working-Class Suburbs of Los Angeles* (Chicago: University of Chicago Press, 2002); Nancy Quam-Wickham, "'Another World': Work, Home, and Autonomy in Blue Collar Suburbs," in *Metropolis in the Making: Los Angeles in the 1920s*, ed. William Deverell and Tom Sitton (Berkeley: University of California Press, 2001), 123–41.

2. Carey McWilliams, *Southern California: An Island on the Land* (Salt Lake City: Peregrine Smith, 1946).

3. Gilbert G. González, *Labor and Community: Mexican Citrus Worker Villages in a Southern California County, 1900–1950* (Urbana: University of Illinois Press, 1994).

4. See essays by Ronald Tobey, Charles Wetherell, Vincent Moses, Anthea Hartig, Margo McBane, Douglas Sackman, and Lisbeth Haas in the special issue of *California History* 74 (Spring 1995).

5. Matt García, *A World of Its Own: Race, Labor, and Citrus in the Making of Greater Los Angeles* (Chapel Hill: University of North Carolina Press, 2001).

6. An exception is Margo McBane, "The Role of Gender in Citrus Employment: A Case Study of Recruitment, Labor, and Housing Patterns at the Limoneira Company, 1893 to 1940," *California History* 74 (1995): 69–81.

7. Barbara Cox, *Latinos in California's Inland Empire: A Demographic Databook for Riverside and San Bernardino Counties* (Claremont: Tomás Rivera Center, Claremont Colleges, 1993), 1–5.

8. George Pozetta and Gary Mormino, *The Immigrant World of Ybor City: Italians and Their Latin Neighbors in Tampa, 1885–1985* (Urbana: University of Illinois Press, 1990); Douglas Flamming, *Creating the Modern South: Millhands & Managers in Dalton, Georgia, 1884–1984* (Chapel Hill: University of North Carolina Press, 1992); Mary Murphy, *Mining Cultures: Men, Women, and Leisure in Butte, 1914–41* (Urbana: University of Illinois Press, 1997); Laurie Mercier, *Anaconda: Labor, Community, and Culture in Montana's Smelter City* (Urbana:

University of Illinois Press, 2001); Elizabeth Jameson, *All That Glitters: Class, Conflict, and Community in Cripple Creek* (Urbana: University of Illinois Press, 1998).

9. Mary Murphy, *Mining Cultures* (Urbana: University of Illinois Press, 1997); Roy Rosenzweig, *Eight Hours for What We Will: Workers and Leisure in an Industrial City, 1870–1920* (Cambridge: Cambridge University Press, 1983); Kathy Peiss, *Cheap Amusements: Working Women and Leisure in Turn-of-the-Century New York* (Philadelphia: Temple University Press, 1994); George Lipsitz, *Rainbow at Midnight: Labor and Culture in the 1940s* (Urbana: University of Illinois Press, 1994); Robin D. G. Kelley, *Race Rebels: Culture, Politics, and the Black Working Class* (New York: Free Press, 1994); Nan Enstad, *Ladies of Labor, Girls of Adventure: Working Women, Popular Culture, and Labor Politics at the Turn of the Twentieth Century* (New York: Columbia University Press, 1999); Susan Lee Johnson, "Bulls, Bears, and Dancing Boys: Race, Gender, and Leisure in the California Gold Rush," *Radical History Review* 60 (Fall 1994): 4–37.

10. Vicki Ruiz, "'Star Struck': Acculturation, Adolescence, and the Mexican American Woman, 1920–1950," in *Building with Our Hands: New Directions in Chicana Studies*, ed. Adela de la Torre and Beatriz Pesquera (Berkeley: University of California Press, 1990), 109–29; Ruiz, *From Out of the Shadows: Mexican Women in Twentieth-Century America* (New York: Oxford University Press, 1998); Douglas Monroy, "'Our Children Get So Different Here': Film, Fashion, Popular Culture and the Process of Cultural Syncretization in Mexican Los Angeles, 1900–1935," *Aztlan* 19 (1990): 79–107; Monroy, *Rebirth: Mexican Los Angeles from the Great Migration to the Great Depression* (Berkeley: University of California Press, 1999); George J. Sánchez, *Becoming Mexican American: Ethnicity, Culture and Identity in Chicano Los Angeles, 1900–1945* (New York: Oxford University Press, 1993)

11. Peter Way, "Rough Humors and Ardent Spirits: The Rough Culture of Canal Construction Laborers," *Journal of American History* 79 (March 1993): 1397–428; Way, *Common Labor: Workers and the Digging of North American Canals, 1780–1960* (Cambridge: Cambridge University Press, 1993).

12. Ava Baron, ed., *Work Engendered: Toward a New History of American Labor* (Ithaca, N.Y.: Cornell University Press, 1991). Ruiz, "'Star Struck,'" 115–23; Ruiz, *From Out of the Shadows*, chap. 3; Monroy, *Rebirth*, 167–81. On the political nature of women's leisure, see Susan Shaw, "Conceptualizing Resistance: Women's Leisure as Political Practice," *Journal of Leisure Research* 33 (2001): 186–201.

13. Gilbert G. González, "Factors Relating to Property Ownership of Mexican Americans and Italian Americans in Lincoln Heights," in *Struggle and Success: An Anthology of the Italian Immigrant Experience in California*, ed. Paola Sensi-Isolani and Phylis Cancilla Martinelli (New York: Center for Migration Studies, 1993), 219–30.

14. On racialized social system in the United States, see Eduardo Bonilla-Silva, *White Supremacy and Racism in the Post–Civil Rights Era* (Boulder, Colo.: Lynne Rienner, 2001), chap. 2; on whiteness and Italian immigrants, see Thomas Guglielmo, *White on Arrival: Italians, Race, Color, and Power in Chicago, 1890–1945* (New York: Oxford University Press, 2003).

Chapter 1: Lemon Capital of the World

1. Janet Williams Gould, *The Golden Circle, 1886–1936* (Corona High School Press, May 1, 1936), 3–44; Janet Williams Gould, "Golden Circle: A Historical Pageant of Corona and the Mesa," Typescript, February 11, 1936, Janet Williams Gould Collection, Box 1, Heritage Room, Corona Public Library, Corona, California [hereafter CPL]; "Nearly 4,500 Enjoy Jubilee Pageant," *Corona Independent*, May 2, 1936.

2. "Mrs. Gould an Eminent Historian," *Corona Independent*, May 4, 1961, 2.

3. C. C. Johns, "Colorful Pageant Depicts Romance of Citrus at Corona Celebration," *California Citrograph*, June 1936, 282. Corona's Cinco de Mayo celebration received local and regional coverage; see "Mexican Fiesta Group Thankful," *Corona Independent*, May 6, 1936, 1; "Corona Fete Climaxed," *Los Angeles Times*, May 6, 1936, B1; "Jubileo de Oro de la Ciudad de Corona, Cal.," *La Opinión*, May 7, 1936, 4.

4. Robert Cleland, *The Cattle on a Thousand Hills* (San Marino, Calif.: Huntington Library, 1941), 117–37; Oscar Osburn Winther, "The Colony System of Southern California," *Agricultural History* 27 (July 1953): 94–98; Carey McWilliams, *Southern California: An Island on the Land* (Salt Lake City: Peregrine Smith, 1946), 215–16.

5. Joyce Carter Vickery, *Defending Eden: New Mexican Pioneers in Southern California, 1830–1890* (Riverside, Calif.: Riverside Museum Press, 1977), 1–86; Albert Camarillo, *Chicanos in a Changing Society: From Mexican Pueblos to American Barrios in Santa Barbara and Southern California, 1848–1930* (Cambridge: Harvard University Press, 1979), 101–41.

6. Judge North is quoted in Thomas Patterson, *A Colony for California: Riverside's First Hundred Years* (Riverside, Calif.: Press-Enterprise, 1971), 19, 139–53; Vincent Moses, "'The Orange-Grower Is Not a Farmer': G. Harold Powell, Riverside Orchardists, and the Coming of Industrial Agriculture, 1893–1930," *California History* 74 (Spring 1995): 24.

7. Robert B. Taylor, *South Riverside: The Queen Colony of Southern California* (South Riverside, Calif.: South Riverside Land and Water Company, 1887), 4; Diann Marsh, *Corona the Circle City* (Encinitas, Calif.: Heritage Publishing, 1998), 32; "Early History of Corona by R. B. Taylor, A Pioneer," *Corona Courier*, April 10, 1913; Frank Rolfe, "A Sketch of the Life of R. B. Taylor," *Historical Society of Southern California* 13 (1924): 29–36;

8. "Locals," *South Riverside Bee*, February 2, 1888, 3; "Keep the Heathen Out," *South Riverside Bee*, August 30, 1888; "Locals," *South Riverside Bee*, January 3, 1889; Harry Lawton, "Denis Kearney among the Orange Groves: The Beginnings of the Anti-Chinese Movement in the Citrus Belt (1879–1880)," in *Wong Ho Leun: An American Chinatown*, Vol. 1 (San Diego: Great Basin Foundation, 1987), 193–203; Alexander Saxton, *The Indispensable Enemy: Labor and the Anti-Chinese Movement in California* (Berkeley: University of California Press, 1971), passim.

9. "South Riverside Changes Its Name," *South Riverside Bee*, June 27, 1896, 3.

10. Charles Holman, "Keeping Faith with the Consumer," *Technical World Magazine* 20 (December 1913): 537; 1913–14 Annual Report, Queen Colony

Fruit Exchange Minutes, Box 1, Orange Heights Orange Association Collection, CPL [hereafter OHOAC]; Tom Patterson, "The Great Freeze of 1913," in *A History of Citrus in the Riverside Area,* ed. Esther Klotz, Harry Lawton, and Joan Hall (Riverside, Calif.: Riverside Museum Press, 1969), 41–44.

11. 1916 Annual Report, Queen Colony Fruit Exchange Minutes, OHOAC; "Corona Is Greatest Lemon Producer," *Corona Courier,* January 30, 1915, 1; F. A. Harlow, "The Exchange Movement in Corona," *California Citrograph,* March 1916, 4; Franklyn Hoyt, "Railroad Development in Southern California, 1868 to 1900" (PhD diss., University of Southern California, 1951), 313–324.

12. T. H. Powell, "Production, Packing, Distributing and Selling Lemons," *California Citrograph,* January 1923, 66, 4; Rahno Mabel MacCurdy, *History of the California Fruit Growers Exchange* (Los Angeles: California Fruit Growers Exchange, 1925), 36–45; Albert J. Meyer, "History of the California Fruit Growers Exchange, 1893–1920" (PhD diss., Johns Hopkins University, 1950), 229–244.

13. "The Lemon," *Land of Sunshine,* 2 (January 1895): 30; G. Harold Powell, *California Lemon Industry,* 9 (Los Angeles: Citrus Protective League, 1913), 8.

14. G. W. Garcelon, *Fifteen Years with the Lemon* (Sacramento: State Printing Office, 1891), 1–13; Hajime Fukuoka, "The Lemon Industry in Southern California" (MA thesis, University of Southern California, 1918), 1–15; Robert W. Durrenberger, "Climate as a Factor in the Production of Lemons in California" (PhD diss., University of California, Los Angeles, 1955), 4–12; Andrew Hamilton, "California's Yellow Gold," *Saturday Evening Post* 229 (September 1, 1956): 52.

15. The club's membership gradually increased from 21 in 1911 to 192 in 1925. Irving Clukas, "History of the Lemon Men's Club," 3, 1969, Box 1, Unpublished Manuscript, Lemon Men's Club Collection, Huntington Library, San Marino, California. "Lemon Men's Club Elects President," *California Citrograph,* July 1925, 323.

16. "Coast District Lemon Men Win Baseball Game 8 to 7," *California Citrograph,* November 1921, 22; "Lemon Men's Club Hold Annual Field Day at Corona," *California Citrograph,* November 1922, 24–25; "Annual Field Day Program Observed," *Corona Independent,* September 23, 1922, 2.

17. Fred Eldridge and Stanley Reynolds, *Corona, California, Commentaries* (Corona: Sinclair Printing, 1986), 34–37; "Those Who Have Achieved in the Citrus Industry: Joy Jameson," *California Citrograph,* November 1919, 11.

18. Meyer, "History of the California Fruit Growers Exchange," 148; A. W. McKay and W. M. Stevens, *Organization and Development of a Cooperative Citrus-Fruit Marketing Agency* (Washington, D.C.: U.S. Department of Agriculture, 1924), 1–5; W. W. Cumberland, *Cooperative Marketing: Its Advantages as Exemplified in the California Fruit Growers Exchange* (Princeton, N.J.: Princeton University Press, 1917), 207–18; MacCurdy, *History of the California Fruit Growers Exchange,* 36–45; Harold G. Powell, *Cooperation in Agriculture* (New York: Macmillan, 1913), 12–15.

19. W. J. Pentelow, "Corona, The Queen Colony," *California Citrograph,* March 1916, 14; Articles of Incorporation, Queen Colony Fruit Exchange Minutes, 1905, Box 1, OHOAC.

20. Powell, *California Lemon Industry,* 8; G. Harold Powell, *Italian Lemon Industry* (Los Angeles: Citrus Protective League, 1913), 11–12; "Present Status

of the Lemon Industry in California," *California Citrograph*, April 1926, 224; Meyer, "History of the California Fruit Growers Exchange," 231–37.

21. "What Was Said in Five Minute Limit on Lemon Tariff Matter," *California Citrograph*, April 1929, 1, 240; "Corona Man Now in Washington Asks Lemon Tariff Increase," *Corona Independent*, January 10, 1921, 1.

22. "Lemon By-Products Plant Makes Record," *Corona Independent*, March 5, 1924, 1; Howard Hall and F. R. Wilcox, "Accomplishments with Lemon Products and Their Effect on Growers Returns," *California Citrograph*, November 1939, 20; Keith Monroe, "1,001 New Lemon Aids," *Collier's*, May 28, 1954; Exchange Lemon Products Company, *Sunkist's History in Corona* (Corona: Exchange Lemon Products, 1958), 1–13; Gloria Scott, "Sunkist Growers Inc., Lemon Products Division," 3, 1985, Typescript, Folder "Exchange Lemon Products Company," CPL; Meeting Minutes, August 13, 1918–September 10, 1918, Exchange By-Products Company, Box 5, OHOAC.

23. "Accomplishments with Lemon Products and Their Effect on Growers Returns," *California Citrograph*, May 1939, 19–21; "Summary of Talk on Lemon By-Products," *California Citrograph*, April 1918, 65. "Sunkist Lemon Plant Here Holds a Position of World Leadership," *Corona Independent*, May 11, 1961, 1; D. C. Fessenden, "The Exchange By-Products Company," *California Citrograph*, March 1916, 35.

24. *"Lemon Capital of the World": The Corona Story* (Corona: Corona Chamber of Commerce, 1961), 12; Exchange Lemon Products Company, *Sunkist Lemonade at Corona* (Los Angeles: Sunkist Growers, Inc., 1953), 1–3.

25. George Stanley, "The Story of the Sunkist Whistle," 2, 1988, Typescript, Folder "Exchange Lemon Products Company," Heritage Room, CPL; Meeting Minutes, August 13, 1918–September 10, 1918, Exchange By-Products Company, OHOAC.

26. John B. Wallace, "Turning Culls into Dollars," *Packinghouse News*, November 1924, 536; Josephine Jacobs, "Sunkist Advertising" (PhD diss., University of California, Los Angeles, 1966), 62–63, 82, 103; Douglas Sackman, "'By Their Fruits Ye Shall Know Them': Nature Cross Culture Hybridization and the California Citrus Industry, 1893–1939," *California History* 74 (Spring 1995): 96; Don Francisco, "Increasing the Consumption of Citrus Fruits," *California Citrus Institute*, May 1, 1921, 105–17.

27. Sackman, "By Their Fruits Ye Shall Know Them," 83–99; Paul F. Starrs, "The Navel of California and Other Oranges: Images of California and the Orange Crate," *California Geographical Society* 28 (1988): 1–41.

28. John Zarate, "Research Paper on the Power Elite of Corona," 6, December 1971, Typescript, Folder "Hispanic Population," CPL; Mike Lunetta interview by Alexi Danieri, May 28, 1981, audiotape C-026, Oral History Collection, CPL; Mike Davis, "Sunshine and the Open Shop: Ford and Darwin in 1920s Los Angeles," *Antipode* 29 (October 1997): 356–78.

29. Patricia Drake, "Land and Water Development in Temescal and Corona" (senior thesis, University of California Riverside, 1964), 19–20; Iris Hayward, *A History of the Temescal Water Company* (Corona: Temescal Water Company, March 1973), 4–19.

30. "T. C. Jameson Active in Life of Community," *Corona Independent*, May 4, 1961, 1.

31. "Joy Jameson Chosen Chamber of Commerce Head," *Corona Independent*, January 7, 1928, 3; Tom Patterson, "Jamesons Tied to Corona History of Citrus Production," *Press-Enterprise*, October 16, 1994.

32. "Chamber of Commerce Endorses Parkridge," *Corona Independent*, April 6, 1925, 1; "One-Time Social Center Now Stands Stark, Lonely and Deserted on Hill," *Corona Independent*, Golden Jubilee Edition, April 27, 1936, 12, 1.

33. By 1929, Los Angeles black businessmen were forced to withdraw their offer and a year later the bank issued a foreclosure of the country club. "Fiery Cross Burns Near Parkridge," *Corona Independent*, August 20, 1927, 1; "Appeal to Parkridge Members," *Corona Independent*, August 25, 1927, 1; "Gilkey Bound Over to Superior Court by Corona Justice," *Corona Independent*, August 27, 1927, 1. On the KKK in citrus belt communities, see Christopher Cocoltchos, "The Invisible Empire and the Search for the Orderly Community: The Ku Klux Klan in Anaheim, California," in *The Invisible Empire in the West: Toward a New Historical Appraisal of the Ku Klux Klan of the 1920s*, ed. Shawn Lay (Urbana: University of Illinois Press, 1992), 97–120.

34. Cletus Daniel, *Bitter Harvest: A History of California Farmworkers, 1870–1941* (Berkeley: University of California Press, 1981), 47; "Farm Labor," *California Citrograph*, September 1919, 1.

35. Philip Scranton, "Varieties of Paternalism: Industrial Structures and the Social Relations of Production in American Textiles," *American Quarterly* 36 (Summer 1984): 235–57.

36. Annual Report of the General Manager, 17–19, October 31, 1921, California Fruit Growers Exchange, Box 1, OHOAC; Edward Beechert, *Working in Hawaii: A Labor History* (Honolulu: University of Hawaii Press, 1985), 179–81, 191–95.

37. "Housing the Employees of California's Citrus Ranches," 4, 1920, Unpublished Manuscript, Box 1, A. D. Shamel Papers, Special Collections, University of California, Riverside [hereafter UCR]. On citrus housing, see Gilbert G. González, *Labor and Community: Mexican Citrus Worker Villages in a Southern California County, 1900–1950* (Urbana: University of Illinois Press, 1994), 36–42; "Housing the Employees of California's Citrus Ranches," *California Citrograph*, March 1918, 96–97; "Housing Employees of California's Citrus Ranches," *California Citrograph*, May 1918, 150–51; "Housing Employees of California's Citrus Ranches," *California Citrograph*, June 1918, 176–77. On the relationship of citrus housing and the CCIH, see García, *A World of Its Own*, 62–64; Don Mitchell, *The Lie of the Land: Migrant Workers and the California Landscape* (Minneapolis: University of Minnesota Press, 1996), 100–102. On housing programs and citizenship, see Sean Purdy, "Building Homes, Building Citizens: Housing Reform and Nation Formation in Canada, 1900–20," *Canadian Historical Review* 79 (September 1998): 492–523.

38. On corporate paternalism as a gendered process, see Andrea Tone, *The Business of Benevolence: Industrial Paternalism in Progressive America* (Ithaca, N.Y.: Cornell University Press, 1997); Janice Reiff, "A Modern Lear and His Daughters: Gender in the Model Town of Pullman," *Journal of Urban History* 23 (March 1997): 314–41; Lisa Fine, "Our Big Factory Family: Masculinity and Paternalism at Reo Motor Car Company of Lansing, Michigan," *Labor History* 34 (1993): 274–91.

39. "J. D. Culbertson," by A. D. Shamel, September 2, 1918, transcript, p. 3, A. D. Shamel Papers, Special Collections, UCR; "The Esthetic Side of the

Orange Growing in the Southwest: An Appreciation of the Jameson Family," *California Citrograph*, May 1932, 297; J. D. Culbertson, "Housing of Ranch Labor," *California Cultivator*, April 17, 1920, 649.

40. George B. Hodgkin, "Survey of the Labor Situation," *California Citrograph*, August 1920, 330; A. D. Shamel, "Housing the Employees of California's Citrus Ranches," *California Citrograph*, February 1918, 26; A. D. Shamel, "Housing Conditions of the Employees on California Citrus Ranches," Unpublished Typescript, 1918, 3, A. D. Shamel Papers, Special Collections, UCR.

41. Ethan Allen Chase Personal Diary, April 10, 1906, Ethan Allen Chase Collection, Riverside Municipal Museum, Riverside, California; Ethan Allen Chase, *Celebration in Honor of the Eightieth Birthday of Ethan Allen Chase* (Riverside, Calif.: Press Printing Company, 1912); Frank Chase, "Biography of Ethan Allen Chase Family, 1933," Chase Collection, Riverside Municipal Museum, Riverside, California; Tom Patterson, "Chase Family Had Ups and Downs in Area Citrus Efforts," *Press-Enterprise*, December 9, 1990, B-5.

42. A. D. Shamel, "Housing the Employees of California's Citrus Ranches," *California Citrograph*, February 1918, 25; "Better Housing, Better Employees," *Corona Independent*, June 20, 1919, 1. On citrus ranch housing patterns, see González, *Labor and Community*, 36–42; García, *A World of Its Own*, 62–77; McBane, "The Role of Gender in Citrus Employment," 73–90; José Alamillo, "Bitter-Sweet Communities: Mexican Workers and Citrus Growers on the California Landscape, 1880–1941" (PhD diss., University of California, Irvine, 2000), 143–94.

43. L. T. Mott to Henry Morton, July 23, 1919, Carton 43, DIR Records, Bancroft Library, University of California, Berkeley. On the CCIH's role in the citrus industry, see González, *Labor and Community*, 115–20; García, *A World of Its Own*, 49, 106–97.

44. "Foothill Lemon Corona's Biggest Citrus Operation," *Corona Independent*, August 18, 1964; Lorne L. Allmon, *The Story of Samuel B. Hampton and the California Citrus Industry, 1887–1918* (Riverside: Citrus Label Society, 1994), 6. On the Limoneira Ranch, see McBane, "The Role of Gender in Citrus Employment," 68–81.

45. Articles of Incorporation, 1911, Box 2, Corona Foothill Lemon Company, OHOAC; "Corona Foothill Lemon Company Is Growing," *Corona Independent*, September 10, 1914, 1; "CHS Students Tour Foothill Lemon Industry," *Corona Independent*, February 13, 1952; Alamillo, "Bitter-Sweet Communities," chap. 4.

46. Iris Hayward, "People Most Important in Foothill Ranch Story," *Press-Enterprise*, November 3, 1978, 5.

47. Edward Willits, interview by author, January 21, 1998, audiotape C-088, Oral History Collection, CPL. On "familiar paternalism," see Scranton, "Varieties of Paternalism," 245–47. On the concept of "negotiated loyalty," see Gerald Zahavi, *Workers, Managers and Welfare Capitalism: The Shoeworkers and Tanners of Endicott Johnson, 1890–1950* (Urbana: University of Illinois Press, 1988), chap. 4.

48. Natividad Cortez, interview by author, April 20, 1998, audiotape C-094, Oral History Collection, CPL. "Last Ranch-Owned Store Closes, Marks End of By-Gone Trade Era," *Press-Enterprise*, July 19, 1967, 5.

49. Janet Williams Gould "Story of Pioneers Provides Inspiration to Troubled World," *Corona Independent*, May 1, 1961, 6.

50. On Santa Paula's lemon industry, see Michael Belknap, "The Era of the Lemon: A History of Santa Paula, California," *California Historical Society Quarterly* 47 (June 1968): 113–40.

51. On the ideal "self-made man," see Michael Kimmel, *Manhood in America: A Cultural History* (New York: Free Press, 1996); Anthony Rotundo, *American Manhood: Transformations in Masculinity from the Revolution to the Modern Era* (New York: Basic Books, 1993); Gail Bederman, *Manliness and Civilization: A Cultural History of Gender and Race in the United States, 1880–1917* (Chicago: University of Chicago Press, 1995).

52. Zarate, "Research Paper on the Power Elite of Corona," 7.

Chapter 2: *Red, White, and Greening of Corona*

1. "Marriage License Issued," *Corona Independent*, July 21, 1915, 1.

2. "Seeks Divorce on Grounds of Cruelty," *Corona Independent*, September 16, 1922, 1; *Corselli v. Corselli*, 11903, 6, September 23, 1922, Court Records Office, Superior Court of County of Riverside, Riverside, California; U.S. Census Bureau, Department of Commerce and Labor, *15th Census of the United States, 1930*, Population Bulletin, City of Corona (Washington, D.C.: U.S. Government Printing Office, 1933).

3. L. Cruz, interview by Helen Ritter, April 3, 1979, transcript, p. 2, Oral History Collection, CPL.

4. David Montgomery, *The Fall of the House of Labor: The Workplace, the State, and American Labor Activism, 1865–1925* (Cambridge: Cambridge University Press, 1987), 58–111.

5. L. Cruz interview.

6. On the extensive social networks among citrus workers in Orange County, see Gilbert G. González, *Labor and Community: Mexican Citrus Worker Villages in a Southern California County, 1900–1950* (Urbana: University of Illinois Press, 1994), 75.

7. On "fraternal culture," see Gunther Peck, *Reinventing Free Labor: Padrones and Immigrant Workers in the North American West, 1880–1930* (Cambridge: Cambridge University Press, 2000), 129–57; Elizabeth Jameson, *All That Glitters: Class, Conflict, and Community in Cripple Creek* (Urbana: University of Illinois Press, 1998), 87–113.

8. On gender and immigrant solos, see Pierrette Hondagneu-Sotelo, *Gendered Transitions: Mexican Experiences of Immigration* (Berkeley: University of California Press, 1994), 7, 142.

9. Juanita Ramírez, interview by author, April 22, 1998, transcript, p. 18 (in author's possession); on medical inspections at Civdad Juarez see Alexandra Minna Stern, "Buildings, Boundaries, Blood: Medicalization and Nation-Building on the U.S.-Mexico Border, 1910–1930," *Hispanic American Historical Review* 79 (1999): 49–81.

10. Mark Reisler, *By the Sweat of Their Brow: Mexican Immigrant Labor in the United States, 1900–1940* (Westport, Conn.: Greenwood, 1976), chap. 2.

11. Elizabeth Broadbent, "The Distribution of Mexican Population in the United States" (PhD diss., University of Chicago, 1941), 1–15; U.S. Census Bureau, Department of Commerce and Labor, *13th–16th Census of the United*

States, 1910–1940, Population Bulletin, City of Corona (Washington, D.C.: U.S. Government Printing Office, 1943).

12. Fred Eldridge and Stanley Reynolds, *Corona, California, Commentaries* (Corona: Sinclair Printing, 1986), 41–43; "Italians Played Key Early Role in Corona Citrus Industry," *Corona Independent*, February 8, 1972, 1.

13. Christian Hans Palmer, "Italian Immigration and the Development of California Agriculture" (PhD diss., University of California, Berkeley, 1965), chap. 1; Andrew Rolle, *The Immigrant Upraised: Italian Adventurers and Colonists in an Expanding America* (Norman: University of Oklahoma Press, 1968); Micaela di Leonardo, *The Varieties of Ethnic Experience: Kinship, Class, and Gender among California Italian-Americans* (Ithaca, N.Y.: Cornell University Press, 1984); Paola Sensi-Isolani and Phylis Cancilla Martinelli, eds., *Struggle and Success: An Anthology of the Italian Immigrant Experience in California* (New York: Center for Migration Studies, 1993), 1–5.

14. U.S. Census Bureau, Department of Commerce and Labor, *13th–16th Census of the United States, 1910–1940*, Population Bulletin, City of Corona (Washington, D.C.: U.S. Government Printing Office). On Italian immigration, see Donna Gabaccia, *Italy's Many Diasporas* (Seattle: University of Washington Press, 2000).

15. Angelo Lunetta, "Non Te Scordate di Mei/Don't Forget Me," 10, 1992, Typescript, Folder "Italian Population," CPL; "Corona's Little Italy Parties of the Early Days Recalled," *Corona Independent*, February 22, 1972, 5. On Italian women's immigration experience, see Donna Gabaccia and Franca Iacovetta, eds., *Women, Gender, and Transnational Lives: Italian Workers of the World* (Toronto: University of Toronto Press, 2002).

16. "Lemon Men in Battle for Life before Interstate Commerce Commission," *Corona Independent*, March 25, 1910, 1; "The Corona Lemon Company," *California Citrograph*, March 1916, 22.

17. C. T. Songer, "Reminiscence of Early Corona," 3, 1965, Typescript, Folder "Corona History," CPL; "Yellow Importations Discouraged," *Corona Independent*, April 27, 1936, 7; Morrison Gideon Wong, "The Japanese in Riverside, 1890 to 1945: A Special Case in Race Relations" (PhD diss., University of California, Riverside, 1977), 1–69. According to Micaela di Leonardo, the presence of American Indians, Asians, and Mexicans in the state "deflected racist sentiment" against Italian Americans; see Leonardo, *The Varieties of Ethnic Experience*, 94. In his study of Italian Chicago, Thomas Guglielmo argues that Italians were "white upon arrival" in the late nineteenth century and remained so through World War II; see Thomas Guglielmo, *White on Arrival: Italians, Race, Color, and Power in Chicago, 1890–1945* (New York: Oxford University Press, 2003), 6–7. On whiteness and manhood see Gail Bederman, *Manliness and Civilization: A Cultural History of Gender and Race in the United States* (Chicago: University of Chicago Press, 1995).

18. Meeting Minutes, 3, March 16, 1920, Box 3, Queen Colony Fruit Exchange, OHOAC.

19. Cletus Daniel, *Bitter Harvest: A History of California Farmworkers, 1870–1941* (Berkeley: University of California Press, 1981); Don Mitchell, *The Lie of the Land: Migrant Workers and the California Landscape* (Minneapolis: University of Minnesota Press, 1996); Devra Weber, *Dark Sweat, White Gold: California Farm Workers, Cotton, and the New Deal* (Berkeley: University of

California Press, 1994); Camille Guerin-Gonzales, *Mexican Workers & American Dreams: Immigration, Repatriation, and California Farm Labor, 1900–1939* (New Brunswick, N.J.: Rutgers University Press, 1994).

20. González, *Labor and Community*; Matt García, *A World of Its Own: Race, Labor, and Citrus in the Making of Greater Los Angeles* (Chapel Hill: University of North Carolina Press, 2001).

21. George P. Clements, "Mexican Immigration and Its Bearing on Calif's Agriculture," *California Citrograph*, December 1929, 3.

22. U.S. Census Bureau, Department of Commerce and Labor, *14th–15th Census of the United States, 1920*, Population Bulletin, City of Corona (Washington, D.C.: U.S. Government Printing Office); "The Picking and Hauling of Lemons," *California Citrograph*, July 1921, 264.

23. Reynaldo Aparicio, interview by author, January 17, 1998, transcript, p. 22 (in author's possession); Frank Salgado, interview by author, January 29, 1998, audiotape C-095, Oral History Collection, CPL; Paul Garland Williamson, "Labor in the California Citrus Industry" (MA thesis, University of California, 1947), 89–90.

24. Luis Hernández was the first Mexican crew leader for the Corona Foothill Lemon Company, with thirty men working under his supervision. Luis Hernández, interview by Helen Ritter, March 15, 1979, audiotape C-012, Oral History Collection, CPL.

25. Cortez interview.

26. Frances Martínez, interview by author, January 22, 1998, audiotape C-090, Oral History Collection, CPL; Pat Murkland, "Heat and Haze: Before Smog, There Was Smudge," *Press-Enterprise*, October 24, 1999, S-15.

27. "What System of Paying Pickers Results in Least Fruit Injury?" *California Citrograph*, July 1921, 310.

28. Santos García, interview by author, July 22, 1999, audiotape (in author's possession).

29. Salgado interview.

30. Aparicio interview; Carl Hercklerath, interview by author, October 19, 1998, transcript, p. 15 (in author's possession).

31. "The Story of the Mission Bridge Brand and the George Gobruegge Family in California Citrus," 8, 1984, Typescript, Folder "Corona Citrus," CPL. One fight broke out between two workers both using pruning shears to inflict wounds on each other. "Mexican Facing Serious Charge in Local Court," *Corona Independent*, July 31, 1929, 1.

32. Salgado interview; Martínez interview.

33. Ruth Cortez, interview by author, March 30, 1998, audiotape C-016, Oral History Collection, CPL.

34. The two highest-paid occupations for Mexican women, according to the 1930 Corona census, were servants (21) and packinghouse workers (47). Ramírez interview; Guadalupe Delgadillo, interview by the author, March 31, 2000, audiotape (in author's possession).

35. García, *A World of Its Own*, 162–74; McBane, "The Role of Gender in Citrus Employment," 78; Gilbert González, "Women, Work and Community in the Mexican Colonias of the Southern California Citrus Belt," *California History* 74 (1995): 62–64.

36. Williamson, "Labor in the California Citrus Industry," 77; U.S. Department of Labor, Women's Bureau, *Employment Conditions in Citrus Fruit Packing, 1939* (Washington, D.C.: U.S. Government Printing Office, 1940), 1–23; U.S. Census Bureau, Department of Commerce and Labor, *14th–15th Census of the United States, 1920,* Population Bulletin, City of Corona (Washington, D.C.: U.S. Government Printing Office, 1933).

37. Martínez interview; Teresa Enríquez, interview by author, June 18, 2000, audiotape (in author's possession). On women's "work culture," see Vicki Ruiz, *Cannery Women, Cannery Lives: Mexican Women, Unionization, and the California Food Processing Industry, 1930–1950* (Albuquerque: University of New Mexico Press, 1987).

38. Alice Rodríguez, interview by author, January 27, 1999, audiotape C-092, Oral History Collection, CPL.

39. Enríquez interview; Martínez interview.

40. Labor Camp Inspection Report, American Fruit Growers, Folder "AL-AM," Carton 31; Labor Camp Inspection Report, "Corona Foothill Lemon Company," Folder "COP-COZ," Carton 37; Labor Camp Inspection Report, "Jameson Company," Folder "JA-JD," Carton 33; Labor Camp Inspection Report, "A. F. Call Estate," Folder "CAA-CAG," Carton 36; Labor Camp Inspection Report, "El Cerrito Ranch Co.," Folder "EL-EQ," Carton 37, all located in the California Department of Industrial Relations, Division of Immigration and Housing, C-A 194, Bancroft Library, University of California, Berkeley; A. D. Shamel, Unpublished Manuscript on "Limoneira Company" 3, A. D. Shamel Papers, Special Collections, UCR.

41. L. Cruz interview.

42. Esperanza Olvera, interview by author, September 30, 1997, audiotape (in author's possession).

43. *1924 Corona City Directory* (Los Angeles: Kaasen Directory Company, 1924), 1–10.

44. "Mexican Population Improving Conditions," *Corona Courier,* August 29, 1919, 1; L. Cruz interview; Mike Villa, interview by William Ritchie, February 22, 1984, audiotape C 050, Oral History Collection, CPL.

45. "Mexican Girls Wanting House, Build Their Own," *Corona Independent,* February 22, 1945, 5.

46. "Better Housing, Better Employees," *Corona Independent,* June 20, 1919, 2.

47. Onias Acevedo, interview by Bill Ritchie, February 20, 1985, audiotape C-058, Oral History Collection, CPL. On racial restrictive covenants directed against Mexican immigrants, see Vesta Penrod, "Civil Rights Problems of Mexican Americans in Southern California" (MA thesis, Claremont College, 1948), 32–47. On public health officials' racial discourse and Mexican housing, see Natalia Molina, "Illustrating Cultural Authority: Medicalized Representations of Mexican Communities in Early-Twentieth-Century Los Angeles," *Aztlan* 28 (Spring 2003): 129–43.

48. "Looking Back: Tales from the Early Days," *Press-Enterprise,* "Corona Centennial" issue, June 29, 1986, 14.

49. "What's the Matter with Corona?" *Corona Independent,* January 5, 1917, 2; "Mexican Quarters Need Cleaning Up," *Arlington Times,* November 15, 1929, 1.

50. "Dr. Herbert Priestly Authority on Mexican Affairs Addressed Peace Congress at Mission Inn," *Corona Independent*, December 7, 1926, 1; on germ theories and Texas Mexicans, see David Montejano, *Anglos and Mexicans in the Making of Texas, 1836–1986* (Austin: University of Texas Press, 1987), 225–28. For a discussion on Anglo American writers and the "Mexican problem," see Gilbert González, *Culture of Empire: American Writers, Mexico, and Mexican Immigrants, 1880–1930* (Austin: University of Texas Press, 2003).

51. "Mrs. Huckins Is for Separation of Foreigners in Schools," *Corona Independent*, March 24, 1926, 2; "Will Ask That Mexicans Be Segregated," *Arlington Times*, June 20, 1924, 1; Meeting Minutes, April 7, 1926, 21, Corona-Norco Unified School District Board, Norco, California; Martínez interview.

52. Meeting Minutes, 5, October 28, 1925, Corona City Council, City Clerk's Office, City Hall, Corona, California; "Looking Back: Tales from the Early Days," *Corona Independent*, June 18, 1926, 6; "Looking Back: Tales From the Early Days," *Press-Enterprise*, Corona Centennial Issue, June 29, 1986; Penrod, "Civil Rights Problems of Mexican Americans in Southern California," 25.

53. Ramírez interview.

54. In Norfolk, Virginia, African Americans turned segregation on its head by creating spaces for congregations "to gather their cultural bearings, [and] to mold the urban setting." Similarly, Corona's Mexican population used public gatherings within a segregated city to redefine their own interests. Earl Lewis, *In Their Own Interests: Race, Class, and Power in Twentieth-Century Norfolk, Virginia* (Berkeley: University of California Press, 1991), 92.

55. *1927 Corona City Directory* (Los Angeles: Kaasen Directory Company, 1927), 10–15; L. Cruz interview; Tony Cruz, interview by Helen Ritter, March 15, 1979, transcript, p. 6, Oral History Collection, CPL.

56. By 1941, only three businesses—a beauty shop, restaurant-bar, and movie theater—were female-owned; see *1927 Corona City Directory*, 8–12.

57. T. Cruz interview.

58. Emilio Zamora, *The World of the Mexican Worker in Texas* (College Station: Texas A&M University Press, 1993), chap. 4; Leon Heredia, "Bajo El Espejo de Opinion," *Revista de Corona*, February 22, 1929, 9.

59. Angelo Lunetta, "Non Te Scordate di Mei/Don't Forget Me," 11.

60. M. Lunetta interview; Domenica Danieri, interview by author, January 10, 2001, audiotape (in author's possession); James Barrett and David Roediger, "Inbetween Peoples: Race, Nationality and the 'New Immigrant' Working Class," *Journal of American Ethnic History* 16 (Spring 1997): 3–44.

61. Martínez interview; A. Lunetta interview. On the similarities between the Mexican and Sicilian languages, see Philip A. Buscemi, "The Sicilian Immigrant and His Language Problems," *Sociology and Social Research* 7 (November–December 1927): 137–43.

62. Olive Kirschner, "The Italian in Los Angeles" (MA thesis, University of Southern California, 1920), 48. See also Carey McWilliams, *North from Mexico: The Spanish-Speaking People of the United States* (Westport, Conn.: Praeger, 1990), 188–205; González, *Culture of Empire*, 1–12.

63. John A. Guirbino, "Things Remembered: A Treasure Chest of Memories," 33–35, 1987, Unpublished Manuscript, CPL.

Chapter 3: *Saloons, Pool Halls, and Bootlegging*

1. "Mexican Is Held under Bonds for Serious Charges," *Corona Independent,* February 7, 1929, 1.

2. U.S. Census Bureau, Department of Commerce and Labor, *13th–14th Census of the United States, 1910–1920,* Population Bulletin, City of Corona (Washington, D.C.: U.S. Government Printing Office). On Mexican working-class masculinity, see Maxine Baca Zinn, "Chicano Men and Masculinity," *Journal of Ethnic Studies* 10 (1982): 29–44; Pierrette Hondagneu-Sotelo, "Gender Displays and Men's Power: The 'New Man' and the Mexican Immigrant Man," in *Theorizing Masculinities,* ed. Harry Boyd and Michael Kaufman (Thousand Oaks, Calif.: Sage, 1994), 200–217; Lionel Cantu, "Entre Hombres/Between Men: Latino Masculinities and Homosexualities," in *Gay Masculinities,* ed. Peter Nard (Thousand Oaks, Calif.: Sage, 2000), 224–43.

3. Peter Way, "Rough Humors and Ardent Spirits: The Rough Culture of Canal Construction Laborers," *Journal of American History* 79 (March 1993): 1403.

4. J. D. Culbertson, interview by A. D. Shamel, 1918, transcript, p. 3, A. D. Shamel Papers, Special Collections. UCR.

5. Mary Murphy, *Mining Cultures: Men, Women, and Leisure in Butte, 1914–41* (Urbana: University of Illinois Press, 1997), chap. 2; Paul Michel Taillon, "'What We Want Is Good, Sober Men': Masculinity, Respectability, and Temperance in the Railroad Brotherhoods, 1870–1910," *Journal of Social History* 36 (2002): 319–38.

6. Oscar Osburn Winther, "The Colony System of Southern California," *Agricultural History* 27 (July 1953): 99–100; Michael Belknap, "The Era of the Lemon: A History of Santa Paula, California," *California Historical Society Quarterly* 47 (June 1968): 129; Carey McWilliams, *Southern California: An Island on the Land* (Salt Lake City: Peregrine Smith, 1946), 224; Michael James, "The City on the Hill: Temperance, Race, and Class in Turn-of-the-Century Pasadena," *California History* (Winter 2001/2002): 186–203; Dana Bartlett, *The Better City: A Sociological Study of a Modern City* (Los Angeles: Neuner, 1907), 142.

7. Jon M. Kingsdale, "The Poor Man's Club: Social Functions of the Urban Working-Class Saloon," *American Quarterly* 25 (October 1973): 472–89; David Brundage, "The Producing Classes and the Saloon: Denver in the 1880s," *Labor History* 26 (Winter 1985): 29–52; Perry Duis, *The Saloon: Public Drinking in Chicago and Boston, 1880–1920* (Urbana: University of Illinois Press, 1983); Madelon Powers, "The 'Poor Man's Friend': Saloonkeepers, Workers, and the Code of Reciprocity in U.S. Barrooms," *International Labor and Working-Class History* 45 (Spring 1994): 1–15.

8. Roy Rosenzweig, *Eight Hours for What We Will: Workers and Leisure in an Industrial City, 1870–1920* (Cambridge: Cambridge University Press, 1983), 64.

9. Kenneth Rose, "'Dry' Los Angeles and Its Liquor Problems, 1924," *Southern California Quarterly* 69 (1987): 51–74; McWilliams, *Southern California,* 157; Bartlett, *The Better City,* 131–45; K. Austin Kerr, *Organized for Prohibition: A New History of the Anti-Saloon League* (New Haven, Conn.: Yale University Press, 1985), chap. 3.

10. Bartlett, *The Better City,* 140–41; "Housing the Employees of California's Citrus Ranches," *California Citrograph,* February 1918, 71; Marlou Belyea, "The

Joy Ride and the Silver Screen: Commercial Leisure, Delinquency and Play Reform in Los Angeles, 1900–1980" (PhD diss., Brandeis University, 1983), 33–37.

11. William McEuen, "A Survey of the Mexicans in Los Angeles" (MA Thesis, University of California, 1914), 83; Emory Bogardus, *Essentials of Americanization* (Los Angeles: University of Southern California Press, 1919), 181.

12. "How It Works in Corona," *Corona Independent*, January 11, 1902, 3; Joyce Carter Vickery, *Defending Eden: New Mexican Pioneers in Southern California, 1830–1890* (Riverside, Calif.: Riverside Museum Press, 1977), 84–85; Powers, "The 'Poor Man's Friend,'" 1.

13. "Communicated," *Corona Courier*, March 14, 1908, 1; "Corona Will Be a Dry Town," *Corona Independent*, December 22, 1900, 2; "County Adopts New Prohibition Ordinance," *Corona Independent*, March 10, 1908, 1; "Saloon Question Hot in Early Corona," *Corona Independent*, May 4, 1961, 5. San Bernardino was the only inland valley town to remain wet while the rest went dry. Sanford V. Smith, "A History of the First Baptist Church of Riverside, California, with Particular Reference to Its Relation to the Community" (MA thesis, University of Southern California, 1950), 51–69, 85–86.

14. Meeting Minutes, 23, January 12, 1912, Corona City Council, Clerk's Office, Corona City Hall, Corona, California; "Mexicans Paid Fines for Card Gambling," *Corona Independent*, April 4, 1912, 1.

15. "Blind-Piggers to Get Theirs," *Corona Courier*, March 21, 1912, 2; "Mexicans and Booze Can't Mix," *Corona Courier*, December 19, 1913, 1.

16. Meeting Minutes, 14, December 22, 1913, Corona City Council, Clerk's Office, Corona City Hall, Corona, California; "Less Shooting in Corona Now," *Corona Independent*, October 2, 1913, 1; "A Need of Legislation," *Corona Independent*, October 21, 1913, 1; "City Marshall Murdered Early This A.M.," *Corona Independent*, December 22, 1913, 1; "Offers Good Suggestion," *Corona Independent*, December 25, 1913, 1; "Italian Has a Few Words on the Local Situation," *Corona Independent*, January 12, 1914.

17. Meeting Minutes, 32, June 9, 1914, Corona City Council, Clerk's Office, Corona City Hall, Corona, California; "Costs Money to Pull Trigger," *Corona Courier*, April 17, 1913; "A Need of Legislation," *Corona Independent*, October 21, 1913, 1; "Mexican Loses at His Own Game," *Corona Independent*, February 11, 1914, 1; Gunther Peck, *Reinventing Free Labor: Padrones and Immigrant Workers in the North American West, 1880–1930* (Cambridge: Cambridge University Press, 2000), 141–42.

18. "Saturday Night Disturbance," *Corona Courier*, March 27, 1913, 1; "Cops Raid Houses in Mexican's Colony," *Corona Independent*, October 27, 1924, 1; "Mexicans Fined, Given 'Floaters,'" *Corona Independent*, March 8, 1924, 1. On the Emerson Hotel, see Iris Hayward, "A House That Was More Than a Home," *Press-Enterprise*, May 3, 1970, B4. Ann R. Gabbert, "Prostitution and Moral Reform in the Borderlands: El Paso, 1890–1920," *Journal of the History of Sexuality* 12 (October 2003): 575–604; Mark Wild "Red Light Kaleidoscope Prostitution and Ethnoracial Relations in Los Angeles, 1880–1940," *Journal of Urban History* 28 (September 2002): 720–742.

19. "Mexicans Attack Woman As She Leaves for Neighbor's," *Corona Independent*, December 8, 1925, 1; "Mexican Slays Friend, Shoots Former Wife; Makes Good His Escape," *Corona Independent*, July 23, 1928, 1; "Mexican Killed Rival for Hand of Local Woman," *Corona Independent*, January 28, 1930,

3. On male violence against working-class women, see Christine Stansell, *City of Women: Sex and Class in New York, 1789–1860* (Urbana: University of Illinois Press, 1987), 78–83.

20. *State of California v. Vasquez,* No. 17593, 23, January 10, 1928, Court Records Office, Superior Court of County of Riverside, Riverside, California.

21. On pool rooms, see Howard Chudacoff, *The Age of the Bachelor: Creating an American Subculture* (Princeton, N.J.: Princeton University Press, 1999), 115–25.

22. Ray Delgadillo, interview with the author, June 25, 2001, audiotape (in author's possession).

23. Ibid.; Simon Ludwig Treff, "The Education of Mexican Children in Orange County" (MA thesis, University of Southern California, 1934), 16.

24. Mary Lanigan, "Second Generation Mexicans in Belvedere" (MA thesis, University of Southern California, 1932), 59–60; Kathryn Camp, "Study of the Mexican Population in Imperial Valley, California," March 31–April 9, 1926, Box 40, Paul Taylor Papers, Bancroft Library, University of Berkeley, California.

25. Meeting Minutes, 34, May 12, 1914, Corona City Council Minutes, Clerk's Office, Corona, California; Meeting Minutes, 67, February 23, 1916, Clerk's Office, Corona City Hall, Corona, California; Arnold Roth, "Sunday 'Blue Laws' and the California State Supreme Court," *Southern California Quarterly* 55(9) (1973): 43–47.

26. "Translation of Circular Distributed in Corona Pool Halls," Folder 1, "Labor," Box 5, OHOAC. On IWW unionization efforts in California, see Cletus Daniel, *Bitter Harvest: A History of California Farmworkers, 1870–1941* (Berkeley: University of California Press, 1981), 71–104; Hyman Weintraub, "The IWW in California: 1905–1931" (MA thesis, University of California, Los Angeles, 1947), 84–98. On the IWW in the citrus industry, see Nelson Van Valen, "The Bolsheviki and the Orange Growers," *Pacific Historical Review* 52 (February 1953): 39–50; "Agitators Causing Trouble among Orange Pickers in South," *California Citrograph,* March 1919, 129.

27. "A Strong Appeal for White Labor," *Corona Independent,* January 10, 1916; "Twelve White Men Arrive on Corona Lemon Co. Job," *Corona Independent,* March 6, 1917, 1.

28. "Mexicans to Join a Labor Union at Once," *Corona Independent,* April 6, 1917, 1. "Mexican Unrest without Reason," *Corona Independent,* April 14, 1917, 1.

29. Meeting Minutes, March 22, 1917, and March 27, 1917, Box 1, Queen Colony Fruit Exchange, OHOAC.

30. Meeting Minutes, March 27, 1917, Box 1, Queen Colony Fruit Exchange, OHOAC; "Pickers Strike a Thing of the Past," *Corona Independent,* February 21, 1920, 1. The pool hall became a battleground between police authorities and labor organizers during the 1928 cantaloupe strike in Imperial Valley; see Paul S. Taylor, *Mexican Labor in the United States: Imperial Valley* (Berkeley: University of California Press, 1928), 48; Charles Wollenberg, "Huelga 1928 Style: The Imperial Valley Cantaloupe Workers' Strike," *Pacific Historical Review* 38 (February 1969): 45–58.

31. "Fails to Salute Flag; Goes to Jail," *Corona Independent,* September 30, 1918, 1; "Mexican Draws 60 Day Sentence in Court Today," *Corona Independent,* October 1, 1918, 4.

32. McWilliams, *Southern California*, 224; "W.C.T.U.," *South Riverside Bee*, April 15, 1893, 2; "Corona's Early Days Recalled," *Corona Independent*, April 1, 1927, 3.

33. Thomas Pegram, *Battling Demon Rum: The Struggle for a Dry America* (Chicago: Ivan Dee, 1998), 1–23; Jack Blocker, *Retreat from Reform: The Prohibition Movement in the United States, 1890–1913* (Westport, Conn.: Greenwood, 1976), 23–56.

34. "Delegates Vote Aid to Wright Act," *Los Angeles Times*, April 30, 1922, B3; "Woman Holds Queer Meeting in Our Gutters," *Corona Courier*, May 5, 1916, 2. Rose, "'Dry' Los Angeles," 62–63; Women's Christian Temperance Union of Southern California, *Annual Report, 1919* (Los Angeles, 1920); Gilman Ostrander, *The Prohibition Movement in California, 1848–1933* (Berkeley: University of California Press, 1975); Wendell Harmon, "A History of the Prohibition Movement in California" (PhD diss., University of California, Los Angeles, 1955), chap 5.

35. Stella J. Platt, "History of the Women's Improvement Club," 3, 1912, Typescript, Folder 35, Box 1, Women's Improvement Club Collection, CPL [hereafter WICC]; "Resolution in Support of the Wright Act," Meeting Minutes, May 19, 1922, Box 1, WICC.

36. Samuel Ortegon, "Religious Thought and Practice among Mexican Baptists of the U.S., 1900–1947" (PhD diss., University of Southern California, 1950), 69–70; "High Class Citizenship Demands Church and Social Features of Life; All Provided for in Corona," *Corona Independent*, November 11, 1920, 6. Mexicans also joined the temperance movement, sometimes creating their own organizations; see Mario García, *Desert Immigrants: The Mexicans of El Paso* (New Haven, Conn.: Yale University Press, 1981), 221.

37. Don Francisco, "Increasing the Consumption of Citrus Fruits," *California Citrus Institute*, May 1, 1921, 114–15; Don Francisco, "A Look Ahead at Lemons," *California Citrograph*, April 1918; Josephine Jacobs, "Sunkist Advertising" (PhD diss., University of California, Los Angeles, 1966), 103. See also W. J. Rorabaugh, "Beer, Lemonade and Propriety in the Gilded Age," in *Dining in America, 1850–1900*, ed. Kathryn Grover (Amherst: University of Massachusetts Press, 1987), 24–46.

38. "No More Booze for Corona," *Corona Independent*, October 13, 1916; "Corona against All Wine Making," *Corona Independent*, October 6, 1919, 1; "Bone Dry Ordinance Is Upheld in Higher Courts," *Corona Independent*, October 24, 1918, 1. After the passage of the Eighteenth Amendment and the Volstead Act, the Bureau of Internal Revenue issued a ruling that held that fruit juices and cider, even though they contained more than 0.5 percent alcohol, could be manufactured in the home in quantities up to two hundred gallons per year. The line between "nonintoxicating" and "intoxicating" homemade wines was a tenuous one, and agents seldom inspected private homes for fruit juices. Nevertheless, these rulings brought relief to the California winemakers who previously had feared their own demise under Prohibition. See John Meers, "The California Wine and Grape Industry and Prohibition," *California Historical Society Quarterly* 46 (March 1967): 19–32.

39. Alma Herman, "WCTU Starts Anew," *Corona Independent*, April 27, 1965, 1; Fred Eldridge and Stanley Reynolds, *Corona, California, Commentaries* (Corona: Sinclair Printing, 1986), 52; Joyce Vickery, "Prohibition in a Dry Town: Some Contending Forces," *Riverside County Historical Quarterly* 2 (1980): 18–24.

40. Clifford James Walker, *One Eye Closed, the Other Red: The California Bootlegging Years* (Barstow, Calif.: Back Door Publishing, 1999), 44.

41. Refugio Lopez, Application for Probation, No. 17455, 1, November 22, 1927, Court Records Office, Superior Court of County of Riverside, Riverside, California. Newspaper reports listed Samuel Feliz, E. Vasquez, Francisco Hernandez, Refugio Lopez, Jesus Yxta, and Juan Maris for Wright Act violations. "Mexican on Liquor Charges Is Re-Arrested," *Corona Independent*, May 7, 1929, 1; "Arestado Bago Quejas de Licor," *Revista de Corona*, May 10, 1929, 5; Walker, *One Eye Closed, the Other Red*, 458–59.

42. Victor Villaseñor, *Rain of Gold* (New York: Dell, 1991), 288, 485.

43. "Dry Squads Land Man and Wife in Second of Raids," *Corona Independent*, August 4, 1918, 1; "Six Months Time Given," *Corona Courier*, July 7, 1928, 3; *State of California v. Carmen Ayala*, No. 18233, June 21, 1928, Court Records Office, Superior Court of County of Riverside, Riverside, California; Manuel Gamio, *The Life Story of the Mexican Immigrant* (Chicago: University of Chicago Press, 1931), 102–3. On female bootleggers, see Murphy, *Mining Cultures*, chap. 2; Julia Kirk Blackwelder, *Women of the Depression: Caste and Culture in San Antonio, 1929–1939* (College Station: Texas A&M University Press, 1984), 158–61.

44. "Mexican Immigration," *Transactions: The Commonwealth* 21 (1926): 5–6; "Sixty Percent of Arrests Are among Mexicans," *Corona Independent*, January 15, 1929, 1; Richard Hadley, "An Analysis of the Southern California Woman's Christian Temperance Union, 1920–1938, As an Expression of Progressivism" (MA thesis, University of Southern California, 1970), 21–58; Gamio, *The Life Story of the Mexican Immigrant*, 71–75; Walker, *One Eye Closed, the Other Red*, 198–99; Oscar Martínez, *Border Boom Town: Ciudad Juarez since 1848* (Austin: University of Texas Press, 1978), 57–59, 78–87; Clifford Alan Perkins, *Border Patrol: With the U.S. Immigration Service on the Mexican Boundary, 1910–54* (El Paso: Texas Western Press, 1978), 83–88. On the racial profiling of Mexican bootleggers, see Kelly Lytle Hernández, "Entangling Bodies and Borders: Racial Profiling and the United States Border Patrol, 1924–1955" (PhD diss., University of California, Los Angeles, 2002), 18–42.

45. "Mexicans Cause Most Trouble to Law Officers," *Corona Independent*, January 14, 1929; Robert O'Brien, *Survey on Mexicans and Crime in Southern California* (Claremont, Calif.: Lawson Roberts, 1927), 5; Walker, *One Eye Closed, the Other Red*, 458–59.

46. "Dry Squad Raids Net Four; Other Complaints Soon," *Corona Independent*, July 29, 1929, 1; "Sensations May Be Expected Here," *Riverside Enterprise*, August 1, 1929; "So the People May Know," *Corona Independent*, August 3, 1929, 1; "Five Boys Tell Court of Liquor Purchases as Witnesses Today," *Corona Independent*, August 22, 1929, 1; "Coronans Guilty in Liquor Cases; Plead for Mercy," *Corona Independent*, September 27, 1929, 1; *California v. Pete De George*, 35, No. 19857, August 9, 1929, Court Records Office, Superior Court of County of Riverside, Riverside, California; *California v. Sam Feliz*, 45, No. 16166, December 13, 1929, Court Records Office, Superior Court of County of Riverside, Riverside, California.

47. "Orange Thief Is Fined in Court," *Corona Independent*, February 1, 1928, 1; "Orange Thieves Stealing Fruit in Local Groves," *Corona Courier*, January 11, 1929, 3; "What Is a Fruit Thief?" *Corona Independent*, January 23, 1929, 1.

48. Frances Martínez interview. Gary Mormino found a similar pattern of police connections among Italian American bootleggers, see his *Immigrants on the Hill: Italian Americans in St. Louis, 1882–1982* (Columbia, Missouri: University of Missouri Press, 2002), 133.

49. "Fight Gun Battle with Rum-Runners," *New York Times*, April 5, 1931, C3.

Chapter 4: Churches, Movie Theaters, and Cinco de Mayo Fiestas

1. Frances Martínez, interview by the author, July 14, 1999, audiotape (in author's possession).

2. For a discussion of domestic ideology and working-class women, see Alice Kessler-Harris, *Out to Work: A History of Wage-Earning Women in the United States* (New York: Oxford University Press, 1982), 45–72; Christine Stansell, *City of Women: Sex and Class in New York, 1789–1860* (Urbana: University of Illinois Press, 1987), 19–37.

3. "Foothill Ranch," Typescript, Box 2, Folder "Corona Foothill Lemon Company," OHOAC, CPL; "Mrs. Lester Hampton Was a Teenager Hayrider," *Corona Independent*, July 19, 1967, 3; "Ice Cream and Oak Trees Accentuate 80 Years of Memories," *Press-Enterprise*, June 9, 1979; "Corona Mexican Woman Has Wonderful Flower Garden," *Corona Independent*, May 31, 1928, 4; "Corona Mexicans Are Good Gardeners," *Corona Independent*, May 17, 1928, 5.

4. On Americanization efforts aimed at Mexican women, see George Sánchez, "Go After the Women: Americanization and the Mexican Immigrant Woman, 1915–1929," in *Unequal Sisters: A Multicultural Reader in U.S. Women's History*, ed. Ellen DuBois and Vicki Ruiz (New York: Routledge, 1990), 250–63; Vicki Ruiz, *From Out of the Shadows: Mexican Women in Twentieth-Century America* (New York: Oxford University Press, 1998), chap. 2; Sarah Deutsch, *No Separate Refuge: Culture, Class, and Gender on an Anglo-Hispanic Frontier in the American Southwest, 1880–1940* (New York: Oxford University Press, 1987), 63–86; Gilbert G. González, *Labor and Community: Mexican Citrus Worker Villages in a Southern California County, 1900–1950* (Urbana: University of Illinois Press, 1994), chap. 5.

5. "Washington School to Give Room for Americanization," *Corona Courier*, October 9, 1925, 1; Meeting Minutes, 2, 1931–1932, Folder "Corona Settlement House," Box 3, WICC; Catherine Joy Mattocks, "Settlement House of Corona," Unpublished Manuscript, Folder "Corona Settlement House," CPL; "Settlement House Committees Have Meeting," *Corona Independent*, May 11, 1921; "Settlement House Serves Many with 'Cast Offs,'" *Corona Independent*, June 26, 1934, 2; "Corona Woman's Improvement Club One of the Most Important Groups in the Community," *Corona Independent*, May 4, 1961, C7.

6. "Corona Hospital History," Typescript, 15, June 1959, Folder "Corona Hospitals," CPL; "Early Rx: Town Doctor, Nurse," *Corona Independent*, May 1, 1986, 22; "Mexican Babies Keep Up State's High Birth Rate," *Corona Independent*, December 24–25, 1930, 1.

7. Jay Dolan and Gilberto M. Hinojosa, eds., *Mexican Americans and the Catholic Church, 1900–1965* (Notre Dame, Ind.: University of Notre Dame

Press, 1994); Timothy Matovina and Gary Riebe-Estrella, eds., *Horizons of the Sacred: Mexican Traditions in U.S. Catholicism* (Ithaca, N.Y.: Cornell University Press, 2002); Roberto Treviño, "La Fe: Catholicism and Mexican Americans in Houston, 1911–1972" (PhD diss., Stanford University, 1993).

8. Bruce Harley, *Centennial History of the Catholic Church in Riverside County, 1886–1986* (San Bernardino: Diocese of San Bernardino, 1987), 1–15; "Catholic Parish Founded in '96," *Corona Independent*, Golden Jubilee Edition, April 27, 1936, 1.

9. Villa interview.

10. On racial and linguistic barriers to Catholic Church attendance, see Alberto Pulido, "Searching for the Sacred: Conflict and Struggle for Mexican Catholics in the Roman Catholic Diocese of San Diego, 1936–1941," *Latino Studies Journal* 5 (September 1994): 37–59; Alberto Carrillo, "The Sociological Failure of the Catholic Church towards the Chicano," *Journal of Mexican American Studies* 1 (Winter 1970): 78–80.

11. Villa interview; Harley, *Centennial History of the Catholic Church in Riverside County*, 14.

12. Martínez interview. On Mexican women as "pillars of the church," see Mary Pardo, *Mexican American Women Activists: Identity and Resistance in Two Los Angeles Communities* (Philadelphia: Temple University Press, 1998), 173–78.

13. Martínez interview.

14. "Gran Jamaica El Proximo Domingo," La Sección Mexicana De Corona, *Corona Daily Independent*, July 10, 1949, 10; Margaret Muñoz, interview by the author, August 2, 2000, audiotape (in author's possession); Jessie Hayden, "La Habra Experiment in Mexican Social Education" (MA thesis, Claremont Colleges, 1934), 32; Roberto Treviño, "In Their Own Way: Parish Funding and Mexican-American Ethnicity in Catholic Houston, 1911–1972," *Latino Studies* 5 (September 1994): 95–98.

15. "Mexican Christmas Customs Portrayed," *Corona Independent*, December 13–14, 1926, 1.

16. "Hold Mexican for Delinquency of Girl," *Corona Independent*, June 24, 1924, 5; Hayden, "La Habra Experiment," 85. On conflicts within Mexican families over courtship and marriage, see Mary Odem, *Delinquent Daughters: Protecting and Policing Adolescent Female Sexuality in the United States, 1885–1920* (Chapel Hill: University of North Carolina Press, 1995), 157–84; Douglas Monroy, *Rebirth: Mexican Los Angeles from the Great Migration to the Great Depression* (Berkeley: University of California Press, 1999), 183–88.

17. For a discussion of Protestant activity in U.S. Mexican communities, see Rodney W. Roudy, "The Mexican in Our Midst," *Missionary Review of the World* (May 1921): 366; R. Douglas Brackenridge and Francisco O. García-Treto, *Iglesia Presbiteriana: A History of Presbyterians and Mexican Americans in the Southwest* (San Antonio: Trinity University Press, 1974); Justo González, ed., *Each in Our Own Tongue: A History of Hispanic United Methodism* (Nashville: Abingdon, 1991); Clifton Holland, *The Religious Dimension in Hispanic Los Angeles: A Protestant Case Study* (South Pasadena, Calif.: William Carey Library, 1974); Gastón Espinoza, "Borderland Religion: Los Angeles and the Origins of the Latino Pentecostal Movement in the U.S., Mexico, and Puerto Rico, 1900–1945" (PhD diss., University of California, Santa Barbara, 1999).

18. Between 1918 and 1929, eleven Mexican Baptist churches and twenty-four missions were established in Southern California. Holland, *The Religious Dimension in Hispanic Los Angeles,* 290–328.

19. Mrs. L. E. Troyer, *The Sovereignty of the Holy Spirit* (Los Angeles: Students Benefit Publishing, 1934), 35–37; Holland, *The Religious Dimension in Hispanic Los Angeles,* 296; "Mexican Baptist Group Dates from 1911," *Corona Independent,* April 27, 1936, 4. On the term "pious paternalism," see Espinoza, "Borderland Religion," 39.

20. Ruth and Cecil Henson, "The Ninety Fifth Anniversary of Corona First Baptist Church, 1891–1986," 5, Typescript, n.d., Folder "Corona Churches," CPL; "Mexican Baptist Church Dedicated," *Corona Independent,* January 19, 1920, 2; "Reaching Mexicans in the United States," *Missionary Review of the World* (January 1927): 51–52.

21. "Mexican Baptist Church Dedicated," *Corona Independent,* January 19, 1920, 2; "Reception Is Held for Pastor at Mission," *Corona Independent,* July 6, 1923. Enríquez interview. On Mexican Baptist ministers, see Ortegon, "Religious Thought and Practice among Mexican Baptists of the United States," 214–15.

22. "Mexican Mission Finishes Third Week at Picnic," *Corona Independent,* July 31, 1925, 1; "New Pastor Here Is Ordained in Mission Church," *Corona Independent,* January 28, 1928, 3; "Many Registered at Mission School," *Corona Independent,* June 30, 1917; Enríquez interview.

23. Enríquez interview. For a study that examines how women converted their Catholic husbands to Protestantism so they might stop drinking and committing destructive forms of masculine behavior, see Elizabeth Brusco, *The Reformation of Machismo: Evangelical Conversion and Gender in Colombia* (Austin: University of Texas Press, 1995).

24. On working-class women and the movies, see Elizabeth Ewen, "City Lights: Immigrant Women and the Rise of the Movies," *Signs* 5 (1980): 45–65; Kathy Peiss, *Cheap Amusements: Working Women and Leisure in Turn-of-the-Century New York* (Philadelphia: Temple University Press, 1994), 142–62; Lary May, *Screening Out of the Past: The Birth of Mass Culture and the Motion Picture Industry* (Chicago: University of Chicago Press, 1980), 43–59; Lauren Rabinovitz, *For the Love of Pleasure: Women, Movies and Culture in Turn-of-the-Century Chicago* (Chicago: University of Chicago Press, 1998), 105–36; Nan Enstad, *Ladies of Labor, Girls of Adventure: Working Women, Popular Culture, and Labor Politics at the Turn of the Twentieth Century* (New York: Columbia University Press, 1999), 161–200. On Mexican moviegoers, see Vicki Ruiz, "'Star Struck': Acculturation, Adolescence, and the Mexican American Woman, 1920–1950," in *Building with Our Hands: New Directions in Chicana Studies,* ed. Adela de la Torre and Beatriz Pesquera (Berkeley: University of California Press, 1990), 109–29; George J. Sánchez, *Becoming Mexican American: Ethnicity, Culture and Identity in Chicano Los Angeles, 1900–1945* (New York: Oxford University Press, 1993), 173–74; Monroy, *Rebirth,* 165–83; Charles Ramirez Berg, "Colonialism and Movies in Southern California, 1910–1934," *Aztlan* 28 (Spring 2003): 1–23; Jan Olsson, "Hollywood's First Spectators: Notes on Ethnic Nickelodeon Audiences in Los Angeles," *Aztlan* 26 (Spring 2001): 181–93.

25. A. Rodríguez interview; Ramírez interview; Iris Hayward, "Early Day Theatergoers Fondly Recall 10 Cent Matinee," *Press-Enterprise*, September 1, 1978, B2.

26. "Coronans Will See 'The Bad Man' Tomorrow," *Corona Independent*, December 27, 1924, 1. On the early film portrayals of Mexicans, see Blaine Lamb, "The Convenient Villain: The Early Cinema Views of the Mexican-American," *Journal of the West* 14 (October 1975): 75–81; Helen Delpar, "Goodbye to the 'Greaser': Mexico, the MPPDA, and Derogatory Films, 1922–1926," *Journal of Popular Film & Television* 12 (1984): 34–41.

27. McEuen, "A Survey of the Mexicans in Los Angeles," 70; Rosalie Fowler, "Motion Picture Shows and School Girls," *Journal of Applied Sociology* 7 (November–December 1922): 76–83; Roy F. Woodbury, "Children and Movies," *Survey* (May 15, 1929): 253–54; Paul Crawford, "Movie Habits and Attitudes of the Under-Privileged Boys of the All Nations Area in Los Angeles" (MA thesis, University of Southern California, 1934), 85.

28. "Prize Fight Pictures Are Prohibited," *Corona Independent*, July 14, 1910, 1; Meeting Minutes, 14, November 9, 1917, Corona City Council, Clerk's Office, Corona City Hall, Corona, California; Alison Parker, "Mothering the Movies: Women Reformers and Popular Culture," in *Movie Censorship and American Culture*, ed. Francis G. Couvares (Washington, D.C.: Smithsonian Institution Press, 1996), 73–96.

29. "Club Members Hear Social Service Worker Tell of Needs," *Corona Independent*, February 9, 1921, 1; Meeting Minutes, 45, May 17, 1921, Folder "Civic Section," Box 5, WICC.

30. T. Cruz interview.

31. "New Theatre Is Being Built by J. Cruz on Main St.," *Corona Independent*, April 16, 1926, 1; "Mexican Theatre Completed with Dedication Tonight," *Corona Independent*, July 28, 1926, 4; *Corona City Directory*, 1927, 7–11. Manuel Cruz, interview by the author, January 14, 1998, audiotape C-104, Oral History Collection, CPL.

32. Enríquez interview; "El Charro del Zarape Rojo at Teatro Chapultepec," *Corona Independent*, August 2, 1926, 1; "Mexican Theatre Completed with Dedication Tonight," *Corona Independent*, July 28, 1926, 8; Nicolas Kanellos, *A History of Hispanic Theatre in the United States: Origins to 1940* (Austin: University of Texas Press, 1990), 17–70.

33. Ruiz, "Star Struck," 109–29; Rena Blanche Peek, "The Religious and Social Attitudes of the Mexican Girls of the Constituency of the All Nations Foundation in Los Angeles" (MA thesis, University of Southern California, 1929), 40–50.

34. Ramírez interview.

35. Viola Rodríguez is quoted in "Corona Building Falling to Mall, and with It Memories of Another Day," *Press-Enterprise*, January 13, 1970, B3.

36. Muñoz interview; Mary Lanigan, "Second Generation Mexicans in Belvedere" (MA thesis, University of Southern California, 1932), 56; Margaret Santos, interview by author, March 16, 1998, audiotape C-096, Oral History Collection, CPL.

37. Martínez interview; "Club Feminino Es Comenzado," *Revista De Corona*, March 8, 1929, 8. On Mexican women organizations, see Emma Perez, *The*

Decolonial Imaginary: Writing Chicanas into History (Bloomington: University of Indiana Press, 1999), 84–98; Cynthia Orozco, "Beyond Machismo, La Familia, and Ladies Auxiliaries: A Historiography of Mexican Origin Women's Participation in Voluntary Associations and Politics in the United States, 1870–1990," *Perspectives in Mexican American Studies* 5 (1995): 1–25.

38. "Corona Theatre Opening Is Outstanding," *Corona Independent,* August 30, 1929, 1; Charles Ellison, "Vista de Corona," *Corona Independent,* March 15, 1937, 3; Charles Ellison, "Vista de Corona," *Corona Independent,* March 25, 1937, 5; Gloria Scott, "Corona Theater: The Landmark Building," 23, August 1987, Typescript, Folder "Corona Theater," CPL.

39. Roberto Cabello-Argandoña, *A Brief History of Cinco de Mayo* (Encino: Floricanto Press, 1993); Laurie Kay Sommers, "Symbol and Style in Cinco de Mayo," *Journal of American Folklore* 98 (1985): 476–82; Richard Griswold del Castillo, *The Los Angeles Barrio, 1850–1890* (Berkeley: University of California Press, 1919); Benedict Anderson, *Imagined Communities: Reflections on the Origin and Spread of Nationalism* (New York: Verso, 1983), 1–13.

40. "Local Celebration of Mexicans Well Attended," *Corona Independent,* May 5, 1919, 1; "Mexicans Have Active Groups," *Corona Independent,* May 4, 1961, C15; "La Comision Was Once Leading Latin-American Group in Corona," *Corona Independent,* May 4, 1961, C14.

41. "Convencion de Comisiónes Honoríficas," *La Opinión,* May 13, 1927, 5; Sánchez, *Becoming Mexican American,* 108–25; Gilbert González, *Mexican Consuls and Labor Organizing: Imperial Politics in the American Southwest* (Austin: University of Texas Press, 1999), 37–81.

42. The theater occasionally performed the play *El 5 de Mayo* as well as *Maximiliano I, emperador de México,* which was performed in Spanish-language theaters throughout the southwestern United States. "Mexican Consul Makes Appeal for Better Cooperation," *Corona Independent,* February 12, 1926; Lisbeth Haas, *Conquests and Historical Identities in California, 1769–1936* (Berkeley: University of California Press, 1995), 142–50.

43. "Cinco de Mayo Es Un Gran Triunfo," *Revista de Corona,* May 10, 1929, 1; "Mexicans Parade in Celebration of Independence," *Corona Independent,* May 4, 1929, 1.

44. "Coronans Asking White Labor Be Given Jobs First," *Corona Independent,* January 15, 1932, 6; "No Local Fiesta for Cinco de Mayo Fete, Old Mexican Holiday," *Corona Independent,* May 4–5, 1934.

45. Howard Pressy, "The Housing and Handling of Mexican Labor at Rancho Sespe," *California Citrograph,* December 1929, 72; "Cinco de Mayo Parade Attracts Huge Crowd," *Corona Independent,* May 5, 1939, 3.

46. Aparicio interview; Onias Acevedo, interview by the author, June 13, 2001, audiotape (in author's possession).

47. A. Rodríguez interview; "Mexican Group Endorses Fiesta," *Corona Independent,* March 30, 1939, 1.

48. M. Cruz interview; Martínez interview; "Enjoyable Event at the Foothill Ranch," *Corona Courier,* March 30, 1931.

49. Teresa Lemus is quoted in "Nostalgia Tugs at Heart of First Queen of Cinco de Mayo," *Corona Independent,* May 4, 1986, 1. On the first Cinco de Mayo queen contest, see "Grand Fiesta for Spanish People Today," *Corona Independent,* May 5, 1923, 1.

50. Emily Delgadillo, interview by author, June 6, 2000, audiotape (in author's possession).

51. Frances Martínez, "Corona As I Remember," *Hispanic Centennial Review, 1898–1986* (Corona: Corona Public Library, 1986), 1.

52. Ruiz, *From Out of the Shadows,* 65–67.

53. Yolanda Tarango, "The Hispanic Woman and Her Role in the Church," *New Theology Review* 3 (November 1990): 58.

Chapter 5: Baseball and Sports Clubs

1. Cortez interview.

2. C. L. R. James, *Beyond a Boundary* (1963; Durham: Duke University Press, 1993), 66.

3. Wallace Thompson, *The Mexican Mind: A Study of National Psychology* (New York: Little, Brown, 1922), 97–100. On the rise of baseball in Mexico, see William Beezley, *Judas at the Jockey Club and Other Episodes of Porfirian Mexico* (Lincoln: University of Nebraska, 1987); Gilbert M. Joseph, "Forging the Regional Pastime: Baseball and Class in Yucatan," in *Sport and Society in Latin America: Diffusion, Dependency, and the Rise of Mass Culture,* ed. Joseph Arbena (Westport, Conn.: Greenwood, 1988), 29–61; Samuel Regalado, *Viva Baseball: Latin Major Leaguers and Their Special Hunger* (Urbana: University of Illinois Press, 1998).

4. George Hodgkin, "Making the Labor Camp Pay," *California Citrograph,* August 1921, 75. On industrial recreation, see Wilma J. Pesavento, "Sport and Recreation in the Pullman Experiment, 1880–1900," *Journal of Sport History* 9 (1982): 38–62; John Schelppi, "'It Pays': John H. Patterson and Industrial Recreation at the National Cash Register Company," *Journal of Sport History* 6 (1979): 20–28.

5. A. G. Spalding, *America's National Game* (New York: American Sports Publishing Company, 1911), 1–5; Howard F. Perry, "The Housing and Handling of Mexican Labor at Rancho Sespe," *California Citrograph,* December 29, 1924, 57; "Rancho Sespi y Hermosa-El Paso Juegan En Sespi Hoy," *La Opinión,* September 16, 1934; "Club Juvenil Figura Para En El Programa," *La Opinión,* June 14, 1933, 5; Hayden, "La Habra Experiment," 20.

6. "Corona Mexican Arrested after Cock Fight Raid," *Corona Independent,* July 13, 1936, 4; Letter to Cecil Forster by Charles C. Teague, June 3, 1930, Microfilm Reel 15, Charles C. Teague Papers, Special Collections, University of California, Los Angeles [hereafter UCLA]. On cockfighting see Jerry García, "The Measure of a Cock: Mexican Cockfighting, Culture and Masculinity," in *I Am Aztlan: The Personal Essay in Chicano Studies,* ed. Chon Noriega and Wendy Belcher (Los Angeles: UCLA Chicano Studies Research Center Press, 2004), 109–40; Charles McCaghy and Arthur G. Neal, "The Fraternity of Cockfighters: Ethnical Embellishments of an Illegal Sport," *Journal of Popular Culture* 8 (Winter 1974): 557–69.

7. Cary Goodman, *Choosing Sides: Playgrounds and Street Life on the Lower East Side* (New York: Schocken, 1979), 33–58; Los Angeles Department of Playgrounds and Recreation, *Annual Report, 1926–27* (Los Angeles: Department of Playground and Recreation, 1927), 20; Emory Bogardus, *The City Boy and His*

Problems: A Survey of Boy Life in Los Angeles (Los Angeles: House of Ralston, 1926), 67–100; Emory Bogardus, *The Mexican in the United States* (Los Angeles: University of Southern California Press, 1934), 59–60; David A. Bridge, "A Study of the Agencies Which Promote Americanization in the Los Angeles City Recreation Center District" (MA thesis, University of Southern California, 1920), 106–108.

8. Katharine Murray, "Mexican Community Service," *Sociology and Social Research* (April 1929): 548. See also "Play for the Mexican Population in Topeka, Kansas," *Playground* 13 (April 1919): 26–27.

9. Cynthia J. Shelton, "The Neighborhood House of San Diego: Settlement Work in the Mexican Community, 1914–1940" (MA thesis, San Diego State University, 1975), 105–9; "La Novena 'Neighborhood House' Gano Campeonato de San Diego," *La Opinión*, May 1, 1932, 3; "Una Novena de Señoritas Debuta Hoy," *La Opinión*, March 1, 1934, 5; Alison M. Wrynn, "Women's Industrial and Recreation League Softball in Southern California, 1930–1950" (MA thesis, California State University, Long Beach, 1989), 40, 66; Susan Cahn, *Coming on Strong: Gender and Sexuality in Twentieth Century Women's Sport* (Cambridge: Cambridge University Press 1994), 142.

10. "Baseball and Racial Harmony in Hawaii," *Sociology and Social Research* (September 10, 1933): 21.

11. "Foothill Takes AFG in Niteball," *Corona Independent*, July 7, 1936, 1; Lorne L. Allmon, *The Story of Samuel B. Hampton and the California Citrus Industry, 1887–1918* (Riverside: Citrus Label Society, July 1994), 1–7; "Foothill Ranch," Typescript, 1925, Box 1, Folder "Corona Foothill Lemon Company," OHOAC.

12. Cortez interview; García interview; Herklerath interview.

13. Zeke Mejia is quoted in a special feature article on the Corona Athletics, Valeria Godines, "Baseball Was the Name of the Game on Weekends," *Press-Enterprise*, June 29, 1996, 20; "Five Mexican Groups Are Operating," *Corona Independent*, April 27, 1936, 6.

14. Workers and managers displayed mutual loyalties that were negotiated and contested; see Gerald Zahavi, *Workers, Managers and Welfare Capitalism: The Shoeworkers and Tanners of Endicott Johnson, 1890–1950* (Urbana: University of Illinois Press, 1988), 605.

15. Frederick Lieb, "Baseball—The Nation's Melting Pot," *Baseball Magazine* 31 (August 1923): 391–93; Samuel Regalado, *Viva Baseball: Latin Major Leaguers and Their Special Hunger* (Urbana: University of Illinois Press, 1998), 36, 50–51, 177.

16. Alan Klein documents the baseball team competitions that crossed back and forth between Laredo, Texas, and Nuevo Laredo, Mexico, in *Baseball on the Border: A Tale of Two Laredos* (Princeton, N.J.: Princeton University Press 1997), 32–65; "Es Probable Que Pronto Este Aqui El Famoso 'San Luis,'" *La Opinión*, June 3, 1930, 6; "Hermosa-El Paso Juega en Hermosillo el 6 y el 7," *La Opinión*, September 28, 1934, 7.

17. "Gran Festiva Prepara La A.D.H.A.," *La Opinión*, July 19, 1927, 5; "El Comite Central Olimpico Mexicano Se Reune En La Ciudad de Mexico Para Pedir La Ayuda De Los Mexicanos Que Vivimos En California," *La Opinión*, May 4, 1932, 7; "Hoy Empieza La Liga De La Asociacion Mexicana," *La Opinión*, December 10, 1933, 3; Douglas Monroy, *Rebirth: Mexican Los Angeles*

from the Great Migration to the Great Depression (Berkeley: University of California Press, 1999), 45–48. On a popular mutualista baseball team, see Albert Camarillo, *Chicanos in a Changing Society: From Mexican Pueblos to American Barrios in Santa Barbara and Southern California, 1848–1930* (Cambridge: Harvard University Press, 1979), 152. On the Oxnard baseball team, see Frank Barajas, "Work and Leisure in La Colonia: Class, Generation, and Interethnic Alliances among Mexicanos in Oxnard, California" (PhD diss., Claremont Graduate University, 2001), 142–44.

18. "Corona Athletics to Enter State Semi-Play," *Corona Independent*, July 19, 1936, 1; "Buen Programa Se Presentara Esta Noche," *Revista de Corona*, March 15, 1929, 8.

19. Mario García, *Memories of Chicano History: Life and Narrative of Bert Corona* (Berkeley: University of California Press, 1994), 85; "Big Boxing Bill for Fistic Fans," *Corona Independent*, July 2, 1928, 1; "Beginning Tuesday No One under 18 Years of Age Allowed," *Corona Independent*, August 17, 1928; "Boxeadores de Corona Se Favorecen El Martes," *Revista de Corona*, March 15, 1929, 7; "Colima Esperado Esta Noche," *Revista de Corona*, February 22, 1929, 8; "El Club Deportivo De Corona Ayuda a Los Compatriotas," *La Opinión*, May 3, 1928, 8; Leon Heredia, "Notas Locales," *Revista de Corona*, February 15, 1929, 8. On boxing and Mexican Americans, see Gregory Rodríguez, "Palaces of Pain—Arenas of Mexican-American Dreams: Boxing and the Formation of Ethnic Mexican Identities in Twentieth Century Los Angeles" (PhD diss., University of California, San Diego, 1999), 23–67.

20. Valeria Godines, "Baseball Was the Name of the Game on Weekends," *Press-Enterprise*, June 29, 1996, 20; Cortez interview; Steven Gelber, "Working at Playing: The Culture of the Workplace and the Rise of Baseball," *Journal of Social History* 5 (1979): 12–15.

21. Fred Eldridge and Stanley Reynolds, *Corona, California, Commentaries* (Corona: Sinclair Printing, 1986), 44–48; Cynthia Alvitre, *Hispanic Centennial Review, 1886–1986* (Corona, Calif.: Corona Public Library, 1986), 1–5; "Derrota a Atleticos de Corona," *La Opinión*, May 12, 1932; "Athletes Defeat Glendale 16–14," *Corona Independent*, January 4, 1933, 5; "Atleticos de Corona Tienen Otra Victoria," *La Opinión*, January 5, 1933; Gilbert Enríquez, "Cara Abierta," *El Imparcial*, August 13, 1949, 1.

22. Valeria Godines, "Baseball Was the Name of the Game on Weekends," *Press-Enterprise*, June 29, 1996, 20.

23. Cortez interview.

24. Delgadillo interview; "Concurso Para Nombrar La Novena," La Sección Mexicana de Corona, *Corona Independent*, April 6, 1949, 8; "Se Formara Una Novena de Muchachas," La Sección Mexicana de Corona, *Corona Independent*, March 11, 1949, 6; "Las Debs Cruzan Sus Bats Con Ontario Hoy En La Noche," La Sección Mexicana de Corona, *Corona Independent*, August 11, 1949.

25. Margaret Zarate, interview by the author, January 7, 2000, audiotape (in author's possession); Annie Bravo, interview by author, September 8, 1999, audiotape (in possession of author). On women softball teams, see Joan Sangster, "The Softball Solution: Female Workers, Male Managers and the Operation of Paternalism at Westclox, 1923–60," *Labour/Le Travail* 32 (Fall 1993): 189–93.

26. Samuel Regalado, "Baseball in the Barrios: The Scene in East Los Angeles since World War II," *Baseball History* 1 (Summer 1986): 57.

27. Simon Ludwig Treff, "The Education of Mexican Children in Orange County" (MA thesis, University of Southern California, 1934), 16; Ed Horner, "A Recreation Director in a Mexican-American Community" (MA thesis, University of California, Los Angeles, 1945), 41–42.

28. "Corona Fete Climaxed," *Los Angeles Times*, May 6, 1936, B2; "Fiesta Dance Closes Jubilee Celebration," *Corona Independent*, May 6, 1936, 5; "Mexican Fiesta Group Thankful," *Corona Independent*, June 6, 1926, 1.

29. George J. Sánchez, *Becoming Mexican American: Ethnicity, Culture and Identity in Chicano Los Angeles, 1900–1945* (New York: Oxford University Press, 1993), 253–69.

30. Jess Uribe, interview by the author, February 20, 1998, audiotape C-097, Oral History Collection, CPL; "Corona Athletics Club's Benefit Dance Saturday," *Corona Independent*, July 10, 1936, 7.

31. Robert E. Copley, *The Tall Mexican: The Life of Hank Aguirre, All Star Pitcher, Businessman, and Humanitarian* (Houston: Piñata Books, 1998), 11; Cynthia J. Wilber, *For the Love of the Game: Baseball Memories from the Men Who Were There* (New York: William Morrow, 1992), 125–31; Gilbert G. González, *Labor and Community: Mexican Citrus Worker Villages in a Southern California County, 1900–1950* (Urbana: University of Illinois Press, 1994), 112–14.

32. Cortez interview; Bobby Perez, interview by author, August 18, 2000, audiotape (in author's possession). "Corona Athletics to Enter State Semi-Pro Play," *Corona Independent*, July 10, 1936; "All Corona Baseball Event Sunday to Be Played at City Park," *Corona Independent*, April 25, 1947; "Cleveland Indians Chief Scout Visits Corona; Seeks Talent," *Corona Independent*, August 11, 1947; "Corona Baseball Stars Signed by Brooklyn Dodgers," *Corona Independent*, June 19, 1950, 1.

33. Bill Cunningham, "Grandstand Grandee," *Collier's* 24 (August 1935): 213; "Las Bandas De Estado Mayor y Jazz de Policia Alegraran Los Juegos," *El Excelsior*, November 25, 1933, 3; "Baile En Honor de Los Almada En El Club Deportivo Chapultepec," *El Excelsior*, December 7, 1933; "U Exito el Homenaje a Melo Almada," *La Opinión*, July 4, 1933, 5; "Almada Honored Today," *Los Angeles Times*, July 23, 1933; Daniel Frio and Marc Onigman, "'Good Field, No Hit': The Image of Latin American Baseball Players in the American Press, 1871–1946," *Revista/Review Interamericana* 2 (Summer 1977): 199–208; Regalado, *Viva Baseball*, 134–46.

34. Cortez interview. "Cortez Wiffs 13 As Athletes Win 22nd of 25 Games," *Corona Independent*, March 7, 1945. On the Mexican Baseball League, see Alan Klein, "Baseball Wars: The Mexican Baseball League and Nationalism in 1946," *Studies in Latin American Popular Culture* 13 (1994): 33–56.

35. Edward Jackson Baur, "Delinquency among Mexican Boys in South Chicago" (MA thesis, University of Chicago, 1938), 131. Frank Ruiz, interview by Gilbert Rivera and Patti Berry, in *Personal Stories from El Monte Communities*, ed. Susan S. Obler (Whittier, Calif.: Rio Hondo Community College, 1976), 92.

36. "Cardinals Defeat Athletics in 12th," *Corona Independent*, April 24, 1939, 5.

37. Michael S. Kimmel, "Baseball and the Reconstitution of American Masculinity, 1880–1920," in *Sport, Men, and the Gender Order*, ed. Michael Mess-

ner and Donald Sabo (Champaign: Human Kinetics Books, 1990), 65–67; Michael Messner, *Power at Play: Sports and the Problem of Masculinity* (Boston: Beacon Press, 1992), 19; Klein, *Baseball on the Border,* chap. 5.

38. R. W. Connell, *Gender and Power: Society, the Person, and Sexual Politics* (Stanford: Stanford University Press, 1987), 1–5

39. Cortez interview; Jess Guerrero, interview by Pat Flores and Jerry Alexander, in *Personal Stories from Pico Rivera,* 30. On Japanese American baseball in Los Angeles, see Yoichi Nagata, "The Pride of Lil' Tokyo: The Los Angeles Nippons Baseball Club, 1926–1941," in *More Than a Game: Sport in the Japanese American Community,* ed. Brian Niiya (Los Angeles: Japanese American Museum, 2000), 100–109. On the Negro Leagues, see Donn Rogosin, *Invisible Men: Life in Baseball's Negro Leagues* (New York: Atheneum, 1983). On Native Americans and sports, see John Bloom, *To Show What an Indian Can Do: Sports at Native American Boarding Schools* (Minneapolis: University of Minnesota Press, 2000).

40. Irene Contreras, interview by author, December 4, 1999, audiotape (in author's possession).

41. "Cubs Ask Sunday Use of City Park Baseball Diamond," *Corona Independent,* August 21, 1946, 52; Uribe interview.

42. Louis Perez Jr., "Between Baseball and Bullfighting: The Quest for Nationality in Cuba, 1868–1898," *Journal of American History* 81 (September 1994): 499.

Chapter 6: *Labor Unionism and the 1941 Strike*

1. Martínez interview.

2. Evan Maxwell, "A Strike's Harvest of Bitterness: Citrus Dispute Took on Aspects of 'Civil War,'" *Los Angeles Times,* January 26, 1975, 1, 4–5; Gilbert G. González, "The Mexican Citrus Picker Union, the Mexican Consulate, and the Orange County Strike of 1936," *Labor History* 35 (Winter 1994): 48–65.

3. On the CIO and Mexican workers, see Zaragosa Vargas, "In the Years of Darkness and Torment: The Early Mexican American Struggle for Civil Rights, 1945–1963," *New Mexico Historical Review* 76 (October 2001): 383–413; Douglas Monroy, *Rebirth: Mexican Los Angeles from the Great Migration to the Great Depression* (Berkeley: University of California Press, 1999), 249–52; Luis Arroyo, "Chicano Participation in Organized Labor: The CIO in Los Angeles, 1938–1950, An Extended Research Note," *Aztlan* 6 (1975): 277–303.

4. Michael Denning, *The Cultural Front: The Laboring of American Culture in the Twentieth Century* (New York: Verso, 1997), 4–21; Mark Naison, "Remaking America: Communists and Liberals in the Popular Front," in *New Studies in the Politics and Culture of U.S. Communism,* ed. Michael E. Brown et al. (New York: Monthly Review Press, 1993), 45–73. On Los Angeles Popular Front groups, see Mario García, *Mexican Americans: Leadership, Ideology and Identity, 1930–1960* (New Haven, Conn.: Yale University Press, 1989), chap. 6; George J. Sánchez, *Becoming Mexican American: Ethnicity, Culture and Identity in Chicano Los Angeles, 1900–1945* (New York: Oxford University Press, 1993), chap 11; Mario García, *Memories of Chicano History: The Life and Narrative of Bert Corona* (Berkeley: University of California Press, 1994); David G.

Gutiérrez, *Walls and Mirrors: Mexican Americans, Mexican Immigrants and the Politics of Ethnicity* (Berkeley: University of California Press,1995), 107–16; and Kenneth Burt, "Latino Empowerment in Los Angeles: Postwar Dreams and Cold War Fears, 1948–1952," *Labor Heritage* 8 (Summer 1996): 6–23.

5. *North Whittier Heights Citrus Association v. National Labor Relations Board*, No. 8819, Federal Reporter, 109 (St. Paul, Minn.: West Publishing, 1940), 75–83; Austin P. Morris, "Agricultural Labor and National Labor Legislation," *California Law Review* 54 (December 1966): 1962–63.

6. "Lemon Men's Club Hears of Various Aspects of Agricultural Labor," *California Citrograph*, November 1937, 32; Stuart M. Jamieson, *Labor Unionism in American Agriculture*, U.S. Department of Labor Bulletin No. 836 (Washington, D.C.: U.S. Government Printing Office, 1945), 40.

7. Vicki L. Ruiz, *Cannery Women and Cannery Lives: Mexican Women, Unionization, and the California Food Processing Industry, 1930–1950* (Albuquerque: University of New Mexico Press, 1987); Robin D. G. Kelley, *Hammer and Hoe: Alabama Communists during the Great Depression* (Chapel Hill: University of North Carolina Press, 1990); Michael Honey, *Southern Labor and Black Civil Rights: Organizing Memphis Workers* (Urbana: University of Illinois Press, 1993); Chris Friday, *Organizing Asian American Labor: The Pacific Coast Canned Salmon Industry, 1870–1942* (Philadelphia: Temple University Press, 1994); Doronty Fujita Rony, *American Workers, Colonial Power: Philippine Seattle and the Transpacific West, 1919–1941* (Berkeley: University of California Press, 2003).

8. *Proceedings*, Third National Convention, UCAPAWA, CIO (1940), 18; Ruiz, *Cannery Women and Cannery Lives*, 41–57; Victor B. Nelson-Cisneros, "UCAPAWA and Chicanos in California: The Farm Worker Period, 1937–1940," *Aztlan* 7 (Fall 1978): 453–74; Devra Weber, *Dark Sweat, White Gold: California Farm Workers, Cotton, and the New Deal* (Berkeley: University of California Press, 1994), 180–99; Dorothy Ray Healey and Maurice Isserman, *California Red: A Life in the American Communist Party* (Urbana: University of Illinois Press, 1993), 65–79.

9. Ruiz, *Cannery Women and Cannery Lives*; Jamieson, *Labor Unionism in American Agriculture*, 168–69, 186–88. On the first CIO citrus union, see "First Citrus Union in San Berdoo-Riverside," *Western Worker*, August 19, 1937, 3. In 1939, San Fernando lemon pickers led a successful strike, winning wage increases and lower rent for company housing. "C.I.O. Demands Lemon Contract," *Los Angeles Times*, August 24, 1938, B3.

10. "District 2 in Drive for 10,000 New Members," *UCAPAWA News*, May 1940, 11; Nelson-Cisneros, "UCAPAWA and Chicanos in California," 469; Proceedings of the Third Convention, UCAPAWA District 2, May 11–14, 1940, Box 3, FTA Collection, Labor Archives and Research Center, San Francisco State University, San Francisco, California.

11. Rudy Ramos, interview by author, February 5, 1998, audiotape C-087, Oral History Collection, CPL; "75 Will Ballot Monday in NLRB Citrus Election," *Corona Independent*, July 20, 1940, 1; "Elections Ordered in Two Citrus Plants," *Corona Independent*, July 5, 1940, 1; "The CIO in Corona," *Citrus Worker News*, July 1940, Folder "Labor Unions," CPL.

12. "Corona Citrus Packing Shed Workers Vote CIO in Labor Board Election," *Newsletter*, July–August 1940, Folder "Committee to Aid Agricultural Work-

ers," 1, FTA Collection, Labor Archives and Research Center, San Francisco State University, San Francisco, California; "The Main Election for Corona," *Corona Independent*, July 18, 1940, 2; "The Stakes Are High," *Corona Independent*, July 19, 1940, 1.

13. "The CIO in Corona," *Citrus Worker News*, July 1940, Folder "Labor Unions," CPL; "C.I.O. Union Wins Bargaining Election," *Corona Independent*, July 22, 1940, 1.

14. "New Picketing Law Introduced before Council," *Corona Independent*, August 7, 1940, 1; Meeting Minutes, September 17, 1937, Box 5, Queen Colony Fruit Exchange, OHOAC.

15. "Pickers Walk off Job; Citrus Strike Looms," *Corona Independent*, February 27, 1941, 1; "40 Jailed in Strike Rioting at Corona," *Riverside Daily Press*, March 22, 1941, 1; "Citrus Employees Hit Council Strike Action," *Corona Independent*, March 19, 1941, 1; Meeting Minutes, February 25, 1941, Corona City Council, City Clerk's Office, Corona City Hall, Corona, California.

16. "Las Tiendas De Raya Son Condenadas," *La Opinión*, March 13, 1941, 1.

17. Ramos interview; "C.I.O. Attempts to Organize Citrus Workers in District," *Arlington Times*, March 14, 1941, 1.

18. José M. Pozos, "Will Any Team Challenge 120?" *UCAPAWA News*, September 1939, 10. On the CIO baseball matches, see "El Equipo CIO Juega Hoy Con Mexico-Nippon," *La Opinión*, June 25, 1939, 1; "Victoria Del CIO Sobre Mexico-Nippon," *La Opinión*, May 27, 1939, 3. During the 1930s, unions and communist-led groups organized sports teams and challenged Jim Crow laws in professional baseball; see Mark Naison, "Lefties and Righties: Communist Party and Sports during the Great Depression," in *Sport in America: New Historical Perspectives*, ed. Donald Spivey (Westport, Conn.: Greenwood, 1985), 129–44.

19. Willits interview; M. Lunetta interview; "Moral Re-Armanent Suggested as Lead to Strike Settlement," *Corona Independent*, March 12, 1941, 1; "Officers Coerce Strikers, Charged," *Riverside Daily Press*, March 17, 1941; "Pickets on Job as Unions Try to Enforce Demands," *Arlington Times*, March 21, 1941, 1.

20. Guirbino, "Things Remembered," 23; Lunetta, "Non Te Scordate Di Mei," 12.

21. Angelo Lunetta, interview by author, June 10, 2001, audiotape (in author's possession).

22. M. Lunetta interview.

23. "Growers to Make Plans to Harvest Fruit," *Riverside Daily Press*, March 15, 1941, 5 (emphasis mine); "Growers to Stick to Open Shop Policy," *Riverside Daily Press*, March 15, 1941, 6; "Riverside Citrus Strikers Battle Associated Farmers Terrorism," *People's World*, March 22, 1941, 3; Martínez interview. The ideology of the "local" was widely used by California growers as a tool to repress labor strikes; see Don Mitchell, "The Scales of Justice: Localist Ideology, Large-Scale Production, and Agricultural Labor's Geography of Resistance in 1930's California," in *Organizing the Landscape: Geographical Perspectives on Labor Unionism*, ed. Andrew Herod (Minneapolis: University of Minnesota Press, 1998), 159–94.

24. "Union Seeks Election in Local Citrus Strike," *Corona Independent*, March 13, 1941, 1, 5; "Growers Blast Union Strike Election Plan," *Corona Independent*, March 14, 1941, 1, 6; "Union Conducts Poll; Growers Hit Tactics," *Corona Independent*, March 15, 1941, 1, 3; "Citrus Ballot Said in Favor of CIO," *Riverside Daily Press*, March 15, 1941, 4.

25. "The CIO in Corona," *Citrus Worker News*, July 1940, 2.

26. Herklerath interview.

27. L. Cruz interview. On subtle acts of resistance waged daily by oppressed people, see Robin D. G. Kelley, "'We Are Not What We Seem': Rethinking Black Working-Class Opposition in the Jim Crow South," *Journal of American History* 80 (June 1993): 111–32.

28. M. Cruz interview.

29. Aparicio interview.

30. M. Cruz interview; "Citrus Strike to Reach Climax Here This Week," *Corona Independent*, March 3, 1941, 2; "Foothill Group Receives Bonus," *Corona Independent*, December 24, 1941, 1.

31. Acevedo interview; Joe Gutierrez, "Strike Grim Chapter of Corona's Past," *Press-Enterprise*, February 4, 1996, B2.

32. "Tent City Will House Strike-breakers Here," *Corona Independent*, May 24, 1941, 3.

33. A. Rodríguez interview. The union negotiation committee was comprised of George Becerra, Heliodoro Medina, Angel Altamirano, Alejandro Muro, Theodore Rasmussen, Alfonso Ortiz, Ralph Smathers, and William Franklin McCarty. "Strikers Move Meeting Center to Home Gardens," *Corona Independent*, March 21, 1941, 1; "Stearns Denies He Has Been Dickering with CIO Group," *Riverside Daily News*, March 12, 1941, 10; "Citrus Packinghouse Workers on Strike," *Riverside Enterprise*, March 7, 1941, 8.

34. Martínez interview.

35. "Woman Arrested during Heckling on Picket Lines," *Corona Independent*, March 11, 1941, 1, 5; "Woman Released in Strike Case," *Corona Independent*, April 2, 1941, 1.

36. "45 Strikers Arrested after Mob Rioting," *Corona Independent*, March 22, 1941, 1; "40 Jailed in Strike Rioting at Corona," *Riverside Daily Press*, March 22, 1941, 1; "Citrus Strike Violence Flares," *Los Angeles Times*, March 22, 1941, C2.

37. "Judge Denies Release of Pickets through Habeas Corpus Writ," *Corona Independent*, March 27, 1941, 1; "Formal Charges Are Filed against Local Strikers," *Corona Independent*, March 26, 1941, 1; Gilson Gray is quoted in "Riverside Citrus Strikers Battle Associated Farmers Terrorism," *People's World*, March 28, 1941, 5.

38. "Workers Give Version of Riot at Citrus Plant," *Corona Independent*, April 30, 1941, 1; "Jury Expected to Take Strike Case by Tonight," *Corona Independent*, May 12, 1941, 1; "Jury Deliberates Fate of Strikers for 24 Hours," *Corona Independent*, May 13, 1941, 1; "Riot Case Dismissed against 27 Strikers," *Corona Independent*, May 17, 1941, 1.

39. *State of California v. Manuel R. Martínez*, No. 33962, 13, 17–19, Court Records Office, Superior Court of County of Riverside, Riverside, California; "Corona Fruit Picker Guilty of Assault," *Riverside Daily Press*, May 28, 1941, 3; "First Testimony Heard in Trial of 45 Strikers," *Corona Independent*, April 29, 1941, 1; "Striker Is Sent to San Quentin," *Corona Independent*, June 10, 1941, 1.

40. "Workers Give Version of Riot at Citrus Plant," *Corona Independent*, April 30, 1941, 1; "Defendants Tell of Strike Fray," *Corona Independent*, May 7, 1941, 1; Martínez interview.

41. Meeting Minutes, May 16, 194, Box 18, LA CIO Council Collection, Urban Archives Center, California State University, Northridge, Northridge, California.

42. Acevedo interview; "Citrus Strike Violence Flares," *Corona Independent,* March 22, 1941, 3.

43. "Tent City Will House Strike-breakers Here," *Corona Independent,* May 24, 1941, 2; "Tent City Provides Citrus Pickers," *Riverside Enterprise,* March 25, 1941, 3. Harry Kaplan is quoted in "46 Face Trial in Mass Terror Drive," *People's World,* April 23, 1941, 2.

44. Healey and Isserman, *California Red,* 75. On the decline of the UCA-PAWA, see Cletus Daniel, *Bitter Harvest: A History of California Farmworkers, 1870–1941* (Berkeley: University of California Press, 1981), 277–28; Victor Nelson-Cisneros, "UCAPAWA and Chicanos in California," 470–73.

45. Vicki Ruiz, *From Out of the Shadows: Mexican Women in Twentieth-Century America* (New York: Oxford University Press, 1998), 72–98; Zaragoza Vargas, "Tejana Radical: Emma Tenayuca and the San Antonio Labor Movement during the Great Depression," *Pacific Historical Review* 67 (1997): 553–80; Margaret Rose, "From the Fields to the Picket Line: Huelga Women and the Boycott, 1965–1975," *Labor History* 31 (Summer 1990): 271–93.

46. U.S. Census Bureau, Department of Commerce and Labor, *16th Census of the United States, 1940,* Population Bulletin, City of Corona (Washington, D.C.: U.S. Government Printing Office, 1943), 343; Matt García, *A World of Its Own: Race, Labor, and Citrus in the Making of Greater Los Angeles* (Chapel Hill: University of North Carolina Press, 2001), 158–59.

47. Packinghouse women mobilized signatures for a petition seeking higher wages. See García, *A World of Its Own,* 170–71.

48. Ruiz, *Cannery Women, Cannery Lives,* 82; "CIO Wins 13 of 29 Citrus Worker Union Elections," *Corona Independent,* April 18, 1945, 1; "Defeats Are Out," *Citrus Organizing Newsletter,* June 1945, 3, Food Tobacco Association Minutes, 1945–1950, Box 4, LA CIO Council Collection, Urban Archives Center, California State University, Northridge, Northridge, California

49. "Ventura Lemon Strikers Put Pickets at Exchange Plant," *Corona Independent,* May 1, 1941, 1; "Cars of Spoiled Lemons Dumped in Huge Piles," *Corona Independent,* May 10, 1941, 1; Charles C. Teague letter to Joy Jameson, May 9, 1941, Box 1, Coll. 137, Reel 10, Charles C. Teague Papers, Special Collections, UCLA; George Stanley, interview by Gloria Scott, November 22, 1982, audiotape C-039, Oral History Collection, CPL; McBane, "The Role of Gender in Citrus Employment," 81.

50. Carey McWilliams to Nelson Rockefeller, October 15, 1941, Folder "Mexican-U.S. International Relations," Box 29, Carey McWilliams Papers 1243, Special Collections, UCLA; Carey McWilliams, *North from Mexico: The Spanish-Speaking People of the United States* (Westport, Conn.: Praeger, 1990), 246–47.

Chapter 7: The Struggle for Civil Rights

1. Acevedo interview. On the life of the Onias "Ace" Acevedo, see Pat Murkland, "Acing Victory: A Former Citrus Worker Wins Election to the Corona City Council," *Press-Enterprise,* October 31, 1999, S7.

2. David Green, *The Containment of Latin America: A History of the Myths and Realities of the Good Neighbor Policy* (Chicago: Quadrangle Books, 1971); Ernest Gruening, "New Deal for Latin America!" *Current History* 45 (January

1934): 466–70; Harvey Levenstein, "Leninists Undone by Leninism: Communism and Unionism in the United States and Mexico, 1935–1939," *Labor History* 22 (Spring 1981): 237–61. On Mexican and U.S. labor activists termed "grassroots Good Neighbors" who helped shaped U.S.-Mexico relations and the treatment of Mexican Americans, see Gigi Peterson, "Grassroots Good Neighbors: Connections between Mexican and U.S. Labor and Civil Rights Activists, 1936–1945" (PhD diss., University of Washington, 1998).

3. Pamphlet, Folder "Southern California Council of Inter-American Affairs," Box 5, Manuel Ruiz Papers, M-295, Special Collections, Stanford University, Stanford, California; Adolf Berle Jr., "Race Discrimination and the Good Neighbor Policy," in *Discrimination and National Welfare*, ed. R. M. MacIver (New York: Harper & Brothers, 1949), 91–98; Carey McWilliams, *North from Mexico: The Spanish-Speaking People of the United States* (Westport, Conn.: Praeger, 1990), 245–48; Gilbert González, "Interamerican and Intercultural Education and the Chicano Community," *Journal of Ethnic Studies* 13 (1985): 31–53.

4. McWilliams, *North from Mexico*, 207–11; Eduardo Obregón Pagán, *Murder at Sleepy Lagoon: Zoot Suits, Race, & Riot in Wartime L.A.* (Chapel Hill: University of North Carolina Press, 2003), 71–97; Peterson, "Grassroots Good Neighbors," 193–239.

5. Manuel Ruiz to SCCIAA, July 13, 1944, Folder "Southern California Council of Inter-American Affairs," Box 5, Manuel Ruiz Papers, M-295, Special Collections, Green Library, Stanford University.

6. On the Mexican government's response to the "Zoot Suit Riots," see Richard Griswold del Castillo, "The Los Angeles 'Zoot Suit Riots' Revisited: Mexican and Latin American Perspectives," *Mexican Studies/Estudios Mexicanos* 16 (Summer 2000): 367–91; Peterson, "Grassroots Good Neighbors," 202–39.

7. John Perez is quoted in Jenny Cardenas, "Victory: Hispanics Went to War, Won a Battle at Home," *Press-Enterprise*, January 5, 1992, B1. On the FEPC, see Clete Daniel, *Chicano Workers and the Politics of Fairness: The FEPC in the Southwest, 1941–1945* (Austin: University of Texas Press, 1991), 164–84; Beatrice Griffin, *American Me* (Boston: Houghton Mifflin, 1948), 256–88; W. Rex Crawford, "The Latin American in Wartime United States," *Annals of the American Academy* 223 (September 1942): 123–31. Between 1943 and 1944, out of the 252 total discrimination complaints based on national origin, 182 were Mexican complaints; see Vesta Penrod, "Civil Rights Problems of Mexican Americans in Southern California" (MA thesis, Claremont College, 1948), 88.

8. "Mexico Fuera de Mexico: Discriminación," *El Tiempo*, February 16, 1945, 3; Hensley C. Woodbridge, "Mexico and U.S. Racism: How Mexicans View Our Treatment of Minorities," *Commonweal*, June 22, 1945, 234–37.

9. "Mexican Fete Draws Throng," *Los Angeles Times*, May 6, 1945, 1; "Habla el Sr. Padilla," *La Opinión*, May 6, 1945, 1; "Corona Group Attends Mexican Affairs Session," *Corona Independent*, May 4, 1945, 2; "Coronans Attend Banquet Honoring Mexican Officials," *Corona Independent*, May 8, 1945, 3. On the liberal pluralistic rhetoric of the Good Neighbor Policy, see David Gutiérrez, *Walls and Mirrors: Mexican Immigrants, Mexican Americans and the Politics of Ethnicity* (Berkeley: University of California Press, 1995), 138–41.

10. "Los Amigos Club Meets Thursday," *Corona Independent*, July 17, 1946; "Los Amigos and El Modelo Clubs Big Factors in Fiesta," *Corona Independent*,

May 6, 1946, 1; "Moreno Addresses Los Amigos Club," *Corona Independent,* December 14, 1945, 3.

11. Martínez interview; "Los Amigos Works to Promote Better Citizenship in Corona," *Corona Independent,* May 4, 1961, 15C; "Fred Eldridge, Wine, Dine and Silver Passes," *Corona Independent,* September 6, 1978, 3.

12. Martínez interview.

13. In 1932, there were only 4 high school graduates of Mexican descent. By 1949, there were 70 Mexican Americans out of 460 Corona High School graduates. "Nuestra Raza Sé Adelanta," La Sección Mexicana de Corona, *Corona Independent,* March 25, 1949, 8.

14. At least five Hispanas served in the New Mexico legislature in the 1930s. See Sarah Deutsch, *No Separate Refuge: Culture, Class, and Gender on an Anglo-Hispanic Frontier in the American Southwest, 1880–1940* (New York: Oxford University Press, 1987), 179; Elizabeth Salas, "Ethnicity, Gender, and Divorce: Issues in the 1922 Campaign by Adelina Otero-Warren for the U.S. House of Representatives," *New Mexico Historical Review* 70 (October 1995): 367–81.

15. José M. Alamillo, "Frances Martínez: Mexican American Political Activist," in *Latinas in the United States: A Historical Encyclopedia,* ed. Vicki Ruiz and Virginia Sanchez Korrol (Bloomington: Indiana University Press, 2006); Adriana Chavira, "Hispanic Activist Nears 90th Birthday," *Press-Enterprise,* August 10, 2002.

16. Martínez interview; Leo Grebler, "The Naturalization of Mexican Immigrants in the United States," *International Migration Review* 1 (Fall 1966): 17–32.

17. Gary Gerstle, *Working Class Americanism: The Politics of Labor in a Textile City, 1914–1960* (Cambridge: Cambridge University Press, 1989), 5–15. On the international dimensions of the Popular Front social movement, see Michael Denning, *The Cultural Front: The Laboring of American Culture in the Twentieth Century* (New York: Verso, 1997), 11–16. U.S. and Mexican activists reinterpreted the Good Neighbor Policy to redefine "American"; see Peterson, "Grassroots Good Neighbors," 10–11.

18. "Americanization Objectives Here Are Outlined: Improving Conditions for Those of Mexican Ancestry Is Aim," *Corona Independent,* April 11, 1945, 1.

19. Martínez interview; Aparicio interview.

20. Martínez interview; Delgadillo interview.

21. González, *Mexican Consuls and Labor Organizing,* 200–204; Peterson, "Grassroots Good Neighbors," 58–61. Appointed by President Cárdenas, Los Angeles Consul De La Huerta assisted the Popular Front group Congress of Spanish-Speaking Peoples; see García, *Mexican Americans,* 150; Mario García, *Memories of Chicano History: The Life and Narrative of Bert Corona* (Berkeley: University of California Press, 1994), 182.

22. Raul Morin, *Among the Valiant: Mexican Americans in WWII and Korea* (Los Angeles: Borden, 1963), 277–78.

23. Acevedo interview; Martínez interview; "Mexican Descent War Vets Meet at St. Edwards Today," *Corona Independent,* June 12, 1946, 1.

24. Aparicio interview; "Dominguez Post Active in Many Civic Affairs," *Corona Independent,* May 4, 1961, 13C; "Legion Post for Mexican Descent Veterans

Planned," *Corona Independent*, June 13, 1946, 1; "New Legion Post Selects Title of 'Joe Dominguez,'" *Corona Independent*, July 10, 1946, 1; "Mexican Descent War Vets Meet at St. Edward's Today," *Corona Independent*, June 12, 1946, 5.

25. On Mexican women's home front activities, see Christine Marín, "La Asociacion Mexicana Hispano-Americana de Madres y Esposas: Tucson's Mexican American Women in World War II," *Renato Rosaldo Lecture Series Monograph* 1 (1985): 5–18; Julie Campbell, "Madres y Esposas: Tucson's Spanish-American Mothers and Wives Association," *Journal of Arizona History* 31 (Summer 1990): 161–82.

26. Esperanza Olvera, interview by author, September 30, 1998, audiotape (in author's possession); Williamson, "Labor in the California Citrus Industry," 82; "Student Pickers Work in Groves and Girls Are Used for the First Time," *Corona Independent*, March 3, 1943, 1.

27. G. Delgadillo interview.

28. On intraethnic conflicts between braceros and Mexican American men, see Matt García, *A World of Its Own: Race, Labor, and Citrus in the Making of Greater Los Angeles* (Chapel Hill: University of North Carolina Press, 2001), 174–88.

29. "Good Neighbors from Mexico," *Corona Independent*, July 7, 1942, 4; "First Group of Mexican Citrus Workers Arrives," *Corona Independent*, March 29, 1943; "Two Mexican Nationals Cut," *Corona Independent*, October 2, 1944, 1; "Many Guns Were Seized in Raid on Camp Temescal," *Corona Independent*, April 22, 1946,1; Meeting Minutes, June 20, 1944, Folder "Corona Growers, Inc.," Box 1, OHOAC; Manuel Muñoz, interview by the author, November 12, 1998, audiotape C-105, Oral History Collection, CPL.

30. R. Delgadillo interview.

31. Gloria Granado, interview by author, December 15, 2000, audiotape (in author's possession).

32. Granado interview; Muñoz interview.

33. "Dominguez Legion Post Enjoyed Yule Party Friday Eve," *Corona Independent*, December 20, 1948; "Joe Dominguez Auxiliary Formed," *Corona Independent*, March 13, 1950, 5; Donald McGaffin, interview with author, March 21, 2002, audiotape (in author's possession).

34. "Queen Contest to Feature May Celebration Here," *Corona Independent*, February 26, 1945, 1.

35. "Mexican Consul to Crown Cinco de Mayo Queen," *Corona Independent*, April 30, 1945, 1; "Mexican Consul Is Speaker at Fiesta," *Corona Independent*, May 6, 1945, 1; "Cinco de Mayo Celebration Will Start Tonight," *Corona Independent*, May 4, 1945, 1.

36. "Plans for Cinco de Mayo Program Are Taking Shape," *Corona Independent*, April 25, 1946, 1.

37. A. Rodríguez interview; "Cinco de Mayo to Present Colorful Program Saturday," *Corona Independent*, May 2, 1946, 1; "Big Cinco de Mayo Parade at 10 a.m. Saturday Feature," *Corona Independent*, May 3, 1946, 1.

38. Martínez interview; "Zoot Suiters Again in Action," *Corona Independent*, February 7, 1944; "Pachucos, Some with Weapons, Found Here," *Corona Independent*, February 19, 1945, 1; "Council Urged to Deny Mexicans Dance Per-

mits," *Corona Independent*, March 3, 1943, 1; "Curfew Ordinance to Be Enforced Again," *Corona Independent*, March 17, 1943, 1.

39. "Fiesta Planned to Boost New Recreation Den," *Corona Independent*, March 12, 1946, 3; Frances Martínez, "Cinco de Mayo Raised $2,500 for Recreation," *Corona Independent*, May 17, 1946, 1.

40. "Recreation Dept. Plans Active 1947 with City Fiesta," *Corona Independent*, January 2, 1947, 1; "Mexican Fiesta, Lemon Festival Here April 25–26," *Corona Independent*, February 18, 1947, 1; "Citrus Drinks to Be Pushed during Fiesta," *Corona Independent*, March 18, 1947; "Fiesta Theme to Feature the Local Lemon Industry," *Corona Independent*, March 18, 1947; "Fiesta Notes," *Corona Independent*, April 7, 1947, 5; "Fiesta and Lemon Festival Activity Begins Tonight," *Corona Independent*, April 25, 1947, 1; "Lemonade Capital of the World," in *The Corona Story* (Corona: Hobart, 1954), 5–6.

41. Martínez interview; Aparicio interview.

42. "Mayor, Mexican Consul Are Grand Parade Marshals," *Corona Independent*, April 24, 1947, 1; "Colorful Fiesta Parade Is Lauded for Fine Floats," *Corona Independent*, April 28, 1947, 1; Lemon Fiesta Pamphlet, "The Purpose of the Lemon Fiesta," 1947, 1–5, Cinco de Mayo Collection, Heritage Room, CPL; "Programa Oficial de 5 de Mayo, 1862–1947," Corona California, Flyer, Cinco de Mayo Collection, Heritage Room, CPL.

43. Lemon Fiesta Pamphlet, "The Purpose of the Lemon Fiesta," 2–3, CPL; "Fiesta Banquet Honors Outstanding Fiesta Workers," *Corona Independent*, April 28, 1947, 5.

44. Lemon Fiesta Pamphlet, "The Purpose of the Lemon Fiesta," 5, CPL; "Emily Delgadillo Inspects Harvill's Plant," *Corona Independent*, April 21, 1947, 1.

45. Hilarion López interview.

46. "Colorful Fiesta Parade Is Lauded for Fine Floats," *Corona Independent*, April 28, 1947, 1. On parades as political rituals, see George Lipsitz, *Time Passages: Collective Memory and American Popular Culture* (Minneapolis: University of Minnesota Press, 1990), 16; Susan Davis, *Parades and Power: Street Theatre in Nineteenth-Century Philadelphia* (Philadelphia: Temple University Press, 1986); Sallie A. Marston, "Public Rituals and Community Power: St. Patrick's Day Parades in Lowell, Massachusetts, 1841–1874," *Political Geography Quarterly* 8 (July 1989): 255–69.

47. "20–30 Club Is Lauded for Work toward Fiesta," *Corona Independent*, April 4, 1947, 1. One Berkeley economist estimated that more than 1.05 million California workers lost their jobs in the immediate postwar years. See Samuel Hays, *The Postwar Unemployment Problem in California, 1945–1947* (Berkeley: Bureau of Public Administration, University of California, Berkeley, 1945), 1–11.

48. "Early Completion of La Casita House Asked of Council: Prevent Rather Than Cure Trouble Mrs. Martínez Asks," *Corona Independent*, April 13, 1949, 1; "Completion of La Casita Center Being Studied," *Corona Independent*, February 24, 1949, 1; "La Casita Sera Construida," La Sección Mexicana De Corona, *Corona Independent*, March 16, 1949, 10.

49. Kenneth Burt, "Latino Empowerment in Los Angeles: Postwar Dreams and Cold War Fears, 1948–1952," *Labor Heritage* 8 (Summer 1996): 6. Cinco de Mayo celebrations were also organized during the 1950s to support progressive

causes. See the "Fiesta de Cinco de Mayo" Flyer, Folder 312, Box 64, Dorothy Healy Papers, Special Collections, California State University Long Beach.

50. "Scenes at Opening of Corona's La Casita Hall," *Corona Independent,* October 2, 1950, 2.

51. López interview; "Zoning Tossed Back into Lap of School Board," *Corona Independent,* September 5, 1944, 1; "Home Gardens May Get School of Their Own," *Corona Independent,* October 10, 1944, 1.

52. On the *Lemon Grove* and *Mendez v. Westminster* court cases, see Gilbert González, *Chicano Education in the Era of Segregation* (Philadelphia: Balch Institute Press, 1990), passim; Ricardo Romo, "Southern California and the Origins of Latino Civil-Rights Activism," *Western Legal History* 3 (Summer/Fall 1990): 359–60.

53. Martínez interview; "Mexicans Offer Zoning Protest," *Corona Independent,* September 5, 1944, 1; "Coordinating Groups to Meet," *Corona Independent,* September 13, 1944; "150 at School Zoning Meeting," *Corona Independent,* September 11, 1944. On Protestant political activists in the Mexican community, see Sánchez, *Becoming Mexican American,* 163.

54. "New Elementary School Zones Are Established," *Corona Independent,* September 28, 1944; "Ask Coordinating Council to Aid Zone Dispute: Mexican Consul Appears before School Board," *Corona Independent,* September 12, 1944. Frances Martínez wrote about Mrs. Hampton helping her set up a children's club at St. Edward's Hall; "Frances Martínez Writes of Corona Folks and Actions," *Corona Independent,* January 8, 1945, 1.

55. López interview; "Home Gardens May Get School of Their Own," *Corona Independent,* October 10, 1944, 1.

56. "Mass Meeting Protests Zoning," *Corona Independent,* October 6, 1944, 1; "Home Gardens May Get School of Their Own," *Corona Independent,* October 10, 1944, 1; Donna Rice, "History of Corona-Norco Unified School District," Typescript, n.d., Heritage Room, CPL. Anglo resistance to integrated schools was commonplace in other parts of southern California. See Becky Nicolaides, *My Blue Heaven: Life and Politics in the Working-Class Suburbs of Los Angeles* (Chicago: University of Chicago Press, 2002), 162–68.

57. "Mexican Americans Want to Find Their Place in the Sun," *Corona Independent,* December 5, 1951; "St. Edward School Dedication," Pamphlet, September 7, 1947, Folder "St. Edwards," CPL.

58. Cipriano Hernandez is quoted in Ilene Aleshire, "Hernandez Recalls Prejudice Shown Him by School Board at Meeting 40 Years Ago," *Press-Enterprise,* April 27, 1977, 6D; Martínez interview.

59. Acevedo interview; "Onias Acevedo Seeks Seat on Corona Council," *Corona Daily Independent,* January 6, 1958, 1; Pat Murkland, "Acting Victory: A Former Citrus Worker Wins Election to the Corona City Council," *Press-Enterprise,* October 31, 1999, S7. The Corona LULAC was founded in 1957, with Ray Delgadillo serving as the first president.

60. "Thinking Out Loud," *Corona Daily Independent,* April 9, 1958, 8.

61. Acevedo interview; "Elect Acevedo, Velthoen and Jameson to CC," *Corona Daily Independent,* January 23, 1958, 1.

62. John Dittmer, *Local People: The Struggle for Civil Rights in Mississippi* (Urbana: University of Illinois Press, 1994), 19–40.

63. Aparicio interview; Fred Eldridge, "Nettie Left a Lot before She Departed," *Corona Daily Independent*, May 26, 1976, B2. In *Lopez v. Seccombe*, the court found that San Bernardino city officials had violated the petitioners' constitutional rights "based solely upon the fact that petitioners [were] of Mexican and Latin descent." *Lopez et al. v. Seccombe et al.*, 71 Federal Supplement 769, February 5, 1944, U.S. District Court for the Southern District of California, Central Division, Records of Superior Court of Los Angeles County; "La Corte Federal Rinde Fallo Permanente en el Pleito de la Alberca Publica de Sa Bernardino," *El Espectador*, December 31, 1943, 1; García, *A World of Its Own*, 228–42; García, *Mexican Americans*, 87–88; Penrod, "Civil Rights Problems of Mexican Americans in Southern California," 26–29. For another court case regarding swimming pools in Pasadena, see Howard Shorr, "Thorns in the Roses: Race Relations and the Brookside Plunge Controversy in Pasadena, California, 1914–1947," in *Law in the Western United States*, ed. Gordon Morris Bakken (Norman: University of Oklahoma Press, 2000), 522–28.

64. Martínez interview; Enríquez interview. Frances Martínez, "Estimado Publico de La Colonia Mexicana," La Sección Mexicana de Corona, *Corona Independent*, March 9, 1949, 8; "Los Mexicanaos de Azusa, Irwindale y Glendora se Abstendran de Patrocinar al Teatro State," *El Espectador*, February 17, 1943. In the nearby community of Ontario, local Mexican Americans, with the assistance of Ignacio López, launched a boycott of the Upland Theater for forcing Mexican patrons to sit in the first fifteen rows. Several weeks later, the boycott proved successful when the theater owner accepted the demand to treat Mexican patrons with "equal consideration." See Enrique López, "Community Resistance to Injustice and Inequality: Ontario, California, 1937–1947," *Aztlan* (Fall 1986): 12–14; García, *Mexican Americans*, 86–87.

65. Martínez interview; "Report Attack by Young Mexicans," *Corona Independent*, January 18, 1943; "Cuttings Mark Mexican Dance," *Corona Independent*, March 1, 1943; "Mexican Youths Admit Robberies," *Corona Independent*, April 12, 1943; "Report Mexican Youth Stabbed by Sailor Here," *Corona Independent*, June 11, 1943. Frances Martínez's articles include "Novena Started in Honor of Our Lady of Guadalupe," *Corona Independent*, January 5, 1945; "Frances Martínez Writes of Corona Folks and Actions," *Corona Independent*, January 8, 1945; "Christenings by Mexicans Events of Importance," *Corona Independent*, January 15, 1945; "Guadalupe Feast Observances at St. Edward Friday," *Corona Independent*, December 10, 1947; and "Mexican Colony Loses Colorful Figure in Death," *Corona Independent*, January 19, 1945.

66. Gilberto Enríquez, "Carta Abierta," *El Imparcial*, August 25, 1949, 1.

67. McWilliams, *North from Mexico*, 248.

68. Ramos interview; Iris Hayward, "Community Center Drive Repeats History, Old-Timers Say," *Press-Enterprise*, March 3, 1976, C3.

69. Cruz interview.

Epilogue

1. Martínez interview; Fred Eldridge and Stanley Reynolds, *Corona, California, Commentaries* (Corona: Sinclair Printing, 1986), 102–3; "Face of Area

Economy Changing; Groves Give Way to Corporations," *Corona-Norco Independent*, May 1, 1986, 18.

2. There were sixty-two new industrial plants by 1962. Reynolds and Eldridge, *Corona, California, Commentaries*, 76–78. "Freeway Leaves Circle Intact," *Corona Daily Independent*, January 23, 1958, 1; Fred Eldridge, "Urban Renewal, A Big Corona Fight," *Corona Daily Independent*, March 12, 1979, B8.

3. Ibid., 67; "Corona Plunges into Citrus Heritage," *Press-Enterprise*, July 9, 1998, B1.

4. "MAPA Opposes Urban Renewal in Corona," *The Voice*, January 20, 1966, Folder 2, Box 20, Eduardo Quevedo Papers, Special Collections, Stanford University, Stanford, California; Kenneth Burt, *The History of MAPA and Chicano Politics in California* (Sacramento: Mexican American Political Association 1982), 1–26; "MAPA in Protest Walk," *Corona Daily Independent*, September 18, 1969, 1; "MAPA's Mejia Warns of 'Volatile Circumstance,'" *Corona Daily Independent*, September 19, 1969, 1; Frances Martínez, "MAPA Youths Strictly a U.S. Product," *Corona Daily Independent*, September 29, 1969,.

5. Martínez interview.

6. Al Varela, interview by author, June 1, 2001, Corona, California, tape recording (in author's possession); Christopher Herbert, "Cinco de Mayo Celebration Points to Past and Future," *Corona-Norco Independent*, May 2, 1997, C2; "Nostalgia Tugs at Heart of First Queen of Cinco de Mayo," *Press-Enterprise*, May 5, 1986; Barry S. Surman, "Corona Celebrates 100 Years of History; Weekend Festival Includes Cinco de Mayo and Founder's Day Events," *Los Angeles Times*, May 3, 1986, 15. The 1999 Cinco de Mayo parade featured the first Anglo grand marshal. Jerry Soifer, "Cinco de Mayo Even Celebrates Diversity," *Press-Enterprise*, May 2, 1999.

7. Jim "Chayo" Rodríguez, interview by author, July 7, 1998, Corona, California, tape recording (in author's possession); Jeffy Soifer, "Chayo Is Corona Landmark," *Corona Daily Independent*, November 11, 1989, B2.

Index

Abalos, Jesus, 65
Abalos Pool Hall, 65
Acevedo, Onias, 2, 47, 95, 133, 137, 142, 149; as member of the Corona City Council, 162–63
A. F. Call Association, 19
African Americans, 184n54
Agricultural Citrus Workers Union (ACWU): Local 342, 128; Local 22342, 139
Agricultural Producers Labor Committee (APLC), 125, 139
Aguirre, Hank, 113
Alexander, Grant, 62
Alf, Edward, 81
All Nations Boys Club, 88
All Nations Girls Club, 90
Almada, Baldomero ("Melo"), 106, 114–15
Altamarino, Angel, 135, 202n33
American Baptist (First Baptist) Church, 84
American Federation of Labor (AFL), 124, 138
American Fruit Growers, 125
Americanization (of immigrant populations), 68, 79, 80, 94, 101, 148;

"Americanized" forms of recreation, 102–3; baseball as an Americanizing force, 106, 118, 119; and missionary work, 85
Anderson, Dee, 110
Anti-Saloon League (ASL), 60, 69
Aparicio, Reynaldo, 42, 95, 133, 148, 155–56, 163
Aranda, Mildred, 91
Asociación Atlética Mexicana del Sur de California, 107
Asociación Deportiva Hispano Americana, 107
Asociación Mexicana de Baseball del Sur de California, 107
Asociación Nacional of Mexico-Americana, 125
Associated Farmers, 124, 126, 127, 139
Atchison, Topeka and Santa Fe Railroad, 17
Ayala, Carmen, 73

Balderas, Silvestre, 106
Balderas, Tony, 129, 135
Bandini, Don Juan, 13
Baptists, 84, 85–86, 97–98. *See also* Mexican Baptist churches

JOSÉ M. ALAMILLO is an assistant professor in the Department of Comparative Ethnic Studies at Washington Sate University.

The Immigrant World of Ybor City: Italians and Their Latin Neighbors in
  Tampa, 1885–1985   *Gary R. Mormino and George E. Pozzetta*
The Butte Irish: Class and Ethnicity in an American Mining Town,
  1875–1925   *David M. Emmons*
The Making of an American Pluralism: Buffalo, New York,
  1825–60   *David A. Gerber*
Germans in the New World: Essays in the History of Immigration
  Frederick C. Luebke
A Century of European Migrations, 1830–1930   *Edited by Rudolph J.
  Vecoli and Suzanne M. Sinke*
The Persistence of Ethnicity: Dutch Calvinist Pioneers in Amsterdam,
  Montana   *Rob Kroes*
Family, Church, and Market: A Mennonite Community in the Old and the
  New Worlds, 1850–1930   *Royden K. Loewen*
Between Race and Ethnicity: Cape Verdean American Immigrants,
  1860–1965   *Marilyn Halter*
Les Icariens: The Utopian Dream in Europe and America
  Robert P. Sutton
Labor and Community: Mexican Citrus Worker Villages in a Southern
  California County, 1900–1950   *Gilbert G. González*
Contented among Strangers: Rural German-Speaking Women and Their
  Families in the Nineteenth-Century Midwest   *Linda Schelbitzki Pickle*
Dutch Farmer in the Missouri Valley: The Life and Letters of Ulbe Eringa,
  1866–1950   *Brian W. Beltman*
Good-bye, Piccadilly: British War Brides in America   *Jenel Virden*
For Faith and Fortune: The Education of Catholic Immigrants in Detroit,
  1805–1925   *JoEllen McNergney Vinyard*
Britain to America: Mid-Nineteenth-Century Immigrants to the United
  States   *William E. Van Vugt*
Immigrant Minds, American Identities: Making the United States Home,
  1870–1930   *Orm Øverland*
Italian Workers of the World: Labor Migration and the Formation of
  Multiethnic States   *Edited by Donna R. Gabaccia and Fraser M.
  Ottanelli*
Dutch Immigrant Women in the United States, 1880–1920
  Suzanne M. Sinke
Beyond Cannery Row: Sicilian Women, Immigration, and Community in
  Monterey, California, 1915–99   *Carol Lynn McKibben*
Merchants, Midwives, and Laboring Women: Italian Migrants in Urban
  America   *Diane C. Vecchio*
American Dreaming, Global Realities: Rethinking U.S. Immigration
  History   *Edited by Donna R. Gabaccia and Vicki L. Ruiz*
Making Lemonade out of Lemons: Mexican American Labor and Leisure
  in a California Town, 1880–1960   *José M. Alamillo*

The University of Illinois Press
is a founding member of the
Association of American University Presses.

Composed in 9.5/12.5 Trump Mediaeval
by BookComp, Inc.
Manufactured by Thomson-Shore, Inc.

University of Illinois Press
1325 South Oak Street
Champaign, IL 61820-6903
www.press.uillinois.edu